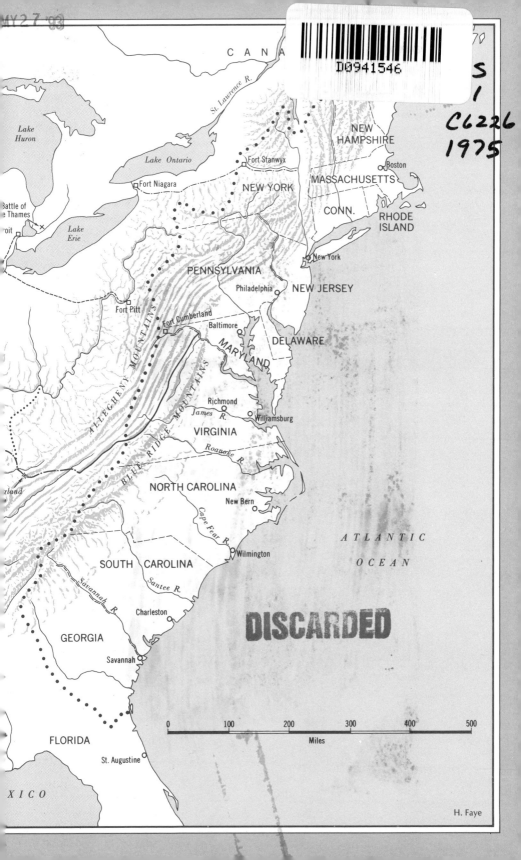

CANADA

Lake
Huron

St. Lawrence R.

Lake Ontario

Fort Stanwyx

NEW
HAMPSHIRE

Boston

Fort Niagara

NEW YORK

MASSACHUSETTS

Battle of
e Thames

Lake
Erie

CONN.

RHODE
ISLAND

roit

PENNSYLVANIA

New York

NEW JERSEY

Fort Pitt

Philadelphia

ALLEGHENY MOUNTAINS

Fort Cumberland

Baltimore

DELAWARE

MARYLAND

Richmond

James R.

Williamsburg

BLUE RIDGE MOUNTAINS

VIRGINIA

Roanoke R.

land

NORTH CAROLINA

New Bern

Cape Fear R.

ATLANTIC

OCEAN

Wilmington

SOUTH CAROLINA

Savannah R.

Santee R.

Charleston

GEORGIA

Savannah

FLORIDA

St. Augustine

X I C O

0	100	200	300	400	500

Miles

H. Faye

A FAIR AND HAPPY LAND

BOOKS BY WILLIAM A. OWENS

Tales from the Derrick Floor
with Mody C. Boatright

*Three Friends: Roy Bedichek,
J. Frank Dobie, Walter Prescott Webb*

This Stubborn Soil

Look to the River

Fever in the Earth

Walking on Borrowed Land

*Slave Mutiny:
The Revolt on the Schooner Amistad*

A Season of Weathering

A Fair and Happy Land

WILLIAM A. OWENS

A Fair and
Happy Land

CHARLES SCRIBNER'S SONS

New York

1 3 5 7 9 11 13 15 17 19 H/C 20 18 16 14 12 10 8 6 4 2

Printed in the United States of America

Library of Congress Cataloging in Publication Data

Owens, William A   1905–   A fair and happy land.
Includes bibliographical references and index.
1. Cleaver family. 2. Owens family. 3. Frontier
and pioneer life—United States. I. Title.
CS71.C6226 1975   929'.2'0973   75–13867
ISBN 0–684–14343–7

THIS BOOK IS GRATEFULLY DEDICATED
to those of my blood who have gone before, men
and women who, enjoined by the Old Testament
to seek a New Canaan, sought it on the American
frontier, who in the midst of both abundance and
danger wittingly coupled, wittingly brought forth
sons and daughters to people the face of a new
earth, to make it indeed a land of milk and honey.
Especially I keep in mind those forebears whose
surnames I am able to record: Cleaver, Smith,
Coleman, James, Chennault, Witherspoon, Hopson,
Edmonds, Duval, and my own.

Contents

[vii]

CONTENTS

On Jordan's stormy banks I stand
And cast a wishful eye
To Canaan's fair and happy land
Where my possessions lie.

REFRAIN:
I am bound for the Promised Land,
I am bound for the Promised Land;
Oh, who will come and go with me?
I am bound for the Promised Land.

—white spiritual

To SAY that the frontier as a force in history
is passé is equivalent to saying that water, air
and history itself are all obsolete and of no
force. The frontier was land, and everything
it contained from grass to gold.

—Walter Prescott Webb

East to West
Up and Down

From my early childhood the question *"Who am I?"* came to me from time to time, especially when I read about people in faraway places or when people who had left Pin Hook came back and talked of people and places they had seen. At home I asked the question often, not in that form but in another: *"Where did we come from?"* In a family of intermittent literacy, a family not given to keeping records, the answers were not satisfactory. My uncle, Charlie Kitchens, for one, when I asked where his folks came from, replied, "The old country." I was greatly disappointed when I learned that for him "the old country" was Mississippi. Dates of births, marriages, and deaths had been written in Bibles by those who could write, but the older Bibles had been lost through fire or flood or carelessness. Memory went back only two generations: to my mother and her mother, with little from my father's side, as he had died soon after I was born. For anything earlier, anyone I could call kin had to fall back on "they say." No amount of looking into myself helped, except that it set me to seeking satisfaction in writing about the question.

When I wrote *This Stubborn Soil* I reported my early life as clearly and as accurately as I could, with a kind of expectation that at least a part of the answer would emerge. I ended the book knowing it had not, and that it could not be found in my immediate family or in Pin Hook, Lamar County, Texas, where my kinfolks had lived and I had spent my early years. I knew I had to look farther back, as far back as I could.

But where? Which of the names I knew from earlier generations might be a place to begin? They had followed different paths and traveled at different times, but they had all come to Pin Hook and

[xi]

signed their names or made their marks on deeds to land. I knew only the "they say" of where they came from and nothing of why they came.

The clearest link to my past was my great-grandmother, Missouri Ann Cleaver, who had seen to it that *Cleaver* was perpetuated in the names of her children, grandchildren, and even great-grandchildren. Her life and mine overlapped two years, but I do not remember her. For me, she appears most vividly in two recollections of those who knew her: she was captured as a spy by Yankee soldiers; she hid Jesse James out after one of his raids.

She was born in Alabama and raised in Arkansas. The Missouri in her name was said to have come from relatives who lived near Hannibal, Missouri. She told my grandmother and my mother that she had Dutch blood, but they did not know from which of her kin. From my grandmother I had some details of her later life. The Civil War—the War for Southern Independence or the War between the States were names more to her liking—had left her destitute and had driven her on to Texas to make some kind of living for her "passel o' young'uns."

With no more facts than I have put down here, but driven by the need to know, I started working back, first with the 1850 United States census for Ouachita County, Arkansas, where my grandmother was born. I found her name and with it the three entries the census taker was required to make: born in Alabama, age fifteen, daughter of Henry Cleaver. Not much, but a start. The names of her brothers and sisters were listed. More important, Henry Cleaver had given Kentucky as his birthplace and I was moved another step farther back along the frontier.

Soon, as time and money permitted, I followed the Cleaver name back, through census records, deeds and wills in county courthouse records, and county and local histories. Gradually the Cleaver journeyings became known to me. I could trace them back state by state: Texas, Arkansas, Alabama, Missouri, Kentucky, West Virginia, Virginia, Maryland, Pennsylvania. Nine states in two hundred years, or in five generations, with each generation on the outer fringe of some new frontier.

My search led me to other members of the Cleaver family, some of them as interested as I in knowing the full Cleaver story. They called me "cousin" and gave me the information they had. It was useful but never enough, chiefly because it was too often narrowly genealogical—names and dates, births, marriages, and deaths—good for building family trees but not for knowing the people behind the names. In libraries and courthouses I met countless others who were working almost feverishly at building family trees. Before long I realized that I had stumbled into a kind of national obsession—genealogy. As a people we were beginning to look back with the hope of saying who we are through what our people were.

One afternoon in the dimly lit stacks of the Columbia University Library I came upon the name of Peter Klever in a history of Germantown, Pennsylvania, and of his wife, Catherine or Gertrude—the records give both—Shoemaker. It was an exciting moment. He was German; she was Dutch. If the tradition of Dutch blood was true, they could be the beginning of the line in America. In any case. I could go no farther back in time or place. I had reached the Atlantic. Their earlier history was hidden in the records of seventeenth-century Europe.

My need at the time was to know them not in Europe but in America, as they made a part of the American experience. I wanted to know what they treasured, what they laughed at, what they believed, what they fought for. I wanted to get as close to them, generation after generation, as I could—to walk on the land they had walked on, to see the rivers and valleys and mountains they had known—to seek out their human essence. That they were human I had learned from long-buried court records penned in old-fashioned letters with a goose-quill pen: one found guilty of profane swearing, another of gambling, another of a challenge to a duel. The time had come for me to reverse my steps.

I set out then to follow them halfway across America, and more, east to west, up and down, taking the routes they took, walking on land they had claimed and cleared and cultivated, immersing myself in what must have been the life of the time and place at each stop on the way, in the kinds of hardships they had endured in the wilderness. Simulation, I found, could be revealing but not exact. I could never recapture the whole of their experience. For instance, on the long stretches where they traveled rough trails by foot or horse or wagon I went by car on superhighways, covering in an hour a distance that took them days, and I did not have to stop to cook bear meat or pick a bait of berries. Nevertheless, as I went, the essential parts of their story emerged, often bolstered by the stories of those who traveled with them.

What I ended up with—the story from which this book is made —is not a single narrative thread. It is episodic and fragmentary. At times it leaps hundreds of miles into a new part of the frontier; at times it tarries in one place the length of a generation. Whether moving or staying, each generation laid down ways of doing things —good and bad—for those who followed. Interweavings of many threads of custom and belief and ethnic origin keep the pattern constantly changing. Only one strong element endures through it all: the frontier.

At last their road took me back to Pin Hook and I arrived there with more than a sketchy knowledge of where we had come from. My father's name is Welsh, but my Welsh blood is so melded that it has a mixture of Dutch, German, French, Scotch, Irish, and English. In religion, my people were more diverse in denominational names than in the beliefs they adhered to. With the exception of one great-grandmother, who was possibly Roman Catholic, they were Protestants: Quakers, Huguenots, Baptists, Christians—seekers lured to America partly by the promise of religious freedom and, having tasted it, fierce in their determination to see it maintained. The sacraments—called ordinances by those most opposed to ritual— they held to were baptism and the Lord's Supper, and with some the public washing of feet. The priest was alien to them; the preacher had no surer way to God than they had in their own hearts.

They were not men of letters. They were people of action, and they often managed to be where the action was taking place, especially if the action was soldiering. For the most part they kept close to the land—men and women who went deeper and deeper into the forest, fording rivers, climbing mountains, until the biggest river of all had been crossed and they had to find new ways to build on the treeless plains. Their toughness of body and mind and purpose, as strong in those who marched with them, changed a wilderness into a country—a country not quite the dream they had dreamed, but better than people like them had ever known before.

I still did not have a satisfactory answer to "Who am I?" I knew, though, that it lay elusively in what made them and what they made, in what they had endured, in their will to survive. This, then, is their story. In a broader sense it is the story of Americans moving west in search of the promised land, of countless people lost to history except for their *X*'s or signatures on deeds to the land they held for a time as they passed through.

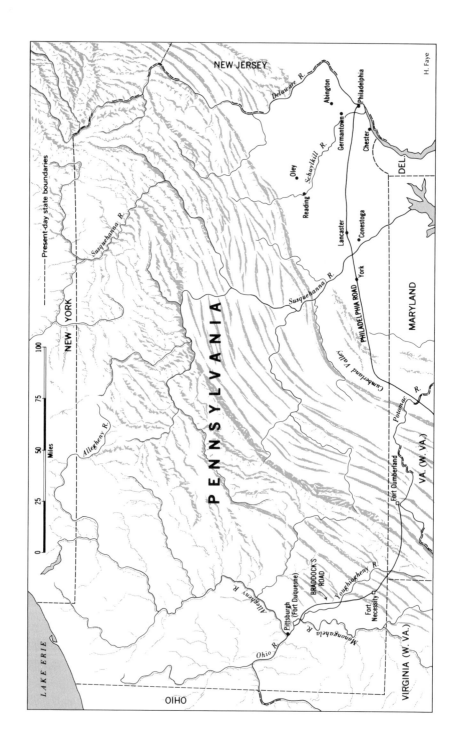

Pennsylvania

THE STORY AS PERCEIVED BEGINS ABOUT 1690 IN PENNSYLVANIA, WITH WILLIAM PENN AND HIS "HOLY EXPERIMENT," AND WITH A HANDFUL OF GERMAN QUAKER IMMIGRANTS, OF WHOM PETER Klever was one. For historical narrative it was a fortunate beginning. By geography alone Pennsylvania was destined to become a main gateway to the West. Through the influence of its founder Pennsylvania became more than a gateway. William Penn, a landed proprietor who put principle ahead of profit, infected those who would listen with the belief that men of all races and religions could live together in peace, brotherhood, and goodwill—a belief that went west with the pioneers and played a considerable part in the development of frontier thought. Penn's story is essential to understanding liberal elements of that thought.

William Penn was a young aristocrat who for reasons of conscience had broken with the Church of England. In his seeking for truth he came to the Quakers, a sect founded by George Fox out of a revelation that came to him in 1647. Their beliefs, as put forth by Fox and others, had been distilled out of the despair of people who had for centuries suffered religious oppression, and out of their hope for personal and religious freedom. They called themselves Friends; in derision the world called them Quakers because they reportedly trembled in the presence of the Lord. Penn came to question their beliefs and remained to worship with them. A man of wealth and influence, he soon determined to make a place for religious freedom in the New World, where Quakers or any others could live together without fear of persecution. He tried in West Jersey and East Jersey, but though Quakers emigrated to these provinces, conditions were not right for him for his "Holy Experiment." In both colonies he had to share control with men not of his religious or political persuasion.

In March 1681, Penn, in payment for a debt owed to his father, secured from King Charles II the grant of land which the King himself named Pennsylvania, Penn's Woods. As sole proprietor, Penn was now free to set up any kind of government he chose. Colonies to the north and south of Pennsylvania, with the exception of New York, had been settled by the English. By 1664, including New York, they were ruled by the English—in a colonial extension of England. The colonies had already become a refuge for members of various dissenting sects that had developed out of the religious and political upheavals in Europe in the seventeenth century. Colonial rule perpetuated dissension. New England had been established for the Puritan way of life and was governed by a modified theocracy. Virginia was England all over again: royalist, Anglican. In either colony a man might be persecuted or harried out for his religious belief. To the Quakers, on the other hand, a man's religion was his own business, a doctrine Penn accepted wholeheartedly. Though Pennsylvania was to be a Quaker colony, he would welcome a Roman Catholic or an Anabaptist as warmly as he welcomed those of his own persuasion, and provide protection for them against religious persecution. He would also be mindful of the rights of the Indians. He set forth the principle that colonists should treat them in a manner "as also to reduce the Savage natives by gentle and iust [*sic*] manners to the love of Civil Societies and Christian Religion. . . ."

This protection was to be rooted in what Penn considered the fundamental rights of all men: right and title of each to his own life, liberties, and property; a voice in the government; and the right of trial by jury. His was not to be absentee ownership. From the beginning he planned to go with his colonists to the wilderness, to share with them any hardship. He sold land on terms favorable to the buyers. He joined with his purchasers in drawing up "The Frame of the Government of the Province of Pennsylvania," a document that because of its guarantee of civil and religious freedom was of considerable importance in the development of American institutions.

The foundations of his colony laid, Penn set sail for Pennsylvania, accompanied by about one hundred passengers, mostly friends from Sussex. His ship, *Welcome*, arrived at Newcastle at the mouth of the Delaware on October 27, 1682, where Penn received from the settlers already established there the solemn "delivery of turf, and twig, and water, and soyle of the River Delaware" as symbols of his owner-ship of the land. Thus he held ownership from king and settlers. As soon as possible, in keeping with his resolve to deal fairly with the Indians, he made a treaty to secure ownership from them, a treaty that was not broken for close to fifty years.

From the beginning of colonization in America by the English, ownership of land was of prime importance. Most of the colonists had never owned land, but they knew the benefits to be derived from ownership. They knew that those who held the land could establish churches, schools, and homes according to their consciences, and that ownership of land gave them rights in government. In the English system land was ultimately owned by the crown. Even in the Pennsylvania charter Charles II retained ownership of the land, for the use of which Penn was to pay a token fee of two beaver skins a year. As lord of the manor, however, Penn could dispose of the land as he pleased, while retaining to himself the rentals he thought just or expedient. He also had the right to establish a frame of government. Thus the land system in Pennsylvania was feudal, as the term was understood in England. Fortunately, the lord of the manor was enlightened, and ambitious to make Pennsylvania a model of government everywhere.

Unfortunately, another European institution was in America ahead of him: slavery. What came to be called "the infernal triangle" was beginning to take shape: British and Yankee ships took rum to the west coast of Africa, where it was traded for slaves to be sold in Barbados for molasses, to be made into rum in Boston, to be traded for slaves in Africa. Indians were also sold as slaves, and occasionally white men, though white men were more often indentured servants who could expect freedom after their time had been served. Penn and his followers protested against slavery from the beginning, but it was a system too profitable to be easily abolished.

The first settlers who came to Pennsylvania brought deeds to land that they had purchased from Penn's agents either in London or in Rotterdam. Later settlers who could afford to bought patents or deeds to land. Those who could not, either rented or indentured themselves for passage and keep. The last knew that once the indenture was over they were free to move farther into the wilderness, where they could take up land not under deed but under what came to be called squatter's rights or tomahawk leases, and claim it for their own. Penn envisioned this as a three-tiered society made up of landowners, renters, and indentured servants. Once in Pennsylvania he encountered a lower tier: Negro slaves, who could never rise even to the lowest of the other three, or own land.

As a colonist, William Penn came fairly late. Captain John Smith had settled Jamestown in 1607. The first African slave was brought to Virginia in 1619, the year before the Pilgrims landed at Plymouth Rock. Harvard College was founded in 1636. By the time Penn arrived at the Delaware, colonies were already stretched out along the Atlantic seaboard: Massachusetts, Rhode Island, Connecticut, New York, Maryland, Virginia, and Carolina. When Penn first set foot in Pennsylvania, the Virginians had already started the westward march toward the Blue Ridge Mountains. Holland Dutch and Swedes had cleared land and built homes along the Delaware and on the site of Philadelphia itself.

Yet the Pennsylvania that Penn came to was a wilderness, and he was free to make of it any kind of colony he chose. Following principles he had laid down in England he made it cosmopolitan— a port of entry to the New World for all who wanted to come, regardless of language or nationality or religion, whether rich or poor, whether educated or unable to read or write. He selected with care the site of his City of Brotherly Love, between the Schuylkill and the Delaware, where the Schuylkill flows into the Delaware, some one hundred miles from Newcastle.

On March 14, 1681, before leaving England, Penn granted Philadelphia a charter. Before the settlers came in numbers, a plan for the city had been made and some surveying had been done, but there had been little clearing of the forest and the new arrivals must have felt set down in the wilderness. Those who came first were English and Welsh Quakers, sober, pious, intent on personal and religious freedom, eager to work at their trades unhampered by the restrictions they had left behind. They came with a lifting of spirit, for most of them had suffered oppression and persecution for their beliefs.

Pennsylvania was becoming what Penn had planned for his "Holy Experiment," a place free of such oppression and persecution. The first General Assembly, held at Chester in 1682, on the "fifth and twentieth day of the second month, vulgarly called April," enacted what came to be called the "Great Law," which gave the colony the first truly representative government in America. The "Holy Experiment" took into account the Quaker belief, the Quaker experience, and opened the way for Quakers to influence the development of civil and religious principles in America. The belief that the word of God sent direct can be found in the human soul gave each person a sense of worth and dignity regardless of his station, or his ability to read or write. The body was the true vessel of the spirit. Since this was so, all men were indeed created equal in the sight of God, and were to be respected as equals. In the early years of their movement deep religious emotions left them quaking in the presence of God— hence the name Quakers, a name that aroused suspicion and hatred and persecution.

Almost from their beginning, Quakers, like the Pilgrims, fled from England to Holland. Some went on to Germany, some to America. In Holland they found acceptance, but not fully in Germany. In the New World, in colonies already established, they again found persecution. In all the colonies except Rhode Island they were whipped and imprisoned. In New York they were tortured. They were driven out of Massachusetts. All this in spite of the fact that physical manifestations of religious feeling had become rare among them, and they had become plain, quiet, pious people, more appropriately called The Religious Society of Friends.

By chance, Penn's "Holy Experiment" was well placed geographically—in the middle of the Atlantic coast, separating the colonies to the north from those to the south. By chance, the easiest routes to the West lay through Pennsylvania. Settlers from New York and New England were welcome to pass through, or to tarry as long as they wished. It was both natural and practical for the settlers, including the Quakers, to look west while they were still clearing their first land and building their first houses of logs cut and shaped only with an ax, the kind of house that a man could build in any part of the wilderness. It was natural for some of them to be infected with a new kind of liberalism before they went.

At thirty-eight William Penn could accept the reality of religious division in America and lead his followers into acceptance of a society built on pluralism. He also recognized the reality of economic structures brought from Europe, and the need for adjusting them to New World circumstances. For him it had to be a practical economy based on productiveness—the productiveness of merchants, artisans, farmers, and laborers alike, with a place for every worker. Pennsylvania was thus nearer than any of the other colonies to a genuine "come one, come all" policy.

Germantown

IN THE NEXT YEAR, 1683, Germantown was founded, six miles to the northwest of Philadelphia. In his years as a seeker William Penn had visited Mennonites—followers of Menno Simons—Pietists, and other evangelical Protestant Christians in Germany, and had found himself in deep sympathy with their struggle for religious freedom. Later, when he had land aplenty in Pennsylvania, he invited them to share both the new land and the new freedom. Leaders of both German and Dutch religious groups accepted, with the assurance that they would be able to practice their beliefs: the Bible as the sole rule of faith, nonresistance, refusal to take oaths, restriction of marriage to members of the same sect.

On March 20, 1682, through an agent, probably at Rotterdam, William Penn conveyed five thousand acres each to Jacob Telner of Crefeld, who was a merchant in Amsterdam, Jan Streypers, a merchant of Kaldkirchen, and Dirck Sipman of Crefeld. On June 21, 1683, he conveyed one thousand acres each to Govert Remke, Lenart Arets, and Jacob Van Bebber, all of Crefeld. A majority of them Mennonites, eager for freedom of worship, they had as their purpose colonization, not land speculation. Wittingly or not, Penn had added considerably to the pluralism of his colony.

Pennsylvania had its William Penn, Germantown its Francis Daniel Pastorius, who came to America as head of the Frankfort Land Company, agent for German settlers whose descendants were to plant the name Frankfort, or Frankford, across the nation. Pastorius was an intellectual from the continent who had turned to the Pietists for reasons of conscience. He was a writer, trained in the law, and before coming to America he had engaged in both theological

[8]

and political debate on the side of personal and religious freedom. In America, as occasions arose, he formulated some of the original documents on which the laws of the nation were eventually based.

Pastorius arrived on the *America* on August 16, 1683. He was then thirty-two and a bachelor. Philadelphia had been laid out, but it was still largely forest, with here and there an open space around scattered houses. To illustrate how much was still wilderness, he reported that he got lost once in the bushes on a journey up from the river to the baker's. Land clearing and house building proceeded slowly. While they built their homes most of these settlers lived in what they called caves—half-houses set in the earth. Pastorius himself lived in a cave until he was able to build his own log house, thirty feet long, fifteen feet wide. There he awaited the arrival of the German and Dutch settlers.

It was not easy to move to the New World. Families had to be broken up; farewells almost certain to be final had to be said. Clothing, tools, supplies had to be baled and bundled, with the settlers selecting, discarding, knowing they could not take enough with them to make a new life. The Dutch and Germans had to get to London, where passage had been arranged by Penn's agents. Then they had to endure a long and hazardous journey at sea. With oppression to drive them, promises to lead them, they left behind what they could not take and went.

On July 24, 1683, thirteen families—thirty-three persons—sailed from London on a ship felicitously named the *Concord*. In the words of James Claypoole, one of the passengers, "The blessing of the Lord did attend us so that we had a very comfortable passage, and had our health all the way." Such a passage was an exception in those days of preclipper ships. It must have seemed a good omen.

They landed at Philadelphia on October 6 and went to work at once. Winter was coming. Land had to be assigned, shelters built. On October 12 a warrant was issued to Pastorius for six thousand acres "on behalf of the German and Dutch purchasers." Penn would not give the land out to individuals. He wanted green country towns, like some he had known in Europe, with the settlers living in clustered houses, farming land outside, on which they did not live. Other advantages were obvious. Living close together, they could build churches and schools, and in times of distress help each other. Fourteen divisions were measured off, with the plots so arranged that they fronted on a winding Indian trail eventually to be called Germantown Avenue. On October 25 at a meeting with Pastorius they drew lots for choice of location, and Germantown came into being.

Up to this time the new arrivals had lodged with Pastorius, with as many as twenty accommodated in his house at one time. Immediately after the division the people began digging cellars and building huts. Many of them were weavers of fine linens, unprepared for the settler's life, or for the cold and hunger that came with winter. For some, conditions became so bad that they called their new home "Armentown," or poor town. But there was no turning back. They cut logs for houses and cleared land for crops, knowing that what they earned by hand or land would not be taken from them for a tithe or a fine. Quaker or Mennonite, they were free—free to wear their hats inside the house or out as they liked, and they could never be compelled to doff them to any man.

They expected to make Germantown a center for weaving. At the same time, they had to turn to farming, to raising Indian corn for bread and hominy, and flax and wool for weaving. Many of the fears they had talked about on the long voyage proved unfounded. The land was fertile and easy to till once the oaks and chestnuts and maples had been cut and burned. There were no wild animals fierce enough to impede their work. There was only an occasional rattlesnake to cause an alarm.

The expected trouble with Indians did not arise, partly because of Penn's treaties and scrupulous purchase of lands, partly because Pennsylvania was only sparsely populated by Indians when the first settlers arrived. The ones who appeared in Germantown were bronze oddities, with their bodies naked except for loincloths, with their faces painted red and blue. They may have looked strange and savage but they were not disturbers of the peace. A Quaker wrote back to England, "We have more distress from spoiled Christians than from the Indians."

Pastorius came and stayed, both as a leader in Germantown and historian of the early years of the settlement. At various times he served as recorder of the courts, compiler of laws and ordinances, bailiff, county judge, and member of the Assembly. To augment his income, he acted as conveyancer and notary. He wrote leases, deeds, marriage licenses, and wills. He maintained the *Germantown Grund und Lager Buch*, the *Germantown Ground and Lot Book*, in which the early land transfers were recorded. For the last twenty years of his life he taught the school in Germantown. Among other things, he wrote a primer, which was the first published textbook in the middle colonies.

Germantown prospered, and so did Pennsylvania. In 1685 Pastorius reported that there were fourteen houses in Germantown. By then, Pennsylvania had a population of approximately nine thousand, excluding Indians, and more settlers were arriving daily.

Among them came Peter Klever, weaver. It is not known when he came or by what route, though he may have come with the German families that included the Shoemakers, Lukens, and Conrads. They arrived in October 1685, on the *Francis and Dorothy*. He was certainly there as early as 1688, for the *Germantown Grund und Lager Buch* records that William Streypers granted fifty acres of land to Peter Clever—the name already partially Anglicized—on the first day of the first month of 1689. He could have arrived in the New World with enough money to purchase land at once, or he could have been here long enough to earn the money.

The spelling of his name did not come from him. In his early years in Germantown he had to make an *X* for his mark on both private and public papers. In later years he managed an awkward *P. C.* The name appears in the records in three spellings: *Klever, Clever, Cleaver.* It means the same in German and English: *cleaver,* one who or that which cleaves, especially like a butcher's cleaver. It is also related to *cliff* and *cleft.* The spellings *Klever, Kleber,* and *Clever* appear in German village records as early as the beginning of the eighteenth century. Cleaver is not an unusual name in England and it had appeared in Virginia long before Peter Klever arrived in Germantown. The spellings *Clever* and *Cleaver* were used almost interchangeably by his descendants into the third generation. Some of the latter have speculated that he came from a family of Cleavers who fled from England to Germany to escape religious persecution. Anything beyond the fact that he came from Germany remains speculation.

He was a German in an English colony, where English was spoken and colonial and other business was conducted in English. Within it Germantown was like a foreign colony, its citizens of Dutch or German nationality, its language spoken and written either Dutch or German. In 1691 there was an attempt to naturalize all settlers not English by birth. Peter Klever, along with some of his Germantown neighbors, presented himself for naturalization, but it was not immediately granted.

Germantown at the time was a village of scattered houses straggling along a dirt road, without a church or school, and too far from Philadelphia to be incorporated into that city. On June 12, 1689, William Penn issued a charter for the incorporation of Germantown, to become effective in 1691. Laws had to be formed, a court set up. Orders were issued for the building of stocks to punish offenders, and for a jail. Unwittingly they set a pattern for people moving west: jails would be built before schools and churches. At the same time trial by jury became a part of the system.

At the first court trial in Germantown, on December 5, 1694, Peter Klever appeared as a juror, serving with men whose names were often to appear in the records with his. Peter Schumaker was a burgess; Peter Keurlis and William Streypers were fellow jurors.

The court was called. Johannes Koster's declaration against Johanes Pettinger was read:

That the said Johanes Pettinger on the 19th day of the 11th month, 1694, at Germantown, did make an assault upon the said Johannes Koster, and did pull, push, and heavily handle against the King and Queen's peace, and to his the said Plaintiff's damage of three pounds, and thereof he brings suit.

Pettinger's response was that there was more in the plea than he had done.

The jury heard four witnesses and, finding Pettinger guilty, allowed Koster two shillings in damages. This was a mild sentence in a time when a person found guilty might receive a sentence of many lashes "well laid on."

Germantown grew and prospered. Weaving became the chief industry, especially the weaving of "very fine German linen." Richard Frame was moved to write a description that proved apt:

Where lives High *German* and Low *Dutch*
Whose trade in weaving linnen cloth is much;
There grows the Flax as also you may know
That from the same they do divide the tow. . . .

The residents could hardly have been more sober. It was said of them, "They would do nothing but work and pray, and their mild consciences made them opposed to the swearing of oaths and courts, and would not suffer to use harsh weapons against thieves and trespassers." Some went so far as to refuse jury or other government service because they would not swear an oath of any sort.

Three institutions imported from Europe were inimical to the development of democratic principles that were beginning to be felt: the Crown, the established church, and slavery. To the Quakers in Germantown Negro slavery became a matter of conscience. On April 18, 1688, Pastorius and others sent to the Friends' Meeting the first protest voiced in America against the holding of slaves, a protest that arose out of obvious circumstances. Slave trade was becoming increasingly profitable; slaves had been sold in Philadelphia; even some Quakers owned slaves. In a written statement, Pastorius made their feelings clear: "In Europe there are many oppressed for conscience sake; and here there are those oppressed which are of a black Colour."

In one of its parts the statement became more prophetic than perhaps Pastorius suspected:

If once these slaves (which they say are so wicked and stubborn men) should join themselves, fight for their freedom and handel their masters & mistresses, as they did handel them before; will these masters & mistresses tacke the sword at hand & war against these poor slaves, licke we are able to believe, some will not refuse to do? Or have these Negers not as much right to fight for their freedom, as you have to keep them slaves?

The resolution was not passed at the first meeting but was put over for further discussion. It was not an easy resolution, rousing as it did arguments for and against slavery not easily settled. English Quakers with large land holdings defended their right to own slaves. Many of them felt that clearing the wilderness was impossible without the use of slaves. Moreover, some genuinely felt that a slave was better off under Christian tutelage in America than he had been in a pagan tribe in Africa. These same arguments had an added point in other colonies: according to the Bible the blacks were the sons of Ham and decreed to be the servants of others.

The resolution came up in other meetings but was never passed, though slavery still lay heavy on many Quaker consciences. Thus quietly began the protest that was to engage people of conscience for the next one hundred and fifty years, a protest that was muted during the early frontier experience until the frontier experience itself brought the problem to the fore. Thus quietly the Quakers established the right of public dissent, a right not so well tolerated in New England and Virginia at the time.

Peter Klever must have been present at some of these meetings, but there is no record of whether he was against or for, or, like some, of no opinion.

On March 26, 1695, Peter Klever married Catharine Shoemaker at Abington Meeting. There is confusion about her name. In the minutes of the meeting she is called Catharine. When Peter Klever and his wife sold land in 1699 his wife signed her mark by the name Gertrud. Whether she had two given names or he had two wives is not known. Gertrud was the daughter of the Peter Shoemaker who came on the ship *Francis and Dorothy.* His name also appears as Shoenmaker and Shumacher. As his deeds to land were written in Dutch he may have been one of the Hollanders who fled to Germany and then to America.

It is certain that Peter Shoemaker suffered persecution in Germany for his Quaker beliefs. William Caton, an English Quaker who visited Kriegsheim in 1657, wrote the following:

> By means of their preaching, some persons there became convinced of the doctrine of the People called *Quakers.* This alarmed the Priests, who excited the Rabble, disposed to evil, to abuse those persons by scoffing, cursing, reviling, throwing Stones and Dirt at them, and breaking their windows.

In 1661, Caton added this statement:

> But above all others they seem to be bent against us as the offensivest, irregularest, and the perturbatiousest People that are of any sect.

The Church called on the Crown to help suppress dissenters. A fine of one shilling sterling was imposed on a Quaker each time he was caught in an assembly for worship. If the shilling was not forthcoming, property could be taken. On one occasion Peter Shoemaker had goods worth two guilders taken from him for religious assembly; on another, a cow. For refusing to bear arms he was fined two sheets worth three guilders. It was twenty years and more after these oppressions before he could go to America, taking with him his son Peter and his daughters Mary, Frances, and Gertrud.

Minutes of Quaker meetings contain considerable information on the marriage customs of the times. They regarded marriage not as a civil affair but as a contract between two persons. It was to be accomplished in the presence of Friends, with the bride and bridegroom taking each other by the right hand and reciting simple vows. There was no need for a more formal ritual, or for priest or magistrate. Their personal vows were enough to make the marriage binding. Not as a requirement, but as an honor, family and friends at the meeting signed the marriage record.

Quakers did not enter into marriage lightly. There was no publishing of banns, but the couples were expected to announce their intentions in meeting. Then a committee was appointed to learn, among other things, whether the man was "clear" of other women, the woman "clear" of other men. A Quaker could not marry a non-Quaker in meeting. If he married outside meeting, he could expect a committee to wait on him and point out the error of his way. After that, two courses were open: the spouse could become a Quaker or the couple could be read out of meeting.

Both Peter Klever and Catharine Shoemaker were Quakers and their marriage was duly accomplished and recorded in the minutes:

> Whereas Peter Cleaver and Catherine Shoemaker having declared their intentions of marriage with each other before two monthly meetings, Enquiry being made and found clear from all others on the account of marriage: Did accomplish their marriage in the unity of Ffriends [sic], as is signified by their marriage certificate.

The home and the community they entered as a married couple were still as much of the Old World as the New, perhaps more. Their manner of dress—not yet the dress approved for "plain" people— was European. The furnishings for their house and the utensils and tools they worked with were brought by ship from Europe. Much of their thinking was European, as if they were only a transplanted European community. Yet subtle changes were beginning to appear, especially in the freer use of thought and the open show of compassion for others oppressed or persecuted.

These are made clear in the story of Peter Cornelius Plockhoy. He was one of the early utopians who saw in America an opportunity to establish a perfect community. In 1662 he settled a group of twenty-five Mennonites on the South (Delaware) River. Two years later the English destroyed the settlement and carried off what belonged to, as they called it, "the Quaking society." They spared Plockhoy's life, but, with nothing left to work with, he was unable to rebuild his community. Then he passed out of sight for a number of years and came at last to Germantown, where the people took him in.

The Germantown *Rathbuch* records for the Third Session, twenty-fifth day, eleventh month [December 6], 1695 contain the following:

> To the blind man, Cornelius Plockhoy, is granted the citizenship free of charge; and is granted permission to reside at the end of the village on the street from Peter Clever's corner upon a lot one rod wide and twelve rods long whereon shall be built a house with garden which shall be his as long as he and his wife are living, but upon their death the property with all its improvements shall return to the community. It is further decreed that Jan Doeden and Willem Rittenhuysen will have charge of building the house.

Further arrangements appear in the record of the Ninth Session:

> At the end of the session, the business brought up by Peter Clever was discussed, which concerned William Streyper, who gave an acre of his land to Cornelius Plockhoy for as long as he and his wife are living. Trees shall be planted around the house; and after they have died or moved, the property shall be evaluated by an impartial committee, its worth determined, and sold. Half shall go to the Community and half to William Streypers; and the latter shall have the right to reclaim the land.

Plockhoy was blind; Klever illiterate. There is no record of conversations between them while they were neighbors. Neither are there records of conversations between either of them and Pastorius. Yet the three men—two of them political thinkers, the third an illiterate weaver—were sharing responsibility in making a community in which personal rights and property rights were protected.

Before the end of the century Germantown had about sixty families and several single persons. It was still a small village straggling along a winding road. For at least twelve years Peter Klever had lived there and worked at the weaver's trade. Like many around him, however, he saw that in America, as in Europe, the future of the artisan was limited, no matter how great his skill. To improve his lot he had to have land for himself and his children—the two already born and any others to come. For that, he would have to move out of the clustered village, onto acreage broad enough to be called a plantation, and he would have to move fast. New settlers were pouring in from Europe, and pressure for space was beginning to be felt in the older settlements. To meet the demand, new land was being opened, tier after tier, up the Delaware, up the Schuylkill.

In 1695 Peter Klever had bought fifty acres of land in Germantown toward Plymouth from William Streypers and then twenty-five acres of the uttermost half-lot on the west side of Germantown granted to John Silans. In 1699 he sold both tracts to Reynier Jansen, the first publisher of books in the middle colonies, for the sum of ninety pounds silver money of Pennsylvania. His name appears on the deed with his mark, and under it "Gertrud Klever" with her mark.

That transaction completed, Peter Klever bought fifty acres from David Potts in Bristol Township, some fourteen miles from Philadelphia, joining on Germantown, a part of the Robert Longshore grant. Soon after, he moved his family to this land, which he called his plantation. Apparently he did not give up weaving, as he still called himself Peter Klever, weaver, but he did devote time to farming and to acquiring more land.

The move from Germantown brought him nearer to Abington Meeting, where he was a member, as the Germantown Meeting had not yet been established. The Abington minutes record many services he rendered, especially as representative to quarterly and yearly meetings—proof of high regard for his piety and loyalty.

Others were moving out of Germantown, including Reynier Hermans Van Burklow, who had married another of Peter Schumacher's daughters. In 1704 he moved to Bohemia Manor, Cecil County, Maryland, next to Kenty County, Maryland, Kent County, Delaware, and across the Delaware River from Salem County, New Jersey, in all of which the Cleaver name survives. Perhaps sons, certainly grandsons of Peter Klever, followed him to Maryland and from there began their way west.

Bristol Township

THE MOVE TO BRISTOL TOWNSHIP, perhaps no more than eight miles, was not significant in distance, but it was a move farther into the forest, away from the cluster of houses in Germantown, to the more self-sufficient living on scattered plantations, the houses and barns set in small clearings. Dependence on Philadelphia was still necessary, more than on Germantown. Philadelphia had become an important seaport. Whatever tools and supplies the settlers had came through Philadelphia. Indian traders sold their furs to European markets through Philadelphia. Settlers brought their surplus corn and wheat and rye to market in Philadelphia. Philadelphia was growing in commerce. It was also becoming a cultural center that before long would surpass New York and compare favorably with Boston.

Bristol Township, probably established before 1684, was a part of Philadelphia County, one of the three original counties William Penn had decided upon before he left England. Bucks and Chester, the other two counties, were given clearly defined boundaries when they were established. Philadelphia, on the other hand, lay between those two and extended beyond them north, northwest, and northeast to some indefinite horizon. The part called Bristol Township when Peter Klever, now husbandman and weaver, moved there was gently rolling country covered with heavy forest.

New land had to be cleared, houses and barns built. Hardships of the earliest days in Germantown were almost a part of the past, but life still was not easy. Clearing land in the German manner was slow. Trees had to be felled and the logs burned. Some settlers left the stumps to rot in the field—to the German mind an obvious waste

[18]

of land. Even with the stumps left to rot a man had to work hard to clear five acres a year. Then with coulter and share he had to plough through the roots. Work horses were almost unknown. Oxen pulled the plows. Hauling was by oxcart. Planting and harvesting had to be done by hand. Wheat had to be cut by scythe or sickle and threshed and winnowed by hand. A man was likely to clear only as much land as he, his family, and his servants could manage. This early, children were an important part of the work force and large families much to be desired.

Peter Klever had four sons, all born too late to be of help in clearing his new land, and three daughters. Like others around him, he must have cleared his land with his own hands, with whatever help he could get from indentured servants and by sharing work with his neighbors. At the same time he kept up his trade as a weaver. That meant he had to work in field and woods by daylight and at the loom by firelight or candle. His wife and children could help at weaving. Flax had to be cut and stripped; wool had to be carded and spun.

Peter Klever taught his sons to be both farmers and weavers. Other education for both boys and girls was scant enough. Soon after 1700 a school was established in Germantown with Francis Daniel Pastorius as teacher. At about the same time a school was founded at Abington. Peter Klever's children may have attended either, or both, though the school at Abington was nearer his plantation. Schoolhouses of the time were likely to be of logs with puncheon floors, rectangular in shape, with log benches and a fireplace for heat. Pupils struggled over reading, writing, and arithmetic, with some results that can still be seen. Peter Klever made his *X* or, later, his *P. C.;* his children signed their names in clear bold hand.

Their religious life was centered in Abington Meeting, as it had been when they lived in Germantown. Abington Meeting had been in existence as early as 1683, first as meetings held in the homes of members, then in a meeting house built about 1699, before Germantown Meeting was established. Records do not show when Peter Klever became a member there. They do show his marriage. They also show that from time to time for the remainder of his life he represented Abington Meeting in quarterly meetings. To do so, he had to meet strict requirements for piety.

Abington Meeting became a kind of way station for Quakers headed west. In 1717, an English weaver, George Boone, Senior, arrived with his family and settled there. Here the Boone and Cleaver families began an association that was to last for generations and to extend a thousand miles and more into the wilderness. Some of the Boone sons were of the age of some of the Cleaver sons and, though born with an ocean between them, they took similar attitudes toward the frontier—that is, they wanted land, and they wanted adventure.

By the time the Boones arrived land in the vicinity of Philadelphia had been divided and subdivided. It was scarce and expensive. The Boones saw they would have to take their chances farther west, and they moved on, but not till George, Senior, had put the minutes of the Abington Monthly Meeting in order, a task that took time and provided an unusual record of Quakers and Quaker practices.

In 1718, George Boone, Junior, took out a warrant of land for four hundred acres in Oley Township, near Reading. Oley, in Indian meaning "hollow among the hills," is a beautiful and fertile valley surrounded by a rim of hills. It was about forty-five miles from Philadelphia by Indian trail, a distance men and women could cover on horseback in a hard day of riding.

At the time there was no Quaker Meeting at Oley. Abington Meeting gave the Boones a certificate to "settle in and towards Oley and join themselves to Gwynedd Meeting," the nearest to them. Until Exeter Meeting was approved at Oley various members of the Boone family continued at Gwynedd. There Squire Boone and Sarah Morgan, the parents of Daniel, were married on July 23, 1720, and the marriage duly recorded in the minutes:

> Ye said Squire Boone Took ye Said Sarah Morgan by ye Hand Did in A Solemn Manner Openly Declare he Took her To Be his Wife Promising To be Unto Her a Faithfull and Loveing Husband Untill Death Should Seperate Them And Then & There In the Said Assembly the said Sarah Morgan did likewise Declare.

The vows said, those present signed the marriage document.

In like manner Peter Cleaver, Junior, married Elizabeth Potts at Abington Meeting August 4, 1722. She was the oldest daughter of his father's friends and neighbors, David and Alice Croasdale Potts. In the record Peter, Junior, was described as a weaver and Alice Potts as a seamstress. Among those present at the marriage was Elizabeth's younger brother, Stephen, who became friend and employee of Benjamin Franklin.

Benjamin Franklin arrived in Philadelphia in 1723. In 1726 he was foreman in a printing house and assigned to teach apprentices, among them Stephen Potts. Potts joined the Junto Club, founded by Franklin, as a charter member; he was an early subscriber to the Philadelphia Library, also founded by Franklin; and he served as Franklin's bookbinder for many years. When he joined the Junto Club Franklin described him as "a young countryman of full age, bred to the same, of uncommon natural parts, and great wit and humor, but a little idle." These latter traits were hardly considered admirable by the Quakers.

In London, in 1758, Franklin learned that two of his old Junto friends had died: Stephen Potts and William Parsons. He wrote to the sender of the news:

Odd characters, both of them. Parsons a wise man that often acted foolishly; Potts a wit that seldom acted wisely. If *enough* were the means to make a man happy, one had always the means of happiness, without enjoying the thing; the other had the thing without ever possessing the means. Parsons even in his prosperity always fretting; Potts in the midst of his poverty always laughing. It seems, then, that happiness in this life rather depends on internals than externals; and that, besides the natural effects of wisdom and virtue, vice and folly, there is such a thing as a happy or unhappy constitution.

In time, some before his death, some after, all of Peter Klever's children were married: John to Elizabeth Taylor, Christian to William Melchior, Eve to a man named Adams, Derrick to Mary Potts, daughter of Thomas, Isaac to Rebecca Iredell, and Agnes to Richard Shoemaker. Only Christian married out of meeting. She and her "worldling" husband were married in Christ Episcopal Church in Philadelphia.

Peter Klever provided land for his sons and three remained on it or near it for a time at least. Peter, Junior, settled in Upper Dublin, only a few miles from his father's home where, like his father, he made his living farming and weaving. John remained on his father's plantation. Isaac, when he came of age, occupied land his father willed him in Cheltenham Township.

Only Derrick ventured west, and then only as far as Oley Valley.

For a quarter of a century Peter Klever prospered in land and goods. On November 10, 1727, he made his last will and testament and scrawled *PC* where the clerk wrote "his mark." Though he was now a man of property he still called himself Peter Klever, weaver. On January 26, 1728, George Shoemaker made "a true inventory of the personall and real property of Peter Cleaver Deceased." The actual date of his death is not known, but it occurred between the signing of the will and the appraisal of the estate. As his wife is not mentioned in the will, she probably died before him.

His will tells a good deal of how he lived and what he lived for. It is true to his religious belief and in the legal formula of the time:

> . . . Being very Sick & weak of Body but of Sound & perfect mind & Memory Praises therefor Given to the Name of Almighty God, Do make & Ordain this my Last Will & Testament in Manner & Form following (That is to say)—first & principally I Commend my Soul into the hands of Almighty God and My Body I Commit to the Earth to be Decently Buried at the discretion of my Executors herein after Named.

After directing the payment of just debts and funeral expenses as soon as possible after his death, he turned to the disposition of "that Temporal Estate as it hath pleased God to Bestow."

The land he had wrested from the wilderness was a first and deep concern. It was to go to his sons, and not to be sold. His daughters would receive their share in money and goods. To his daughters Christian and Eve he left each "ye sum of Twenty pounds Lawful money of Pensilvania" to be paid at the end of two years after his death, *if* the money could be raised "without selling any of my Lands or Tenements." Otherwise they were to receive only the interest. To his daughter Agnes he left ten pounds, one feather bed and furniture, one cow, and another ten pounds from the residue of the estate.

Though Pennsylvania was under English law and primogeniture was still the rule of inheritance in England, Peter Klever willed his land not to the eldest son nor to one son alone. Peter, Junior, and Derrick, having acquired land of their own, and in other townships, received shares of money but no land. The plantation went to John, who apparently lived on it at the time.

To Isaac, his minor son, he left another tract of land, also with explicit restrictions:

> I give & bequeath unto my Son Isaac Cleaver all that piece or parcel of land which I purchased of John Edwards situate in the Township of Chelten-

ham in the said county of Philadelphia Containing one hundred acres to hold to him & his heirs and assigns for ever he paying to My Son Peter Cleaver Derrick Cleaver and my daughter Agnes Cleaver the sum of thirty pounds to be equally divided & paid in three equal shares when my sd son Isaac Cleaver shall attain the full of twenty one years.

This last payment was to be made only if he could make it "without Straitning so much that he Shall be forced to Sell the sd Land or any part thereof."

A further provision demonstrates foresightedness in the use of land. His executors were to let the land to such persons as they thought convenient "upon such terms as the tenant or tenants shall not Sow any part thereof with Corn so often as to Impoverish the sd Land or any part thereof or to Destroy the Timber."

Peter Klever knew this land. The soil was moderately good when the settlers came. When it was first cleared it bore well for a few years. After that, it had to be cared for or it wore out. When it wore out the people had to move on if they expected to make a living from it. The ones who stayed could expect no more than a bare existence, the effect of overcropping and overclearing.

One person was left to be cared for: his indentured servant Mary. In terms of the times his bequest was generous: "It is my will that my servant Woman Mary shall have taken from & abaited of her term of servitude which by indenture she is obliged to serve one whole year and that she shall serve the residue of the term with my son Peter."

The inventory of Peter Klever's estate indicates some of the essentials of household living, and of his two occupations: weaving and farming. The house was furnished with five feather beds and furniture to go with them, five pairs of sheets, sixteen pillow cases, and five bolster cases. There were also tables and chests and fifteen chairs. For cooking and eating there were various iron pots and pot racks and three brass kettles, as well as pewter plates and dishes and drinking cups.

For weaving, there were a loom and equipment belonging to it, with some of the materials for work: fifty pounds of flax yarn and thirty-seven pounds of tow yarn, a rough yarn similar to that used in tow ropes and tow sacks. There were also products of the work: twenty-three yards of "linsewolsey"—a coarse cloth made of linen and wool—six yards of striped linen, and eight yards of tow linen.

The inventory listed three horses and two mares, with two saddles and two bridles, eight head of cattle, twenty-two sheep, and nine hogs. Farm tools included a wagon, two plows, a harrow, numerous hand tools, and a grindstone. Wheat, oats, and rye in stacks were appraised at about thirty pounds.

Peter Klever had lived in Pennsylvania about forty years. The land had been good to him. In the Quaker manner his body was committed to the earth with no mound or marker to show where, or when, he made his return to the land.

Oley Valley

DERRICK WAS THE FIRST of the Cleavers to travel the long road they were to follow west and his journey took him only as far as Oley Valley. In the earliest days of Pennsylvania, Quakers and others had expanded rapidly north into Bucks County and south into Chester County. By 1700 they were moving up the Schuylkill as well, pushing farther and farther into the west-running wilderness, often before the land could be formally purchased from the Indians.

Settlers were easily induced to go on up the Schuylkill. It was fertile country, well wooded, well watered, with gently rolling hills and broad valleys that stretched beyond as far west at the Susquehanna River and the Blue Mountains. The land was chiefly good for farming, but there were swift streams to turn the wheels of grist mills and saw mills. There was also limestone to be burned in primitive kilns, and iron ore in pockets waiting for digging. It was the presence of iron and lime that first drew the Philadelphia blacksmith, Thomas Potts, Derrick Cleaver's father-in-law.

News of the rich new land and the Quakers' tolerance reached the German Mennonites who had fled to England and also to those who had remained behind in Germany. By 1710 the Mennonite migration had begun, a migration that grew in numbers until they almost turned Pennsylvania into a German colony, a migration of people who paid their passage when they could, who indentured themselves when they could not, a migration of people attracted by the prospect of a good living in a land where they neither would have to pay tithes nor make forced contributions. Those unable to buy land moved on west and took it by squatters' rights. They were called "Pennsylvania Dutch" and honored for their thrift.

[25]

The Germans were followed by the Scotch-Irish from Northern Ireland, descendants of the Scots and English who had gone to Northern Ireland a hundred years earlier to put down the rebellious Irish. Among them there were also Highland Scots. The Germans were pacifist by temperament. The Scotch-Irish were warlike, with their instincts sharpened by generations of border warfare in Scotland and a century of fighting the Irish. They were Presbyterians still smarting from the Penal Act of 1704, which excluded all Presbyterians from civil and military service. Scots, just as warlike, though secure in their Presbyterianism, suffered from other discriminatory acts, including the loss of their living through inclosure, an act by which common lands and small farms were fenced in to make larger grazing areas for sheep. Pennsylvania promised them the personal and religious freedom they sought and they came by the thousands, only to find that the best land had been taken up by the Germans. The Scots had to take up hilly land or move on.

What was a boon to the oppressed in Europe was turned to profit by the Philadelphians. Pennsylvania, as a proprietary colony, was for the first fifty years free of levies from the Crown for defense, even when there were rumors of trouble from the French and Indians on the frontier toward the Ohio. The port was expanded. In 1733, Philadelphia built the "Great Road" to the mouth of the Conestoga River to accommodate the wagon traffic of new settlers going west, and of the corn and wheat and other products they shipped back to market. The Conestoga wagon, built on the Conestoga, became a symbol for the movement west; the "Great Road," or the "Philadelphia Road," as it was more often called, became the gateway.

As the Quakers moved away from Philadelphia they secured permission to set up other meetings, first in homes and then, as they could be built in meeting houses, among them Plymouth, Gwynedd, Horsham, and Upper Dublin. For a time Gwynedd Monthly Meeting, established in 1716, served the families farther up the Schuylkill and into Oley Valley. For a time it was the meeting place for the Boones, Lincolns, Hankses, and some of the Cleavers. On August 25, 1726, a minute was recorded: "Derick Clever produced a certificate on his own behalf and his wife from Abington Monthly Meeting In order to join with this meeting which was red & well received."

By now Quakers, who had been predominant until about 1720, found themselves outnumbered by "worldlings," and their political control threatened. After William Penn's death in 1718 Pennsylvania remained a proprietary colony and the rights passed to his heirs. Quakers, concentrated chiefly in Philadelphia, continued to control the colony by controlling the Assembly—a control they managed to maintain up to 1755, but with difficulty. Some of the new frontiersmen were anti-Indian, belligerent, so land hungry that they were willing to grab what they could without the formality of treaty or purchase. The goodwill that William Penn had so patiently built could hardly withstand their onslaughts. Ill feeling between Quaker and "worldling," as well as between white and Indian, marred Penn's "Holy Experiment."

To distinguish themselves from these "worldlings," and to separate themselves from the vanities of the times, Quakers dressed in sober gray, with broad-brimmed hats for the men and bonnets that half-hid the face for the women. Their neighbors, the Mennonites, also wore distinctive clothes—the women and girls long black dresses and black bonnets, the men and boys flat black hats. Considering buttons a show of vanity, they fastened their clothing with invisible hooks and eyes, or at times with a thorn. The men and boys cut their hair in what came to be called the "Dutch bob," and the men, after they were married, shaved only the upper lip.

In Philadelphia, outside these groups, European styles in clothes and manners prevailed. As the people moved west, however, a change was perceptible. Those who had fine clothes brought them out rarely. Those who did not, turned more to the rough fabrics like tow and linsey-woolsey. Men wore heavy boots, women rough shoes, all of their own making, but they had to be far into the wilderness before they would stoop to wearing Indian moccasins.

In the early days of Germantown, German Quakers and German Mennonites were almost indistinguishable, their worship at times held in common, their general mien that of sober piety. As the Mennonites increased in numbers and formed their own communities they came to be regarded as something different, at times odd. Slow to learn English, they spoke their form of Low German, which was soon called "Pennsylvania Dutch." Language remained a barrier, with the result that even English and Welsh Quakers came to regard them as "dumb Dutch" and to point to the brightly painted hex signs on their barns as evidence of superstitious belief.

No matter how one group regarded the other, however, they were all hard at work shaping the Pennsylvania countryside to the special characteristics it has kept for two hundred and fifty years: stone houses built from memory of stone houses in Germany, great barns, well-cared-for fields, herds of cattle and sheep. By hand they cleared the land of trees and stones and sowed their crops. With scythe and sickle they cut the grain, and threshed it with flail or the tread of horses' hooves. The land had to produce enough for them to live on, with some left over to be taken by packhorse or canoe to Philadelphia for exchange for the things they had to buy.

Derrick Cleaver was one of those farmers. He also became part owner of the Pine Forge on the Manatawny and through it developer in a small way of the iron industry on the Pennsylvania frontier. Iron works had been in operation in Virginia as early as 1715. Swedes on the Delaware before Penn arrived knew that some of the Pennsylvania hills and valleys were rich in minerals, especially iron. William Penn exploited this possibility for wealth in some of his advertisements. About 1716, mining prospectors leaped ahead of the settlers who were farmers and began the development of the iron industry. Thomas Rutter, a blacksmith and Peter Klever's neighbor and friend, moved to Manatawny Creek and built a furnace. He was soon joined by Thomas Potts, Derrick Cleaver's father-in-law, and then by Derrick Cleaver.

Thomas Potts, whose family gave the name to Pottstown, was born in England about 1680, and arrived in Germantown in 1698. He could not read or write, though he did learn how to sign his name. At first he was a miller and then sheriff of Germantown. He married Martha Keurliss, daughter of Peter, who was head of one of the original Germantown families. She was probably a pupil in the Germantown school taught by Francis Daniel Pastorius. After his marriage, Thomas Potts moved to Philadelphia, where town records show him as a butcher and victualer. Having prospered there, he bought two hundred and fifty acres of land from Thomas Rutter. There he built his mansion, "Popodickon," on Iron Stone Creek—a building still standing, not as a mansion but as a boarding house.

This purchase was made in 1730, but the Potts family had moved to the area perhaps as early as 1726, when Derrick and Mary Potts Cleaver were granted permission to change their membership from Abington to Gwynedd. They may have been there as early as 1720, when Potts, Rutter, and others built the Colebrookdale Furnace, named for Colebrookdale in England, on Iron Stone Creek.

The location was good. There were deposits of iron ore on Iron Stone Creek, swift streams for waterpower, and plenty of wood for burning charcoal. The process was primitive, but it helped many people earn a living. A farmer in slack times could cut wood and burn charcoal in an earth-covered mound with an opening at the top. Once the kiln was burning, he could tend it while working at other chores, watching only for gray smoke or blue: gray smoke, burning well; blue smoke, the wood turning to ashes from too much draft. Or he might dig ore from surface pockets and take it by pack horse or wagon to the furnace. Or he might, as the records show Derrick Cleaver did, burn limestone in a kiln on his farm and sell it by the wagon load to the furnace.

Furnace men burned charcoal, ore, and limestone together in a furnace, a stone kiln with a stone chimney high as a house. Heat from the charcoal fire melted the iron ore and limestone. The limestone rose to the top, taking with it most of the impurities from the ore. The liquid iron was then drained into wooden troughs, called "pigs," where it cooled into "pig" iron. Some of it was drained into molds for pots and other utensils. Most of it went on to forges for further refining.

Waterpower played an important part in this next step. Pigs of iron were heated over charcoal fires in the forges until they were soft enough to be shaped. Then they were placed under forge hammers —heavy pieces of cast iron on beams raised and lowered by waterpower. With the aid of these hammers iron workers could beat out remaining impurities and shape the iron into strips and rods, ready for use by blacksmiths.

Iron making did much to change the lives of settlers. Previously, iron and other metal products had to be imported from England, at such prices that farmers often had to shape their tools out of wood. Now there was iron at home for ploughshares and harrows, coulters and froes. There was iron to cast into stove plates to improve fireplaces, plates soon embellished by Scripture and proverbs and other bits of learning to be absorbed by the head while the body absorbed heat. There was iron for the invention and manufacture of the "Pennsylvania fireplace," more commonly called Franklin's stove. Most important for settlers going farther into the wilderness, there was iron for the manufacture of the gun called "the Pennsylvania rifle," "the long rifle," and then, after it was carried across the Alleghenies, "the Kentucky rifle." It was a long rifle—Daniel Boone's Tick-Licker was about five feet—a muzzle loader, slow to reload but of deadly accuracy.

The iron industry developed rapidly in spite of some grumbling from English manufacturers and shippers. In 1740 Thomas Potts built the Pine Forge on the Manatawny, with Derrick Cleaver and George Boone as part owners. Day books show the lively business of the commissary, payments made for loads of limestone and other products brought in by farmers, payments for pigs of iron shipped out. Its importance cannot be overemphasized. For the settlers moving west it provided three essentials: gun, ax, and cooking pot.

Settlers in Pennsylvania encountered for the first time what New Englanders had encountered years before—serious Indian trouble. William Penn had tried to forestall it through fair purchases and treaties, but the flood of immigrants was too great. He had no control over those who rushed beyond treaty boundaries and settled on Indian lands. When the Indians tried to drive them off they fought back. The Indians retaliated with attacks on older settlements. Though Penn's son, Thomas, had purchased the land that included Oley Valley in 1732, Indians ignored the purchase, as they had ignored other peace attempts.

In March of 1728 George Boone wrote to Governor Gordon in Philadelphia:

Our condition at present looks with a bad Vizard, for undoubtedly the Indians will fall down upon us very suddenly, and our Inhabitants are Generally fled, there remains about 20 men with me to guard my mill, where I have about 1000 bushels of wheat and flour; and we are resolved to defend ourselves to ye last extremity. . . . Wherefore I desire the Governor . . . send some Messengers to ye Indians and some arms and ammunition to us. . . .

Strange words for a Quaker pacifist, but the hardships and dangers were great. Those who fled had to go back toward Philadelphia, leaving the products of their labor to destruction by wandering bands. Those who stayed might suffer the tomahawk and scalping knife.

The first conflict came the following May. A party of Indians from outside the region came to houses in Amity and terrified the people, when "having been rude in several houses where they forced the people to supply them with victuals and drink, some of the inhabitants, to the number of twenty, a few of whom were armed with guns and swords" went in search of the Indians and killed their leader. The affair was settled without further loss, but fifty residents of Colebrookdale signed a petition to the Governor in which they did "humbly beg your excellency to take into consideration and relieve us, the petitioners hereof, whose lives lie at stake with us, and our poor wives and children, that are more to us than life."

Indian traders were as responsible as the land grabbers for the trouble. Against any better judgment they sold rum to the Indians. Manatawny, in Indian, means "where we drank liquor"—perhaps translatable into "where we got drunk with the traders." Indians, unfortunately, could not resist the temptation of "fire water." In 1731 a chief asked the Governor "that no Christians send any rum to Shamokin . . . to sell; when they want any they will send for it themselves; they would not be wholly deprived of it, but they would not have it brought by Christians. . . ."

Traders continued to sell them rum. Sometimes they also sold them guns and ammunition and scalping knives.

Indian trouble in Pennsylvania was minor, however, up to the outbreak of the French and Indian War in 1754. Whites cleared land and built homes; Indians moved their villages farther back. By purchase the Penns continued to legalize ownership of land grabbed by the settlers. Indian bands roamed through the settlements, with enough frequency to keep settlers afraid of Indian raids. Fortunately they needed each other for trade. As long as they had to barter with each other, some kind of communication was kept open. Also the time and place provided for the training of young men of the rising generation—Daniel Boone's—who would be the scouts and front men of the next migration in the ways of the Indians and of survival in the wilderness.

Derrick and Mary Cleaver were among the first members of Exeter Meeting in Oley Valley. With them were the Boones and Lincolns. In 1727, Mordecai Lincoln, ancestor of the President, with Benjamin Boone and others was appointed viewer of Tulpehocken Road from the Schuylkill River to Oley. He had moved from Chester County, where he had been in the business of mining and forging iron—in a company eventually sold to Rutter and Potts—and settled at Amity. Neighbors, but not solidly Quakers by affiliation, were the Hankses, who were in some way related to Nancy Hanks, the President's mother.

Exeter Meeting, through the detailed records kept, illuminates many of the religious problems of the frontier, including those of denominational discipline. In New England the advance into new territory was accomplished slowly, usually as new congregations could be formed and parsons appointed. In Pennsylvania and on west there was leapfrogging, more by individuals than by communities, and usually with little regard for religious affiliation. Unlike Puritan New England and Anglican Virginia, Pennsylvania, though founded as a Quaker colony, maintained religious tolerance as a basic principle. William Penn invited settlers of all religious persuasions, including Roman Catholics and Jews, and they came in numbers: Presbyterians, Anglicans, Lutherans, Moravians, and Amish. Separatism based on pluralism came into being with artificial barriers in religion and natural barriers in language.

Quakers, like others, struggled to keep their identity, an identity developed through about a hundred years. Quakers in Pennsylvania prospered and flourished; they built meeting houses, plain but permanent, as the need arose. Yet as they moved out on the frontier, farther from their centers in the eastern counties, as they rubbed shoulders more and more with "worldlings," they felt a need to draw closer together in discipline. Members in meeting were constantly reexamining their spiritual state, for themselves and for the reports they had to submit to quarterly and yearly meetings. Some found the discipline too rigid. At Gwynedd a member was disowned after he stated that he "owned the Discipline established amongst us" but acknowledged the way "too straight for him to walk in." The young were in danger of departing from the ways of their parents; parents were found wanting for not enforcing the doctrine on the young. Marriage outside of meeting, called "outward walking," became an increasing problem, especially in areas where the Quaker community was small, the "worldling" community large.

Minutes of the Exeter Monthly Meeting report both moral and doctrinal judgments. They begin in 1723 when George Boone was appointed by the Gwynedd Monthly Meeting to keep the record of births and deaths at Oley. They become more detailed in 1737, when a monthly meeting was allowed at Oley and the plain stone building now known as Exeter Meeting was erected. They record both complaint and settlement, the latter at times by arbitration, at times by confession of wrongdoing.

Not unusual is the following minute recorded in 1741:

These are to certify that I John James of Oley in the county of Philadelphia, being a professor of Truth, but not keeping it, did Deface the Head of a grey fox so that I received Pay for a red one, to the scandal of my profession: which I am sorry for, and do freely condemn the same, as witness my hand.

Derrick Cleaver had complaint made against him in the meeting for an affair depending between him and Rebekah Potts, an affair apparently financial. Two Friends were appointed to speak with Derrick Cleaver and they did. The minute is clear:

The friends appointed to speak with Derrick Cleaver report that they accordingly did; but as he seems slack in satisfying the Widow Potts, the Meeting therefore appointed James Boone and John Hughes to speak with him; and if he refuses to satisfy her, he must appear at next meeting to show his reasons for so doing.

James Boone was Squire's brother, Daniel's uncle.

The complaint dragged on from August to the next April, with Friends speaking to him from time to time. Then Derrick Cleaver presented in meeting a receipt in full account.

More often the complaints were doctrinal and few families escaped entirely.

Various members of the Boone family were complained of, most notably Squire, Daniel's father. In 1742 his daughter Sarah was "treated with for marrying out" and there were rumors that she was with child before she was married. Friends were appointed to speak to Squire and then to Sarah. The women appointed to speak to Sarah reported that she had indeed married a "Worldling" and from the looks of her not a day too soon. Squire answered the complaint as well as he could in meeting:

Squire declareth, that he was no ways Countenancing or Consenting to the said Marriage; but, confesseth himself in a Fault in keeping them in his House after he knew of their keeping Company, (but that he was in a great streight in not knowing what to do, seeing he was somewhat Sensible that they had been too Conversant before) and hopeth to be more Careful for the future.

Five years later he had to come before the meeting again for a "disorderly marriage" because his son Israel had married a girl who was not a Quaker. This time Squire stood for personal freedom. He insisted on his son's right to marry whom he pleased. Friends tried to "bring him to a sense of his Outgoings," but he did not change his mind. He was disowned, though his wife and others in his family remained members.

Derrick Cleaver's daughter appeared in the minutes in 1758: "Elizabeth Cleaver has gone out in marriage with one not of our Society, having been precautioned; therefore Friends can do no less than Testify against her, and appoints Jane Hughes and Deborah Boone to get a Testimony drawn against next meeting."

This was a formidable committee. Deborah Boone, the wife of George, Junior, was a preacher in the Quaker faith and often charged to counsel with straying members. She reported that the committee had tried to see Elizabeth Cleaver but had failed. In spite of their efforts she did not come before meeting to confess her fault. Later minutes refer to her as "Elizabeth Cleaver (alias Curtz)," proof that her marriage had not been recognized, and therefore she had been disowned. Moreover, she had apparently married into the Pennsylvania Dutch, a graver error in the sight of some of her English neighbors. By the time her children were born the name had been changed from *Curtz (Kurtz)* to *Short,* an exact translation.

On the frontier complete separatism was not possible; neither was total absorption. Religious and ethnic groups had to settle into a kind of coexistence, an easier state as lines drew thin farther west, and now south.

This turning southward was probably predictable from the founding principles of Pennsylvania—personal freedom and religious freedom—and the promises of land. These principles were affirmed in the Pennsylvania Charter, known as the Charter of Liberties, which was approved by the General Assembly on October 28, 1701. The most democratic in all the American colonies, this charter contained three highly significant articles: the right of freedom of worship, the election of officials by vote, and the right of the individual to have "any Complaint, Matter, or Thing" heard in a court of justice. These principles persuaded settlers to come and settlers, having known them, carried them as precious rights when they moved on.

At first any government business required a trip back to the seat, to Philadelphia, at first on horseback and later, as roads were built, by wagon or buggy. Then, as distances became too great, county

government moved to the frontier. To the three original counties—
Bucks, Chester, and Philadelphia—others were added: Lancaster in
1729; York, 1749; and Cumberland, 1750, all on the direct way west
from Philadelphia. In 1752, Berks County, in which the Oley Valley
lies, was formed from Philadelphia County. As government moved,
roads developed. By 1750 the Philadelphia Road offered passage all
the way to the Yadkin River in North Carolina.

In 1736 the Penns had negotiated a deed with the Indians "for
all the River Susquehanna with the lands lying on both sides thereof,"
eastward to the head of its branches, westward "to the setting of the
sun." This deed extended from Berks County across the Susquehanna and downward through the Cumberland and opened a
way into Virginia. Settlers who had been prevented from continuing
the straight line west by mountains and hostile Indians could now
turn south through the Cumberland Valley and across the Potomac.
In 1738 Virginia and North Carolina promised religious freedom to
Presbyterians and the stream of Scotch-Irish gratefully accepted
their invitation to take up land. They soon found, however, that
Germans who were willing to become nominal Anglicans or to pay
the Anglican head tax had already taken up the best valley land. The
Scotch-Irish were forced to take their land on the ridges and in the
hollows and add their part to the beginning of Appalachia.

Derrick and Mary Potts Cleaver watched members of the
Cleaver family leave old Pennsylvania settlements for these new
frontiers. They watched friends and neighbors pack up and go. John
Lincoln, the great-grandfather of the President, left about 1750 and
went through the Valley of Virginia to the present Rockingham
County, where he settled permanently. At about the same time the
Hanks family, whose relationship to Nancy Hanks is claimed, left
Berks County and settled for a time on the South Branch of the
Potomac River. Squire Boone, who had been disowned by the Quakers of Exeter Meeting, disgraced, sold out and began the long trek
south that eventually brought him to the Yadkin River in North
Carolina. His son Daniel, sixteen or seventeen at the time, already
schooled somewhat in the ways of the wilderness and the Indians
who inhabited it, continued his schooling along the way, not in books
but in the mountains and valleys they passed through.

Derrick and Mary Cleaver had land and part ownership in the
iron works. They stayed. Others—some with land as good, some with

land already wearing out through erosion and overcropping—went. The reasons beyond the search for new land are complicated. A restlessness seems to have driven men and women to risk certain hardship, certain death for some of their number, to new parts of the frontier. The desire to look beyond the next river, the next mountain, was like a scourge. And the thought of a New Canaan was often with them, the thought of a place of milk and honey, a place with land, water, timber untouched by human hands—if possible, never before seen by eyes of white men. Such a place was theirs, they believed, if they were willing to travel far enough south and west by the Philadelphia Road.

Mary Cleaver died about 1757. On October 25, 1767, Derrick Cleaver, able now to call himself a yeoman-freeholder—made his will and signed it with a shaky hand. He died the next February. The preamble, in words carried over from Old England, is like a statement of faith:

Be it remembered that I Derrick Cleaver of the Township of Douglas, in the County of Berks and Province of Pennsylvania, Yeoman, being now far advanced in years, but yet of sound Mind and Memory for which Mercy and favor, may I ever Praise the great Author of my Being; And at times feeling the Simptoms of Mortality, through the decay of Nature, but Relying on the Merits of my Redeemer, hope for a happy change from this Life, to that which is to come of Eternal Peace and Rest, And in Daily Expectation of such a Change, Do make and Ordain this My last Will and Testament in manner & form following.

This formula says a great deal about the character of early Pennsylvania people, especially their piety, their dependence on God, their belief in a life to come. Eternal *peace* and *rest*. Such rewards were obviously sustaining for pioneers who could expect little of either on the frontier.

Items of bequest show how well Derrick Cleaver—farmer, lime burner, appraiser of estates—had prospered. To his son John he left three hundred pounds current money of Pennsylvania, together with all his wearing apparel, one-half of his corn, and one-half of his hay.

To his daughter Mary, unmarried at the time, he left one hundred and fifty pounds, together with his riding mare and one cow, which she was to choose, all of his pewter and two iron pots of her choice, plus one-half of his corn and one-half of his hay. To the last he adds a touching note: ". . . And it is my will that my son shall harvest and thrash out her shear of the corn and carry it upstairs for her."

No other children are named in the will, but sums of money were left to grandchildren: John and Nathan Hatfield, sons of Adam and Martha Cleaver Hatfield; Mary Keely; and John and William Short. Mary Keely's parents are not known, but her father may have been the Valentine Keely who witnessed the will with his mark. John and William Short were no doubt the sons of Elizabeth Cleaver, who married a Kurtz out of meeting. It is possible that some of his children—some reports say he had nine or more—had already gone west to make their own clearings in the wilderness.

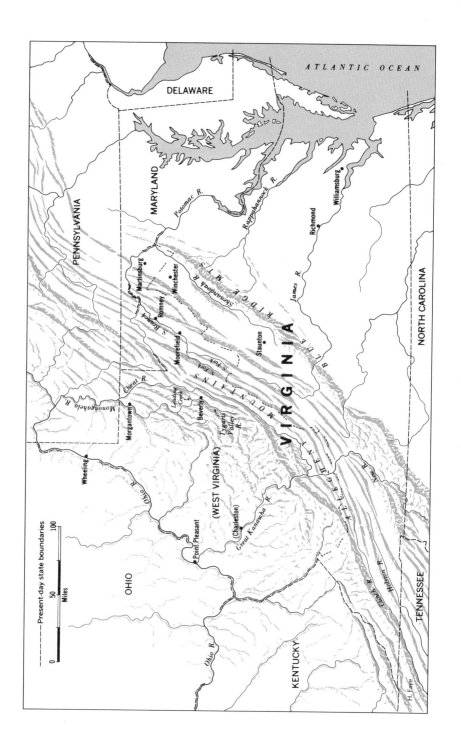

ATLANTIC OCEAN

DELAWARE

MARYLAND

PENNSYLVANIA

Potomac R.

Rappahannock R.

Williamsburg

Richmond

James R.

Martinsburg

Winchester

Romney

S. Branch

Moorefield

BLUE RIDGE MTS.

Shenandoah R.

Staunton

S. Fork

N. Fork

Cheat R.

Monongahela R.

Morgantown

Leading Creek

Beverly

Tygarts Valley R.

VIRGINIA

Wheeling

(WEST VIRGINIA)

Ohio R.

Point Pleasant

(Charleston)

Great Kanawha R.

New R.

ALLEGHENY MOUNTAINS

NORTH CAROLINA

OHIO

Clinch R.

Holston R.

KENTUCKY

Ohio R.

H. Faye

TENNESSEE

Present-day state boundaries

100

50

Miles

0

Virginia

ONCE THEY LEFT THE CUMBERLAND VALLEY THESE SETTLERS FROM PENNSYLVANIA ENCOUNTERED A WAVE OF MIGRATION MOVING ACROSS THE BLUE RIDGE MOUNTAINS FROM THE OLDER SETtlements of Virginia. Land had been their chief concern in going to Virginia, and land they found. They also found a more stratified society and the pronounced presence of the Crown, the Anglican Church, and Negro slavery. They also found a culture different from their own, a culture cohesive enough—English enough—that to an extent they were shaped by it, loosely structured enough that they in turn helped shape it. They had gone from the comparative freedom of Penn's "Holy Experiment" to a colony in which laws were decreed to conform as nearly as possible to those of England, in which both colony and county were ruled by aristocrats, directly or indirectly appointed by the Crown. They had gone from the congregationalism of nonconformist churches to the rule of the hierarchy of the Anglican Church, to the power of bishops and of parish vestries privileged to fill their own vacancies. The people had no more voice in the church than they had in government, a condition that had existed in Virginia in varying degrees since the beginning on May 24, 1607.

On that date Captain John Smith was one of one hundred and forty-four colonists who entered Chesapeake Bay and founded Jamestown, the first permanent settlement in the colonies and a base for westward expansion through Virginia. This expansion, largely agricultural, was slow. As new generations came of age they cleared new land and built new homes, usually on the fringes of older, established communities, rarely in the deeper solitudes of the wilderness.

Instead of the log houses of the rapidly moving frontiers, they built brick homes, many of them substantial, a number of them manorial and named, as was the English custom. Government and the Anglican Church, traveling hand in hand, kept up with this slow progress. In 1700 the colonial government was moved to Williamsburg. At about the same time settlers moved farther up the rivers into the Blue Ridge Mountains. They had taken a hundred years to travel about a hundred miles.

There were rumors of better land beyond the Blue Ridge. In 1670 the first white men, traders with the Indians, had crossed over. Before them lay the broad Valley of Virginia, a vast rich land, uninhabited, used by the Indians only for hunting. Beyond rose another wall of mountains, the Alleghenies, taller than the Blue Ridge, more forbidding. Some of these traders found what is now called the New River and, thinking that the western ocean lay just a little farther on, measured the water for tidal rising and falling. Others went up the Potomac River and discovered that it made a gap through the Blue Ridge, and farther on a gateway to the West. Eventually hunters, long hunters, followed the upper branches of the Potomac and then Indian trails, which they followed till they came to west-flowing rivers and knew they had found pathways to the middle of the American continent. Not settlers themselves, these traders and hunters brought back stories of fertile valleys and vast unclaimed plains, stories that whetted the appetites of the land hungry in Virginia and Pennsylvania.

In 1716, with the aim of exploring new territory for settlement, Governor Alexander Spottswood of Virginia led an expedition on horseback over the Blue Ridge and across the Shenandoah River. Leaving scouts to explore as far as the foot of the Allegheny Mountains, he claimed the land in the name of King George I and made a slow return journey to Williamsburg. There he gave lavish descriptions of this beautiful valley, a settler's dream.

The significance of his exploration was obvious to Spottswood and he sought to memorialize it. In respect to his companions and the many horseshoes they wore out on rocky trails, he established "The Transmontaine Order, or Knights of the Golden Horseshoe." To all who had accompanied him he gave a gold horseshoe inscribed *Sic jurat transcendere Montes,* which can be translated, "Thus he swears to cross the Mountains." These words had little meaning among people on the edge of the wilderness, even if they heard them, but that did not matter. Looking at the mountains towering before them, they did not need a motto. They had their own will to see what lay on the other side, first of the Blue Ridge and then of the Alleghenies.

Land speculation followed almost immediately, a speculation that yielded to two population pressures: one in Virginia east of the Blue Ridge, the other in Pennsylvania. Spottswood's first concern was for the Virginians, the ones who had been slowly advancing up three rivers—the Roanoke, the James, and the Rappahannock. These rivers had provided waterways for canoes, land passages for pack-horses, and men on foot. Now they provided gaps through the mountains for settlers waiting for the chance to cross.

They had to wait no longer. They were now invited to cross over and were offered special inducements such as exemptions from taxes and other public obligations. Like their fathers before them, they could acquire land under the headright system, but now the system was made more favorable to the settler. He could buy a headright of fifty acres on the payment of five shillings and there was no limit to the number of headrights he might purchase.

A system even more attractive to land speculators was devised in 1730. It provided that those receiving grants could prove them by settling one family to each one thousand acres. A part of the aim was to promote rapid settlement, a part to form a buffer against the French, who were expanding their operations in the Ohio Valley. Speculators were there aplenty, chiefly from Virginia and Pennsylvania. So were the potential settlers, especially those passing through Pennsylvania—a flow rising almost to a tide as German Mennonites, Scotch-Irish Presbyterians, dissenters under various names from Ireland and Scotland came on foot or on horseback, lured by the promise of land, by the promise not of religious freedom but at least of religious tolerance. The Toleration Act of 1689 had made it possible for Presbyterians and others to settle in Virginia without first securing permission. Permission had to be secured for any public worship other than that of the Anglican Church.

Many of the speculators from Virginia were men of means— landed gentry, lawyers, merchants, clergymen—some of them educated in England, others nurtured in English manners and customs remnant in Virginia. Many of them moved to the frontier with their families, their indentured servants, their Negro slaves, and built plantation homes in the style of those they had left behind. In as orderly a manner they transported church and government to the frontier, to the part that was Virginia east of the Alleghenies. Thus their frontier was in sharp contrast to that of the backwoodsmen who rushed around them and ahead of them, carrying with them no particular order of society, allowing order to develop only as need became imperative.

The Valley
of Virginia

THE FIRST GRANTS of headrights west of the Blue Ridge were made on June 13, 1728. Before the settlers could claim their land, however, a dispute arose over title, especially over lands that agents of Thomas, Lord Fairfax, insisted lay within his boundaries. This grant, which descended to Fairfax in 1722, included all the land between the Rappahannock and Potomac rivers to their headwaters. A part of the problem of ownership was that no one had defined the head of the Potomac or of the Rappahannock. In 1735 Fairfax arrived in Virginia to settle the boundary question. Because they could not agree on procedure, the governor appointed one commission, Fairfax another, with instructions that each commission would select its own surveyors and make its own survey. The surveyors, including Peter Jefferson, father of President Jefferson, for the Crown and Thomas Lewis for Fairfax, began their surveys on September 26, 1736. Ten years later, after a court had decided in favor of Fairfax, they found and marked the spot where the rainfall divides, part flowing east into the Potomac, part flowing west into the Cheat and on down the Mississippi. There they set up a stone, called the Fairfax Stone. Then they drew a line, the Fairfax Line, from the north branch of the Potomac to the Conway, a tributary of the Rappahannock. This line marks the western boundary of the Northern Neck, and the Fairfax Stone marks the meeting place of two states, Maryland and West Virginia, and of four counties. Through this settlement Fairfax came into possession of an area that at present embraces twenty-five counties, six million acres of land, a major portion of the Shenandoah Valley.

Before and while the boundary dispute was going on Fairfax and his agents were encouraging settlers to take up land. The first settler in the Valley of Virginia was probably Adam Miller, a German who settled there with his family and some friends about 1727. He was soon followed by the Van Meters, Isaac and Joseph, and Jacob Stover. In 1731 Joist Hite settled with sixteen families from Pennsylvania near the present Winchester, Virginia. In 1730 Alexander Ross and Morgan Bryan of Pennsylvania settled a colony of Friends who built Hopewell Meeting House in 1734, a stone building about six miles to the north of Winchester. This was probably the first congregation in the valley and to it the Cleavers went as they moved west.

Of the early settlers in the valley, approximately one-third were Virginians from east of the Blue Ridge, the other two-thirds mostly from Pennsylvania, mostly German and Scotch-Irish, with a sprinkling of New Englanders. Streams of westward migration were now apparent. New Englanders, especially those from Connecticut, came across New York and into the part of Pennsylvania they claimed for Connecticut. Those who wanted to go farther west found themselves confronted by mountains and hostile Indians. They had little choice but to join those already flowing through Pennsylvania down the Cumberland Valley and across the Potomac. There they began to meet the Virginians who had moved from Tidelands to Piedmont and from the Piedmont over the Blue Ridge into the valley.

Some stayed on the first land they could take up. Others going farther south merged the two streams and traveled the road together. By 1750 the road was there for traveling, called sometimes the Philadelphia Road, sometimes the Great Road, on the northern end marked and cut and used for half a century, toward the southern end at times no more than a blazed trail. Mile by mile, four hundred and fifty miles all told, the road had been opened west as new settlements came into being—Lancaster, York—across the Susquehanna, across the Potomac, down the Valley of Virginia between the walls of the Blue Ridge and the Alleghenies, till at the lowest part it veered east into the Yadkin Valley of North Carolina, to admit another migrant stream flowing west from the Carolinas. The road itself was becoming a kind of dividing line between frontiers, joined with the Alleghenies a geographical boundary that also separated by character, by temperament the settlers to the west of it from the settlers to the east of it—boundary but as well a timetable of westering. Before it, settling new frontiers was step by step, up rivers, along Indian trails—new farms added tier after tier only as the population increased, as the wilderness was cleared. With it, settlers were able to make long leaps, to thrust themselves into the wilderness, deeper than their forebears had dared to go. It was also a lifeline. With it they could reach out, reach back to Philadelphia, their center of trade, their market for hides, tobacco, corn, and whiskey. Because of it a person who could write and was of a mind to could send letters back and, if he stopped long enough in one place, expect a reply.

On this road Germans who had prospered in Pennsylvania traveled in ease, in wagons or on horseback, stopping at homes that were gradually being turned into inns, eating and drinking well. There were also Virginia gentlemen acquainted with Williamsburg life, of which it was said, "They live in the same neat manner, dress after the same modes, and behave themselves exactly as the gentry in London; most families of any note having a coach, chariot, berlin, or chaise."

The servants, on whom such a life depended, were English, Scotch, or Negroes—the latter likely to be slaves, and slaves traveled the road with their masters. These men, Pennsylvanian or Virginian, were likely to be educated. Some brought books with them—books that at least reminded them of Europe.

On the same road came the poor, walking, carrying everything they owned, living off the land, sleeping out at night, enduring whatever came to them for the hope of a home of their own. Countless numbers of these were Scotch-Irish, a people displaced once, from Scotland to Ulster, to form a buffer between the English and the Irish, unwittingly to become a kind of buffer between the colonies and the Indians. They had lived with border warfare and were used to hardships as severe as anything they would find in the wilderness. Among them were indentured servants, men and women who had agreed to serve seven years for their passage—most of whom had served and been freed, others who had simply been unwilling to work out the time and had headed toward that window of escape for any who did not conform—the wilderness. Among these, chiefly from Virginia, were convicts from English jails, sent out to save their keep and to relieve overcrowding.

These, if they brought a book at all, brought the Bible, and few among them were able to read it, though many of them carried Bible stories and a sense of the Gospel in their minds. They also carried in their heads rhymes from childhood, religious songs, ballads, fiddle tunes—some straight from England, some from Scotland to Ireland

and then to America—music and words to pass the time and bring back thoughts of home as they traveled the wilderness the lower length of the Appalachian Mountains, all the way down to the Yadkin, the Holston, the Clinch.

Land speculation created new settlements at a rapid pace. New settlers in such numbers forced the creation of new counties west of the Blue Ridge: Frederick and Augusta in 1745 and Hampshire in 1754. It also led to the organization of companies for the purpose of land speculation. Of these, the Ohio Company, organized in 1747, was historically the most important. The company secured a five-hundred-thousand-acre tract across the Allegheny Mountains and between the Great Kanawha and Monongahela rivers. Their purpose was to develop a new province to be called Vandalia in honor of Queen Charlotte, who was supposedly descended from the Vandals. Theirs was a favored grant: they were exempt from quitrent and other duties for a period of ten years and then would pay quitrent only on lands under cultivation.

They began recruiting settlers among the Germans in Pennsylvania. However, when the Germans learned that in order to settle in Virginia they had to become members of the Anglican Church or pay the head tax laid on dissenters, they refused to go. Moreover, the British were reluctant to see a fourteenth province added to the thirteen already in existence. Though the Ohio Company engaged the interest of many prospective settlers in their project, Vandalia never came into being. Virginia had looked on it as a buffer colony on the west slopes of the Alleghenies. Instead they had only the scattered squatters who grabbed land and held it with the rights granted by long knife and long rifle.

Among the Quakers who came into the Valley of Virginia there were enough in Frederick County to set up meetings at Hopewell, Opequon, Apple Pie Ridge, and Crooked Run. They wanted land, but following William Penn's example, insisted that it should first be acquired from the Indians by fair purchase and deed. On the twenty-first day of the fifth month, 1738, Thomas Chaukely, a Quaker minister, set forth the principles that he thought should guide the Quakers in their dealings with the Indians:

To the friends of the monthly meeting at Opequon:
Dear friends who inhabit the Shenandoah and Opequon:

Being in years heavy, and much spent and fatigued with my long journeyings in Virginia and Carolina, makes it seem too hard for me to perform a visit in person to you; therefore I take this way of writing to discharge my mind of what lies weighty thereon; and

First: I desire that you be careful (being far and back inhabitants) to keep a friendly correspondence with the native Indians giving them no occasion for offense; they being a cruel and merciless enemy where they think they are wronged or defrauded of their rights. . . .

Second: as nature had given them and their forefathers possession of this continent of America, or this wilderness, they had a natural right thereto, and no people, according to the law of nature and justice, and our own principle which is according to the glorious gospel of Christ, ought to take away or settle on other men's lands or rights without consent, or purchasing the same agreement of parties concerned; which I suppose in your case is not yet done.

Third: Therefore my counsel and Christian advice to you is, my dear friends, that the most reputable among you do with speed endeavor to agree with and purchase your lands of the native Indians or inhabitants. . . .

Fourth: Who would run the risk of the lives of their wives and children for the sparing of a little cost and pains? I am concerned to lay these things before you, under an uncommon exercise of mind, that your new and flourishing little settlement may not be laid waste. . . .

Fifth: Consider that you are in the province of Virginia, holding what rights you have under that government; and the Virginians have made an agreement with the Indians to go as far as the mountains and no farther; and you are over and beyond the mountains and therefore out of that agreement. . . .

Sixth: If you believe yourselves to be within the bounds of William Penn's patent from King Charles the Second, which will be hard for you to prove, you being far southward of his line; yet if that done, that will be no consideration from the Indians without a purchase from them. . . .

This was the Quaker conscience speaking—conscience and practicality, but little heed was paid to it, partly because there was little sympathy for such a sentiment in Williamsburg, partly because of the attitude of a majority of the settlers, especially the Scotch-Irish, toward Indian rights. In their opinion Indians had no concept of ownership of land. Tribes came and went over it, using it when they wanted to, abandoning it when they felt like it. Individuals did not stake out claims to any part of it; they had no way to hold it in fee simple. Vast tracts, in the settlers' point of view, lay unused. They moved easily to the argument that they were fully entitled to take the land.

Anyway, Quakers with their strange ways and strange speech were not welcome in Virginia. They became the object of "An Act for Suppressing the Quakers," which begins as follows:

Whereas there is an unreasonable and turbulent sort of people, commonly called Quakers, Who Contrary to the Laws do Dayly gather together unlawfull assemblys and Congregations of people, teaching and publishing lies, miracles, false visions, prophecies, and doctrines which have influence upon the Communities of men, both Ecclesiasticall and Civil, endeavoring and attempting thereby to destroy religion, laws, communities, and all bonds of civil Societies leaving it arbitrarie to everie Vaine and Vitious person Whether men shall be safe, laws established, and Governors rule, hereby disturbing the Publique peace and just interest. . . .

In spite of such anti-Quaker enactments, Quakers continued to move into the valley. Because the seat of provincial government was far away and county government was often indifferent, at times sympathetic, they knew that enforcement was well-nigh impossible. There were not enough government men to patrol every remote cove and valley; they could nominally become Anglicans and worship as they pleased; neighbors who also cherished religious freedom likely would not turn them in. Then relaxation of such enforcements came. In 1752, the House of Burgesses of Virginia offered Protestant settlers west of the Alleghenies ten years' exemption from taxes, an exemption later increased to fifteen years.

In that same year Ezekiel Cleaver, third son of Peter Cleaver, Junior, and grandson of Peter Klever, received a grant of a thousand acres of land from Lord Fairfax on the southeast slope of Bear Garden Mountain, on Mill Creek, not far from the present Capon Bridge. He was then thirty-two years of age and father of a family, living in a log hut west of Winchester, off the main road from Winchester to the Potomac, but not out of reach of Cleaver relatives and friends in Hopewell. In the same year his father owned land on the head branches of Hog's Creek in Frederick County.

These Cleavers were at the outer edge of the frontier.

Westward expansion, especially through such land schemes as that of the Ohio Company, inevitably brought English settlers up against French claims and French forces. Differences between English and French methods of colonization became more sharply defined. For the most part the French had been content to get their use of the land out of profits from trapping furs and from the Indian trade. English settlers, on the other hand, wanted to live on the land and eventually conquer the wilderness. They were willing to buy the land when they could; when they could not they simply squatted on a place that pleased them and staked out a "tomahawk claim." Log cabins appeared farther and farther from settled areas. It became quite clear that the more of the wilderness the English conquered the less the French had left to them.

Alerted to these British encroachments, the French began to stir up the Indians, who sided with them because they also resented settlers on land that had been their hunting ground. The time seeming right, the French began to press for control of the Ohio territory, including land that Virginia claimed by charter. The French began building a line of forts that was to stretch from Lake Erie to the forks of the Ohio. Alarmed at this move, Governor Dinwiddie of Virginia ordered George Washington, then a twenty-one-year-old lieutenant, to meet the French and warn them that they were on Virginia territory. With a small party of men he met the French in December 1753, and was told in no uncertain terms that they meant to take and hold the Ohio.

Even more alarmed, Dinwiddie, in January 1754, ordered the construction of a fort at the Forks and sent a work party to do the job. These were to be followed by a force of one hundred and fifty men under Washington who would occupy the fort. At Will's Creek, at present Cumberland, Maryland, Washington met the work force and learned that the French were already building Fort Duquesne at the forks. Washington moved toward the forks and built what they called Fort Necessity, where they were defeated by the French on July 3, 1754, and forced to surrender. This gave the French control of the Ohio and marked the beginning of the Seven Years' War, on the frontier more appropriately called the French and Indian War.

Fearing that the whole of the western territory would fall to the French, Governor Dinwiddie prevailed upon Whitehall to send two Irish regiments of five hundred men each under the command of General Edward Braddock. They arrived at Alexandria, Virginia, in late March 1755, and the slow, discouraging process of organizing the campaign began. After delays and slow marches he assembled at Winchester a force of some fourteen hundred British regulars and four hundred and fifty colonials under the command of then Lieutenant Colonel George Washington. These colonials were for the most part recruited from settlements on the edge of the frontier. A contemporary document reads, "One of the Cleavers has gone off to fight with Braddock."

On June 5 Braddock wrote to Whitehall from Fort Cumberland, Will's Creek:

On the 10 of May I arrived at this place and on the 17th the Train joined me from Alexandria after a March of twenty seven days, having met with many more Delays & Difficulties than I had even apprehended, from the Badness of the Roads, Scarcity of Forage and a General want of Spirit in the People to forward the Expedition.

I have at last collected the whole Force with which I propose to march to the attack of Fort Duquesne, amounting to about two thousand effective Men, Eleven hundred of which Number are Americans of the Southern Provinces, whose sloathful & languid Disposition renders them very unfit for Military Service; I have employed the properest Officers to form and Discipline them, and great pain has and shall be taken to make them as usefull as possible.

The colonials had their shortcomings; they were also experienced in wilderness warfare. In the official report of the campaign there was this complaint: "The frequent Conversations of the Provincial Troops and Country people was that if they Engaged the Indians in their European manner of Fighting they would be Beat. . . ." British officers ignored these conversations.

In the face of what must have seemed well nigh insurmountable difficulties Braddock began his march toward Fort Duquesne, taking time as he went to build a good wagon road. He advanced thirty miles in eight days. After another eight days, on receipt of a report that Fort Duquesne was about to be strengthened, he pushed forward with twelve hundred men, some cannon, wagons, and packhorses. On July 8 he reached a ravine only eight miles from Fort Duquesne, beside a height that would give them a vantage point. The first alarm was given by fire on the advance guard, from some nine hundred French troops and Indians who had occupied the height and flanked them on both sides. The battle that followed is classic in annals of warfare—in the differences between Europe and frontier, in the difference between red-coated British soldiers who marched forward in battle line and colonials who fought from bank to bank, tree to tree in the way they had learned from the Indians. The result was graphically recorded in the official report:

... That an order was then given to the main Body to advance; that they accordingly marched forward in good order and with great alacrity but when they had advanced to a particular place, they were ordered to Halt with a design of forming into a Line of Battle, but when that was attempted, it proved ineffectual, the whole falling into Confusion and all the endeavours of the Officers could not get them into any Regular Form and being by this time within reach of the Enemy's Fire, they appeared struck with Panock, and tho' some seemed willing to Obey, when ordered to form, others Crowded upon them broke their order and prevented it; and this irregular manner they expended a great part of their ammunition; notwithstanding this Confusion, there were several parties advanced from the main Body in order to Recover the Cannon, but were fired upon from the Rear by our own People by which many were Killed and a great many of them discharged their Pieces even in the Air.

Braddock, mortally wounded, ordered a retreat that had already turned into a ragged flight. Braddock was buried in the middle of what came to be called Braddock's Road and his grave was disguised to keep his body from mutilation and scalping by the Indians. Washington led the remnants of troops back to Fort Cumberland. Of those who went into battle, no more than half escaped death or wounds. No record can be found of the Cleaver who had joined them, but Daniel Boone took a horse from the wagon he was driving and escaped.

This defeat turned the settlers to bitterness and hatred against the French and even more so against the Indians. Many of their sons had been killed or wounded, and they had no fighting men to spare. Fear increased. There was scant protection against marauding Indians who lurked in the woods until the time was right and then descended on lonely settlements to burn houses and butcher or take captive women and children. Those who could fled to forts, but there were not enough forts to house them, and the weaker forts were easily overrun. Families abandoned their cabins and crops and fled back to the older settlements. In some places the frontier was pushed back as much as a hundred miles.

For the next eight years the conflict sporadically interrupted life on the frontier, on a ragged line that stretched from the Bay of Fundy to Augusta in Georgia, first with the advantage to the French and then, after the fall of Quebec, to the British. By 1760 the war was virtually over in America as far as the French were concerned, but it dragged on in Europe until 1763, when it was finally brought to a close by the Treaty of Paris. By this treaty France ceded Canada to Great Britain and gave up claim to all territory east of the Mississippi with the exception of New Orleans.

The Indians, however, were far from subdued. Before the French and Indian War had ended Pontiac's War had begun. Pontiac, chief of the Ottawa Indians, tried to recapture Detroit after it had fallen to the British. Then he took to warfare on a wide scale and destroyed all the British forts west of Niagara with the exception of Detroit, and over it he maintained a siege. Settlers found themselves again unprotected. Indians destroyed settlements on the Monongahela. Shawnee warriors penetrated deep into Virginia and left behind blood-chilling stories of death and depredation. In an early form of germ warfare, British officers suggested that blankets infected with smallpox germs be sent among the Indians, but the suggestion was never carried out, perhaps because they feared the germs would not be able to distinguish between white and copper skins. The Indians pressed eastward until Fort Pitt itself was in danger. Then on August 2, 1764, British and colonial soldiers met the Indians in battle at Bushy Run, to the east of present Pittsburgh. The Indians were defeated at heavy cost. In November Pontiac lifted his siege of Detroit and his rebellion was over.

In the years immediately before and after the Treaty of Paris whites continued to clear land and build houses in what the Indians regarded as their territory, some venturing as far west as the Ohio. Indians retaliated with burnings and killings. In an attempt to mollify them the government issued the Proclamation of October 7, 1763, forbidding settlements beyond the headwaters of rivers flowing into the Atlantic until such a time as the Indian boundaries could be determined. Settlers could legally go to the crest of the Alleghenies but not down into the valleys on the other side. Those who had settled west of the Alleghenies were ordered to pull back. A general pacification of the tribes was also initiated. Both measures had only limited success.

Then in the Treaty of Fort Stanwyx in 1768 Iroquois Indians, disposing of land to which they had no right, permitted revision of the boundaries defined in the Proclamation of 1763 so that they extended to the Ohio.

Half a century earlier Spottswood had proclaimed the motto "Thus he swears to cross the mountains." The Alleghenies were higher, more forbidding than the Blue Ridge, the Indians more aroused to trouble. Yet there were men and women by the hundreds waiting to cross over in search of a new Canaan.

For some the reality had already dissipated the dream. Among them was Ezekiel Cleaver. Life on Bear Garden Mountain was hard, discouragements many. Ezekiel tried for a time to make a go of it and then went back to Gwynedd in Pennsylvania, leaving his son Ezekiel, Junior, in charge of the land.

Twenty years after the land was taken up Ezekiel the son was writing a letter to Ezekiel the father, a selection from which appears as he wrote it:

In hopes the disagreeableness of my way of living will grow better after it gets to the hight I believe it is not in the power of Man alone to live satisfied for I am very uncontented discontent grown I see no way to remedie it I am most dishearted but reconsidering that I have often seen how much wors things might have been altho I yet & now believe it might have been much better with me if I never seen this tract of land but as I have made an attempt for a living I believe it best to continue here til I may see a way to leave it reputable that my labour may be of a little advantage to thee or I as yet it is none at all to either of us it has hurt both my body & mind. . . .

In spite of near insurmountable difficulties he remained diligent in the practice of his Quaker faith:

. . . This winter is trying one on the account of attending meetings I have mist rare now within two months then I have this four years it being most impossable to attend on account of the depth of the snow and the ice I have sixteen dangerous fords to cross in going to Mount Pleasant I having got hors rough shod but for all would not do he had many dangerous falls I have went afoot till my feet was so frost bitten & sore that I could not do it any more. . . .

There still remained the relationship between an obedient son, a stern father:

I dont intend to leave the place I pray thee dont grieve or think hard of my thus informing thee but be glad that we both have done the best according to our knowledg, it will be a great relief to me if I may see my way clear to leave it and loos my three years work if thee would favour thy son so much as to take all that I have done for thy growing demand I am willing to go poorer in mind flesh and cloathing from it then when I came to it. . . .

His father's reply can be surmised, for the son died at his place on Bear Garden Mountain in 1787.

South Branch
of the Potomac

THE MAIN MIGRATION ROUTE through Virginia followed the Philadelphia Road south and crossed over the Blue Ridge Mountains into North Carolina. A second route, minor by the number of settlers that traveled it before the Revolution, major because it eventually opened land for settlement all the way to the Ohio River, followed tributaries of the Potomac generally along the Maryland line into Virginia, with a branch swinging northwest along Braddock's Road to the Monongahela, a fork of the Ohio. Settlers going south through the Valley of Virginia saw the Alleghenies as a long, protective wall broken only by the gap made by the New River, a gap that opened the way to western waters but through mountains rugged, uninviting. Settlers going west came to the crest of the Alleghenies and paused before crossing over. Only the hardiest dared face the dangers of moutain travel, hostile Indians, French soldiers ready to fight for their claim to La Belle Riviére, soon to be called the "River of Blood."

Eager for land they came, predominantly Germans and Scotch-Irish from Pennsylvania, Maryland, and Virginia, the way shown as early as 1750 by Thomas Cresap and three years later by Christopher Gist. Even earlier, settlers had crossed into the valley of the South Branch of the Potomac to take up land offered by Lord Fairfax, some of the tracts surveyed by George Washington.

The South Branch has its headwaters in Highland County, Virginia, and flows through the present counties of Pendleton, Grant, and Hardy in West Virginia. It is fed by many tributaries, the largest being the North Fork of the South Branch, which joins it in Hampshire County. The valley formed by the South Branch and its tributaries is remarkably beautiful and fertile, with bottoms at times narrow, at times widening into broad plains between sloping hills, with clear, swift-flowing streams.

First explorations in South Branch Valley were made as early as 1720. The first settlement was made in 1735 by a group of families led by a John Coburn and including Howards, Walkers, and Woods. In 1736 a larger settlement was made at a place called Old Fields because the land had been cultivated by Indians. It included a number of Germans, originally from Pennsylvania but more recently from the Shenandoah region. These early settlers probably followed a road along the Maryland line to the mouth of the South Branch, a road of which George Washington said in 1748, "I believe the worst road that was ever trod by man or beast."

At that time Washington was sixteen years old and a chain bearer on a surveying party sent out by Lord Fairfax to lay out two areas that he called manors: the South Branch Manor of fifty-five thousand acres and the Patterson's Creek Manor of nine thousand acres. The party reached the South Branch near Colonel Thomas Cresap's home at Old Town, Maryland, on March 21, 1748. From there they crossed Patterson's Creek to Abraham Johnson's place and went on to Solomon Hedges' home and then the home of Henry Van Meter. From there they went up the South Branch through Frosty Hollow and over Scott's Ridge to Looney Creek and on to the site of present-day Petersburg. They continued up the North Fork to Meadows and the home of James Rutledge. Returning by way of Looney Creek, they continued by way of present-day Masonville and across South Fork Mountain, across the Great Cacapon, and back to Winchester. In less than a month the surveying was completed. Washington's diary gives details of the journey plus descriptions of who the people were and how they lived.

In his fifth entry, written before they had left Winchester, he wrote:

. . . We got our Supper and was lighted into a Room, and I not being so good a Woodsman as the rest of my Company stripped myself very orderly and went in to the Bed, they called it, when to my Surprise I found it to be nothing but a Little Straw—Matted together—without Sheets or any thing else but one thread Bear Blanket, with double its Weight of Vermin, such as Lice, Fleas, etc. I was glad to get up (as soon as the Light was carried from us). I put on my Clothes and Lay as my Companions. Had we not been very tired I am sure we should not have slept much that night. I made a Promise not to sleep so from that time forward, choosing rather to sleep in the open air before a fire. . . .

Of an Indian dance he wrote on March 23:

Rained till about two o'clock, and Cleared, when we were surprised at the sight of thirty-odd Indians coming from War with only one scalp. We had some liquor with us, of which we gave them Part. It elevated their spirits, put them in the Humor of Dancing, of whom we had a War Dance. Their manner of dancing is as follows: Viz., They clear a Large Circle and make a Great Fire in the middle, then seat themselves around it. The Speaker makes a grand speech telling them in what Manner they are to Dance. After he has finished the best Dancer jumps up, as one awaked out of a Sleep, and runs and Jumps about the Ring in a most comical Manner. He is followed by the Rest. Then begins their Musicians to Play. The Music is a Pot half [full] of Water with a Deerskin Stretched over it as tight it can, and a gourd with some Shott to Rattle, and a piece of an horse's Tail tied to it to make it look fine. . . .

On Saturday, March 26, Washington made an entry that shows how few worldly goods even a man of some importance might have:

Travelled up the Patterson's Creek to Solomon Hedges, Esquire, one of his Majesty's Justices of the Peace for the County of Frederick, where we camped. When we came to Supper there was neither a cloth on the Table nor a knife to eat with, but as good luck would have it we had knives of [our] own.

On Monday, April 4, he wrote of the Pennsylvania Germans among the settlers:

We did 2 Lots and was attended by a great Company of people—Men, Women and Children that attended us through the woods as we went, showing their Antic tricks. I really think they seemed to be as Ignorant a Set of People as the Indians. They would never speak English, but when spoken to they speak all Dutch.

A tract of land surveyed by Washington at this time or later was granted to Nicholas Friend, a Pennsylvania German, on September 4, 1761. On February 27, 1768, he entered into a contract:

. . . Witnesseth That the said Nicholas Friend for and in consideration of the Sum of Five Shillings Current Money of Virginia to him in Hand paid by the said Lawrence Hass the Receipt whereof is hereby acknowledged He the said Nicholas Friend Hath Granted Bargained and by these Presents Doth Grant Bargain and Sell unto the said Lawrence Hass all that Tract or Parcel of Land on Potomack River about Two Miles below the Mouth of little Cacapahon in the county of Hampshire and bounded on by a Survey thereof made by Mr. George Washington. . . .

Lawrence Hass had possessed the use of the land at least as far back as the previous December. For this privilege, the indenture continues:

Yielding and Paying therefore one ear of Indian corn in and upon the Feast of Saint Michael the Arch Angel (if demanded) To the Interest that by Virtue of these Presents and by Force of the Statute for transfferring of Uses into Possession. . . .

The deed transferring the tract from Nicholas Friend to Lawrence Hass was signed the next day. The tract of one hundred and forty-two acres "with the Rights Members and Appurtenances thereof and all Houses Edifices Buildings Orchards Gardens Lands Meadows Trees Woods Underwood Ways Paths Waters Water courses Easements Profits Commodities Advantages Herediments" are specified in the deed. Lawrence Hass was to receive "full third Part of all Lead Copper Tin Coale Iron Mine & Iron Ore that shall be found thereon. . . ." For this Hass had paid one hundred and forty pounds current money of Pennsylvania. In addition,

. . . The Said Lawrence Hass his Heirs or Assigns therefore Yielding and Paying to the Right Honorable Thomas Lord Fairfax Proprietor of the Northern Neck his Heirs or Assigns or to his certain attorney or attornies Agent or Agents or to the certain Attorney or Attorneys of his Heirs and Assigns Yearly and every Year on the Feast of Saint Michael the Arch Angel the Fee Rent of One Shilling Sterling for every Fifty Acres of Land hereby Granted.

Payment of this quitrent to Lord Fairfax was required of all who held land in the northern neck of Virginia and was already a matter for dissatisfaction. Eighteen years earlier, in 1754, the House of Burgesses had petitioned the king to

grant his lands to the west-ward of the great mountains in small parcels, exempt from the payment of rights and quitrents, for the space of ten years, which will be an encouragement to foreign Protestants to settle thereon; and thereby be the most effectual means of securing our frontiers, and cultivating friendship with the Indians.

In the same year the king ordered remission of both quitrents and the charge of five shillings for rights upon each fifty acres, the remission to extend for a period of ten years. He also provided that one person could not take up more than one thousand acres in his own name or in another name in trust for him. The incentive to cross the mountains was thus enhanced, for the settlers in South Branch Valley and for newcomers bound through the Valley of Virginia.

Quitrents ended but not the quaint customs observed in taking possession of land. On May 29, 1761, Jonas Friend purchased from Mary Wood and James and Moses Green of Culpepper County a tract on the North Fork of the South Branch of the Potomac. The deed contains a "memorandum that livery and seisen of the within tract of land was given the said Jonas Friend by the said Mary Wood James Green and Moses Green by delivering to him a Twigg."

In the meantime life was not so peaceful in South Branch Valley, or in any part of this western frontier. Braddock's defeat had exposed the settlers to raids from the Indians and their French allies. George Washington, who had assumed command after Braddock's death, wrote the Governor of Virginia on October 11, 1755:

> The men I hired to bring intelligence from the South Branch returned last night with letters from Captain Ashby, and other parties there. The Indians are gone off. It is believed their numbers amounted to about 150, that 71 men are killed or missing, and several houses and plantations destroyed. ... Captain Waggoner informed me that it was with difficulty he passed the Blue Ridge for crowds of people who were flying as if every moment was death. He endeavored, but in vain, to stop them. They firmly believed that Winchester was in flames.

In a letter dated April 22, 1756, Washington reported the following:

> Your Honor, you may see to what unhappy straits the inhabitants are reduced. I see inevitable destruction in so clear a light that unless vigorous measures are take by the Assembly, and speedy assistance sent from below, the poor inhabitants that are now in fort must unavoidably fall, while the remainder are flying before the barbarous foe. . . .

The name of the Shawnee Chief Killbuck brought terror to the South Branch. In the spring of 1756 he headed about sixty warriors on a raid up the South Fork. At a home they killed and scalped one woman and took another woman prisoner. This woman managed to escape and alert the fort. The Indians moved on to what is called "The Trough," a seven-mile canyon with steep mountains on either side. Here a party of sixteen or eighteen white men tried to trap them between the mountain and the river. The Indians, however, alerted by a dog barking at a rabbit, slipped around the whites and trapped them. In the battle that ensued, called "The Battle of the Trough," nearly half the whites were killed. The wounded were mercilessly tomahawked.

Stories of death and torture, of whites burned to death, among them a twelve-year-old boy, of white women forced by their captors to bear illegitimate children, were told all along the South Branch, some of them rumors, but more of them anchored to the names of the martyred. It was a hardening experience, the settlers knew. They knew also that over the mountains they would be even more exposed to the Killbucks and their warriors. They could have found land in the Valley of Virginia and lived and prospered in comparative safety, but that was not the way to the Ohio.

Jonas Friend was notable among those who waited a time on the South Branch and then pushed on over the mountains. So was Ebenezer Zane, the founder of Wheeling, West Virginia, the explorer of Zane's Trace in Ohio, the man for whom Zanesville was named. Where Red Stone Creek empties into the Monongahela the Linn family lived in one of the few cabins in this far outpost. In their move west they had tarried for a time in Kent County, Maryland, next to Kent County, Delaware. In both counties the name Cleaver was known. Three of the Linn sons—William, Nathan, and Benjamin —became scouts and Indian fighters. At seventeen Benjamin lived for months with Indians in Ohio Valley. Two of the sons—Nathan and Benjamin—were to be bound by flesh and blood to the family of William and Hannah Cleaver.

At some time after 1761 this William Cleaver brought his family to South Branch Valley or to some nearby route over the mountains. How he arrived there can only be surmised. There is belief among his descendants that he was born in what is now Montgomery County, Pennsylvania, about 1730, and that he had Dutch blood. The first of his dates that can be documented is January 29, 1751, the birth of his son Benjamin in Maryland; the next is the birth of his son William, Junior, in Pennsylvania; the next, the birth of his son Stephen on May 20, 1766, in Virginia. These dates and places follow a general pattern of westward migration, but two other pieces of information break the pattern. William's son David claimed to have been born in New Jersey in 1770. William also had a son Joshua. A Joshua Cleaver married Margaret Nelson in Philadelphia on May 17, 1773. It may be that William Cleaver, like many other pioneers, went out and back again several times before making his final move out west.

Since this William Cleaver's name does not appear on land records in South Branch Valley, he probably did not remain there long enough to purchase land. He was, however, in the area long enough to join four others—Joseph Donoho, Jonas Friend, Jesse Hamilton, and Edward Skidmore—in the purchase of a tract of land on the west side of the Allegheny Mountains. How or when he met these four is not on record. Apparently most of them or their families originally came through Pennsylvania. All their family names appear on land records in Augusta or Frederick County, Virginia, or both. Some were among the earliest settlers along the Shenandoah and the Potomac. Whatever the circumstances of their meeting, the five men bought a thousand acres of land that had been granted to James Walker, possibly the James Walker who was an early settler at Old Fields.

The survey was made by Thomas Lewis, who with Peter Jefferson, President Jefferson's father, had run the Fairfax Line. As recorded in the Augusta County courthouse the survey and the deed that followed it show both the manner and problems of land transfer at the time. The survey begins as follows:

In pursuance of a warrant under the Hand & Seal of the Right Honorable John Earl of Dunmore the 17th Dec 1773 I have surveyed for John McClenahan assignee of James Walker 1000 acres of land lying on the Monongehela River in Augusta County Being a part of a Warrant for 3000 acres which the said James Walker is entitled to by his Majesties Proclamation of the year 1763.

The survey, dated March 7, 1774, was embodied in the deed, which was not finally sealed until November 1, 1782. The survey and deed taken together give clues to the origin of suits over land titles that were to embroil landowners on the frontier a hundred years or more. The deed also bears scrutiny, both for what is said and the manner of saying it:

Benjamin Harrison Esquire Governor of the Commonwealth of Virginia to all to whom these presents shall come, Greeting. Know ye that in consideration of military service performed by James Walker in the last war between Great Britain and France there is granted by the said Commonwealth unto William Cleaver, Jonas Friend, Edward Skidmore, Joseph Donoho, and Jesse Hamilton assignees of John McClanahan [who] was assignee of James Walker a certain tract or parcel of land containing one thousand acres being part of three thousand acres granted to said Walker, surveyed the eighth of March one thousand seven hundred and seventy four lying and being in the County of Augusta in the Monongalia River and Bounded as followeth to wit. Beginning at a hickory and whiteoak saplin on the river bank on the west side and runneth thence North fifty degrees west one hundred and fifty poles to a white Oak. and thence North eighty degrees west one hundred and forty eight poles to a poplar and North five degrees west twenty six poles to a Chesnut and Gum on the river bank thence up the river and the several courses thereof crossing it two hundred and eighty two poles to two hickoreys on the river bank and thence North seventy four degrees forty four poles to a thorn Bush and a Cherry tree and thence South eighty degrees east twenty eight poles to a whiteoak and east forty eight poles to a white Oak and South seventy five degrees and fifty six poles to two white Oaks and North fifty six degrees east one hundred and forty four poles to two white oaks and South thirty five degrees east forty eight poles to two white Oaks and thence South sixty four degrees east seventy four poles to a white Oak and south thirteen degrees east eighty poles to a white Oak and South twenty six degrees east fifty two poles to two white Oaks and North seventy two degrees east one hundred and twenty four poles to a white Oak and south seventy two degrees east thirty six poles to two white Oaks and south twenty six degrees west one hundred and thirty poles to two red Oaks on the river Bank thence down the river and the several courses thereof six hundred and sixty poles to the Beginning with the appurtenances to have and to hold the said tract or parcel of land with its Appurtenances to the Said William Cleaver Jonas Friend Edward Skidmore, Joseph Donoho and Jesse Hamilton and their heirs forever In witness whereof the said Benjamin Harrison Governor of the Commonwealth of Virginia hath hereunto set his hand and Caused the lesser Seal of the said Commonwealth to be affixed at Richmond on the first day of November in the year of our Lord One Thousand seven hundred and eighty two and the Commonwealth the Seventh.

Chances are that neither seller nor surveyor ever saw this tract of land. For some military service James Walker was awarded three thousand acres of his own choosing in the lands across the mountains. Without locating the tract he sold it to John McClanahan, a land speculator, also of South Branch Valley, who in turn sold it to the five men. There is no record of how or when William Cleaver and his friends located the particular spot or how they established claim. The survey does not mention the name of a mountain or a stream other than the Monongahela River. It is specific only in that it begins "at a hickory and whiteoak saplin on the river bank on the west side." Other markers are trees—poplar, hickory, red oak, chestnut—and a thorn bush, not any distinguished by chops or slashes or names of settlers. The land might have been on any part of the Monongahela. The survey could have been made hundreds of miles away. It could have been as careless as those George Washington complained of, or as fraudulent. It was on land already granted to Thomas Lord Fairfax and to the Ohio Company. It could as easily be possessed by a squatter as by a purchaser.

Through scouting themselves or on the reports of hunters and traders William Cleaver and his friends found a place that suited them, where Leading Creek flows into the Tygart's Valley River, a tributary of the Monongahela. It had a natural beauty that must have appealed to them—the clear mountain stream, the level bottom land, the hills surrounding them on all sides, making a valley no more than a mile wide, shut in by Rich Mountain and Laurel Hill, overshadowed by Cheat Mountain in the distance.

By the time William and Hannah Cleaver went over the mountains another William Cleaver had settled in South Branch Valley, in Hampshire County. Perhaps they were related, perhaps not. Records are sketchy. His estate was appraised on March 20, 1788, and the settlement recorded on June 11, 1789. The estate in goods and cash amounted to no more than forty-five pounds. The larger amount went to William Cleaver's heirs, a smaller to P. Cleaver's heirs. Of livestock he had one horse, one cow and two heifers, and sixteen head of sheep. Household goods included two bedsteads, pewter, knives and forks, one sifter, and an iron pot and hooks. His personal effects were few: wearing apparel, one pair of shoes and buckles, and a gold ring. He also had a pistol and a shot bag, and, strangely enough, books, with no titles given but with a value of about two shillings.

Sketchy as the records are, they indicate that the P. Cleaver of the will was descended from Peter Klever, weaver.

Tygart's Valley

FIVE MEN COVENANTED to risk themselves and their families for land west of the Allegheny Mountains, to cross over the high and forbidding Allegheny Front, to follow streams down the western slope deeper and deeper into the wilderness to a piece of land that pleased them, there to join in mutual defense, labor, sharing—cut off from the older settlements, from family, church, schools, in a way from government itself, backwoodsmen in the truest sense, before a backwoodsman was an image to be laughed at; there unhampered by tie or tithe to church or state to find their own thoughts and manners. They did not go alone. A few had blazed trails ahead; numbers struggled along behind.

Of those who went ahead, Robert Files, or Foyle, and David Tygart seem to have been the first to settle on the Monongahela River in what is now West Virginia. The valley in which they settled was named for Tygart; the river was in turn named for the valley. Files, with his family, settled at what is now Beverly, on Tygart's Valley River. Tygart settled farther up the valley. They were there as early as 1753, or perhaps a year earlier. They were there at least early enough to raise corn in the summer of 1753, but the yield was not enough to furnish bread until another crop could be made. Short on corn, worried by the increasing hostility of the Indians, they decided in late December or early January to give up and go back to the older settlements. Unfortunately they had delayed too long. Indians returning from a raid on the South Branch went to the Files cabin and killed him, his wife, and five children. One son, who was not at the house, escaped and managed to warn the Tygart family.

Tygart fled with his family and the Files son back to the comparative safety of the South Branch of the Potomac. Eighteen years passed before another settlement was attempted in Tygart's Valley. Then, in 1772, a number of settlers pushed up the Monongahela River to the headwaters of its various tributaries. Names still familiar in the region began to appear in land records in Tygart's Valley: Westfall, Stalnaker, Crouch, Cunningham, and many others. William Cleaver and his friends may have gone as early as 1772; they were certainly there by 1774. The flood of people was such that in a short time they had taken up all the level land in the river bottom and were beginning to reach up the gentler slopes.

William Cleaver's group, if they followed the usual pioneer fashion, left their women and children behind on the South Branch and went ahead to prepare a place for them. Whenever possible, travel was in the summer, after a crop had been made, early enough for shelters to be built, trees cut or girdled, land readied for planting before winter bound them in. On their first journey into the wilderness the men traveled light, burdening themselves only with a gun and ammunition, an ax, a little dried venison, some shelled Indian corn for parching. For other food they shot game and gathered nuts and berries, or chewed roots and bark.

There were no wagon roads into Tygart's Valley. Packhorse trails were too far to the north or south. Those coming from the South Branch had to walk, following streams and Indian trails, up steep mountains—five of them the nearest way—to the crest and down again, over one hundred and fifty miles, keeping their rifles loaded, their long knives at hand, ready for Indians or any other kind of danger. They probably traveled an old Indian trail, called by them the Shawnee Path or Trail because over it the Shawnees, notably Killbuck's bands, came to raid settlements on the South Branch. It was also called the Seneca Trail because it followed Seneca Creek down to its mouth, where it joined the North Fork of the South Branch. Settlers from the South Branch went up Seneca Creek to the Allegheny summit. On the way down they crossed branches of the Cheat River, eventually west-flowing waters, above the mouth of Horse Camp Creek, and at last picked up speed down into the valley, some of them by the Leading Creek Trail along Leading Creek. Any topographic map of the region will show the rugged terrain; it will not show the heavy growth of laurel the pioneers had to work their way around or hack their way through.

The valley they came to was rich and beautiful, and made ready for their coming by a bountiful nature. David Crouch, who was born on the south branch in 1767 and went to Tygart's Valley while still a young boy, said this of the bounty:

It was the beautifullest country for wild fruit I ever saw. Had it not been for the fruit and game, that country could not have been settled as it was. Of the fruit—in kind, there were sarvice berries, growing on a tree as thick as your leg, and high as the joice, on a common log house, with a bark resembling that of the maple; the fruit round, and red, but not like the haws. Spread under the tree a sheet and shake down a half bushel. Whortleberries and cranberries. Three miles of cranberry swamp, by Westfall's. Five hundred bushels could be gotten there.

William Cleaver's group walked through the still forest; there was only the stillness of heavy growth to greet them when they came to their land, where the quiet waters of Leading Creek flow into the quiet waters of Tygart's Valley River. Then there was the sound of axes as they blazed trees to mark boundaries and cut poles to make shelters, or of a gun when they needed meat. Their first shelters were half-houses, open on one side, with dirt for the floor and a pile of leaves on the ground for a bed. These had to do until ground was cleared and dug with a stick for planting. Then those who could built cabins of round poles, notched and fitted to make corners, the cracks between chinked with strips of wood and daubed with clay. For heating and cooking they built pole chimneys and fireplaces daubed with clay mixed with grass or straw. Roofs were made of long strips of wood, rived out with froe and wooden maul, laid on in layers, weighted in place by heavy poles. Floors were made of split logs called puncheons. Doors and windows were no more than openings over which animal skins could be hung or timbers laid in time of danger. But, as settlers fresh from Scotland and Ireland recalled, the houses they had left behind were little better: small, dark, some of stone laid without mortar.

The time came when six shelters were ready, when the women and children also had to cross the mountains, on journeys of incredible hardships. They still had no wagons, though they may have had a few packhorses. Beginning about this time horses packed salt and other goods over the Shawnee Trail. "Horse creatures," as they were sometimes called, were more valuable for packing than for riding. Most of the early settlers went over the mountains on foot, carrying children too small to walk, carrying clothes and pots for cooking, the tools for clearing, the seeds and shoots for planting the wilderness. They walked and drove their cattle and hogs before them, traveling slowly, leaving time for grazing as they went, with no way to pen the stock at night, to keep them from escaping into the wild. Their thoughts as they went were not recorded, but some clues may be found in the songs they passed on to their sons and daughters. Five generations later, Cleavers were singing a song picked up somewhere along the frontier:

> Hog drovers, hog drovers, hog drovers we air,
> A-courting your daughter so rare and so fair;
> Oh, can we get lodging here oh here?
> Oh, can we get lodging here?
>
> Oh, this is my daughter who sits by my side
> And any hog drover can make her his bride
> By bringing me another one here oh here,
> By bringing me another one here.

They traveled knowing they were making the biggest leap yet made into the wilderness. It was no longer a matter of clearing land for new farms, tier on tier, with the distance from the old to the new no more than an hour's walk over a new road to new ground. They went knowing they were leaving home and family and friends, that for most the farewells were final, that most of them would never again turn their faces east, any more than countless settlers from Europe had done. A mixture of English, Welsh, Scotch, Scotch-Irish, German—some three generations in the new world, some who had walked straight from the boat into the wilderness—they carried memories old and new of the heartbreak of setting forth. Some of them carried songs in their minds of a young man who wanted to strike out on his own, of his sweetheart who could not bear to leave her loved ones behind. It was a universal story among frontier settlers. For the Germans it was "Muss i denn"; for the French, "Le Breton." Generations later, Cleavers were singing "Nora Darling," which belonged either to the Irish or Scotch-Irish, or both:

> I am going far away, Nora darling;
> The ship is at anchor in the bay;

And before tomorrow's sun you will hear the signal gun,
So be ready and I'll take you far away.

I'd go with you there, Barney darling,
But I've often told you the reason why;
It would break my mother's heart if from her I had to part
And go roaming with you, Barney McCoy.

They left their living. They left their dead. They traveled themselves in constant fear of death: a rattlesnake beside the trail could
be as deadly as an Indian warrior. The difference: rattlesnakes killed
but did not mutilate or scalp. Sickness brought fear, especially on the
trail, when there was no time to stop, where the only medicine had
to come from "yarbs" and the right ones could not be found. Sickness, death, burial might come within the time from sun to sun. Trails
west were strewn with unmarked graves of those who did not make
it.

  The Cleavers left no record of their journey to Tygart's Valley.
That it was not easy is clear. A letter written twenty years later from
Samuel Allen back to his parents in Connecticut suggests how diffi-
cult it might have been:

  You doubtless remember I rote in my last letter that Prentice was taken
ill a day or two before he continued verry much so until the 10th of July when
he began to gro wors the waggoner was hired by the hundred weight &
could not stop unless I paid him for the time that he stoped & for the
Keeping of the horses that I could not afford to do So we were obliged to
keep on We were now on the Allegany Mountain & a most horrid rode the
wagon golted so that I dare not let him ride So I took him in my arms and
carried him all the while except once in a while Mr Davis would take him
in his armes & carry him a spell to rest me. a young man that Mr. Avory hired
at Allexandria a joiner whose kindness I shall not forgit he kep all the while
with us & spared no panes to assist us in anything & often he would offer
himself. our child at this time was verry sick & no medical assistance could
be had on this mountain on the morning of the 13th as we was at breackfast
at the house of one Mr Tumblestone the child was taken in a fit our company
had gone to the next house to take breakfast which was one mile on our way
we were alone in the room & went & asked Mrs Tumblestone to come into
the room she said she did not love to see a person in a fitt but she came into
the room Polly ask her if she new what was good for a child in a fitt she said
no & immediately left the room & shut the door after her & came no more

into the room when that fitt left him there came on another no person in the room but Mr Tumblestone who took but little notis of the child tho it was in great distress Polly said she was afraid the child would die in one of them fitts Mr Tumblestone spoke in a verry lite manner and sayes with a smile it will save you the trouble of carrying it any farther if it does die We then bundled up the child and walked to the next house ware we come up with our company I had just seated myself down when the child was taken in a fitt again when that had left it it was immediately taken in another & as that went off we saw another coming on the Man of the house gave it some drops that stoped the fitt he handed me a vial of the dropps—gave directions how to use them the child had no more fitts but seemed to be stuped all day he cried none at all but he kept a whinning & scouling all the while with his eyes stared wide open his face and his eyes appeared not to come in shape as before When we took dinner it was six mile to the next house the waggoners said they could not git through thro that night we did not love to stay out for fear our child would die in the woods so we set off & left the waggon I took the child in my arms and we traveled on Mr Davis set off with us & carried the child above half of the time here we traveled up & down the most tedious hills as I ever saw & by nine oclock in the evening we came to the house the child continued stayed all the night the next morning at break of day I heard it make a strange noise I perceived it grew worse I got up and called the women ware with us the woman of the house got up & in two hours the child dyed Polly was obliged to go rite off as soon as his eyes was closed for the waggoners would not stop I stayed to see the child burried I then went on two of the men that was with me were joiners & had their tools with them they stayed with me & made the coffin Mr Simkins the man of the house sent his Negroes out & dug the grave whare he had burried several strangers that dyed a crossing the mountain the family all followed the corps to the grave black & white appeared much affected.

William Cleaver was more than forty years old when he came to Tygart's Valley. He had lived on several parts of the frontier, as farmer, qualified surveyor, and appraiser of estates. His wife Hannah, who survived him, may have been the wife who crossed the mountains with him. There are no records to the contrary. However, men and women widowed on the trail often married again quickly, in an unusual case on the same day. A man could hardly get along without a wife, a wife without a husband, especially where there were young children to be cared for.

Hannah Cleaver no doubt knew the hardships that faced her when she turned toward the mountains. It was a separation almost as final as death from family and friends, from the old settlements and the comforts they could give her. It was going into a part of the wilderness where few white women had dared to go, to bear her children on a leaf bed, or no bed at all, with a neighbor woman to sit with her, or with no help at all, with nothing better for the pain than a knotted rag to clamp her teeth on. No wonder pioneer women took to slipping an ax under a birthing bed to cut the pain in two.

The journey over, in their cabin at the mouth of Leading Creek, she had to make their home and cook their food, with never a time for the pot to get cool. Frontier wisdom taught them that meat had to be boiled—that meat without broth brought on sickness. She also had to work outside. Women and children dug holes with sticks, planted corn by hand, and watched their precious cows and hogs to keep them from being driven away by Indians. Men cleared under-brush, girdled trees, and worked the patches of corn with wooden tools. They hunted for the pot, and for furs that could be sent by traders back over the mountains to the Philadelphia market, or down one river after another until they reached New Orleans.

Tygart's Valley was one of the "little Wests" that came into being as settlement leapfrogged settlement. At first there was a cluster of cabins along the creek and river, perhaps six in all, one no more than a mile from the others, each in a little clearing surrounded by woods. The Cleavers had neighbors: their son Benjamin and the families that came with them, the Donohos, Friends, Hamiltons, Skidmores. Beverly was a settlement six miles away. Other families had cabins up and down the valley. An Indian holler, sounds of a horn, a rifle shot could bring people together or warn them to flee from danger. Thick woods lay between, but houses could be out of sight of each other but still close enough for a man to borrow a chunk of fire if his fire had died out.

The people had to depend on each other. They had gone many miles beyond the last line of frontier forts and could count on no protection from the Indians except what they could provide themselves. Every able-bodied man had to be a soldier. Many learned to use the tomahawk and scalping knife. Boys learned how to load and fire a rifle and to use the bow and arrow. Men and women, boys and girls—all learned to look for Indian signs and to listen for Indian sounds.

The Cleavers had help of their own: Benjamin in a cabin nearby, Joshua and Charles at home. William, Junior, was thirteen; Stephen, eight. James and David were infants, born somewhere on the way west. A man with seven sons had an advantage on the frontier.

Tygart's Valley was in the backwoods. Settlers there were backwoodsmen, and they were endowed by at least some of the defects that made them subjects of ridicule and satire back East, especially in the cities back East: crude speech, rude manners, rough dress, to name a few. Their virtues, rarely recognized by those who poked fun at them, were also strong in them: individualism, desire for freedom, devotion to democratic principles, and a creative genius that permeated how they lived as well as how they made their living.

Individualism, especially the belief that rights and responsibility originate in individuals, not in society as a whole, was central to their makeup. Settlers in Tygart's Valley, who had left established forms and manners east of the mountains, had no restraints on individualism. Those who had come to the New World in search of freedom—personal, political, religious—had found less of it than they liked in the older settlements, especially religious freedom. New England Puritans drove the Baptists out; Anglicans in Virginia, they well knew, enforced a head tax on non-Anglicans. Roman Catholics in Maryland and elsewhere were preached against in a song brought from England, "The Romish Lady":

> There was a Romish lady,
> Brought up in popery,
> Her mother always taught her,
> The priest she must obey.
> "O pardon me, dear mother,
> I humbly pray thee now,
> But unto these false idols
> I can no longer bow."

Quakers, Shakers—whatever the belief, the practice—members of any sect could expect some curtailment of freedom in any colony except Pennsylvania. So might those who claimed no religious belief at all.

William Cleaver's family were in Augusta County, Virginia, when they set out from the South Branch of the Potomac. They were still in Augusta County in Tygart's Valley, still nominally under the discipline of the Anglican Church, though the priest and vestry charged with it were east of the mountains and unable to maintain it. Some Anglicans were among them. There were also Presbyterians, Baptists, Quakers, Mennonites, and splinter groups of some of these. At first there were not enough of any sect to build and maintain a church and, to worship at all, they had to come together. Meetings were held in their cabins or out under the trees. Preachers were itinerant. Services could be held only when one happened to be passing through, or when a local man felt the call to preach and exhort his neighbors.

Inevitably there were reports of a godless people being raised on the frontier. Francis Asbury, the first Methodist bishop in America, a man who tirelessly sought souls up and down the frontier, could write in 1776 of a community in Virginia, "Ignorance of the things of God, profaneness and irreligion then prevailed among all ranks and degrees. So that I doubt if even the form of godliness was to be found in any one family of this large and populous parish."

Not the form but the spirit of worship was coveted by the makers of this new freedom, this new religious democracy. Liturgical forms were forgotten or ignored. Rituals, often hardly recognizable as such, were adjusted to circumstance. Emotionalism, release perhaps from the rigors of frontier life, ran unrestrained. There was nothing to prevent preacher or layman from expressing his religious fervor as he pleased—even in shouting and dancing and talking in unknown tongues.

From another part of the frontier Bishop Asbury wrote the following in his diary:

There is another thing which has given me much pain—the praying of several at one and the same time. Sometimes five or six, or more, have been praying all at once, in several parts of the room, for distressed persons. Others were speaking by way of exhortation, so that the assembly appeared to be all in confusion, and must seem to one at a little distance more like drunken rabble than the worshipers of God.

It is well to remember that this "drunken rabble" was drunk on religion and that, reports to the contrary, there was an intense religious feeling among many of the frontiersmen, coupled with a native genius for religious expression. It is true that even among those who had Bibles many could not read them, including some of the self-called preachers. Hymn books were rare. Congregations sang songs from memory or they "lined out" from the Bible: the leader would set a tune, read a line of Scripture, and lead the congregation through a passage, reading, singing, with the meaning often not made clear till the end of the passage.

A new kind of religious song—the white spiritual—was coming into being, inspired by tricklings of song from New England, recorded in shaped notes brought by Mennonites from Pennsylvania. On the frontier it was clearly the product of religious fervor, of the desperation of lives lived in fear and desolation, and of the promise of heaven at last; and it was often sung to a doleful tune set in modal form or minor key and unrelieved by harmony or instrumental accompaniment. One of these early spirituals sustained Cleavers generation after generation:

> Come, ye sinners, poor and needy,
> Weak and wounded, sick and sore,
> Jesus ready stands to save you,
> Full of pity, love and pow'r.
>
> I will arise and go to Jesus,
> He will embrace me in his arms,
> In the arms of my dear Savior,
> O there are ten thousand charms.

Book learning took a place considerably down the scale from religion. Books were rare, teachers rarer. Time for book learning was almost as rare. Clearing land and raising crops took up the days from sun to sun. There were jobs for the children, in the fields planting and gathering, in the woods picking berries and nuts, in the cabins keeping fires going. A pioneer had to count on his children, his work force. He could rarely afford them time for study other than in ways for survival in the wilderness.

Childhood itself was brief. There are many accounts of girls who were brides at twelve, a few at eleven. At an age when they might have been learning reading and writing they took on the burden of bringing up a family in a log cabin. A few learned to sign their names. The majority never went beyond the letter X. On the rare occasions when a wife had to join her husband in signing a legal document, like a land deed, she could watch him put an X where the clerk had written "his mark" and then make her own X beside "her mark."

In education, boys had an edge over girls, but not much.

Boys or girls learned to read, write, and cypher at home, or not at all. A boy who wanted to learn a skill or a trade had to learn it from his father or from someone else in the settlement. Children made orphans by disease or by Indian depredations became charges of the county court. A fairly common solution for the care of a boy was to apprentice him, no matter his age, to someone who could teach him a trade. It is a matter of record that a two-year-old boy was apprenticed to a hat maker "to learn the art and mystery of hat making." Others were apprenticed to learn the art and mystery of blacksmithing, weaving, leather making, and farming. Since several children might be apprenticed to one man, the courts were in effect supplying cheap labor.

William Cleaver, a surveyor, could provide apprenticeship for his sons at home. When or where he learned his trade is not known. It could have been through apprenticeship, or through studying one of the available books on surveying. In its charter of 1693 the College of William and Mary was given the power to examine and certify surveyors. Though he was appointed surveyor in Augusta County, Virginia, and his name does not appear on the certified list, he may have been certified in Maryland, Delaware, or Pennsylvania, where records of certification were not kept. He taught surveying to at least two of his sons: Benjamin and Stephen. He also managed to give his children an education, at least to the extent that they did not have to sign their mark with an *X*.

Whatever was created in song or story or legend was retained not in print but in memory, to be handed down, sometimes in exact repetition, sometimes garbled beyond recognition. Yet the creating and the handing down went on, and the knowledge they labeled "they say" became the larger, broader, richer knowledge of Appalachia and succeeding frontiers—the knowledge and the laughter, for the backwoodsman was as ingenious at creating humor unmistakably American as he was at creating spirituals out of the frontier experience, at first grafting it on to something borrowed from Europe, later letting it flow in language and form rough as the lives they lived. In storytelling, because it was hard to surpass reality, they outdid themselves, and there were plenty of stories to tell—serious stories of the hardships suffered crossing the mountains, exaggerated stories of outlandish characters, humorous stories sometimes harsh, sometimes gentle about men and women who were a part of their daily lives. There was mimicry of language, especially of the Pennsylvania Dutch, and the making up of words to bring forth a laugh.

In settlements like Tygart's Valley the first winter was likely to be the hardest. There was not enough time to prepare a log cabin to withstand the intense cold in the mountains, or to lay in enough food to last until spring. They needed a full summer to get ready for winter. They needed the winter to get ready for spring.

As snow began to fall and the cold to close in the settlers had one comfort: Indians rarely raided when snow was on the ground. Their trail was too easy to follow. So the men, after they had brought in wood and water and meat for the pot, could turn the cabin into a workshop for making the tools they needed. In winter a cabin was a crowded place as all the activities of living went on, and there was no privacy, even at night, for the fire had to be kept going and there might be enough darkness to cover a face but not a body. The William Cleavers, seven of them, lived and worked in such a cabin.

Clothes wore out and had to be replaced. Whites, for the first time, went over to Indian dress, the men willingly enough, the women reluctantly. A man's outfit was likely to be a leather tunic half-thigh length and belted in the middle, leather breeches and leggings, and Indian moccasins, all usually made of doeskin. A favorite hat was made of hickory splints shaped into a crown and woven around with beaver fur. All of his clothing came from the wilderness and he was usually the maker, from skinning the animal and tanning the hide, to dyeing it a reddish brown with red-oak bark ooze he had boiled in the cooking pot, to cutting and sewing it into shape with leather thongs. A woman's garb was simpler, a loose garment that hung from neck to floor, low enough to hide the shapeless moccasins on her feet. The lucky ones had linsey-woolsey undergarments, which separated flesh from the cold of the leather. Men and women both sometimes decorated their leather garments with beads as the Indians did.

Tools had to be made. At first they were of wood, chopped out with an ax, shaped with the same long knife that was a weapon in the woods, a carving knife at the table, sometimes smoothed with a drawing knife—tools made not from a pattern or design but from an image the pioneer had brought over the mountains in his mind. If the image was not clear, the tool might be rough and shapeless indeed; if the mind was sharp, on the other hand, the tool might come out better than anything known before. For splitting blocks or riving out shingles the settlers made wedges of hickory and called them gluts. To season them hard like iron they laid them on the ledge where the fireplace joins the chimney. More difficult to shape were the wooden hoes and rakes and cradles for gathering grain. Later they were able to carry in steel blades and shares, but they still had to make crude handles and frames, and there was little time to give grace to a curve or to decorate even with color.

Inevitably, corn ran out before winter was over and the settlers were reduced to living only on the game they killed. Even when they had nothing but meat to eat, they could make a joke: they had venison dressed with bear meat. They made tea from sassafras roots, dug and stored before the ground was frozen. When the sap began to run they tapped sugar trees and boiled down a syrup that relieved their hunger for both sugar and salt.

Spring came at last to the mountains and valleys, bringing the first shoots of poke and ramp and dandelion. The diet became varied again. So did the settlers' way of living. They could move out of the cramped cabins and roam the woods in search of greens and, as spring advanced, berries and other fruits. It was not carefree roaming. Again everyone had to be on the lookout for Indians on the prowl for a cow or a pig or a scalp.

While the settlers in Tygart's Valley were working to conquer their part of the wilderness they were gradually being drawn into a broad conflict over new territory and, ultimately, over control of the colonies. Authority of the Crown was seriously threatened.

From 1764 to 1774, in spite of sporadic raids and rumors of raids, the Indians on the western frontier were relatively peaceful, though watchful of the whites and strong in their demands for compensation for lands taken. Then, as new settlers came in and more of what had been hunting ground was cleared, a new tension developed. Land speculators were at the bottom of it—land speculators and that part of Virginia called Kaintuck or Kentucky.

Long hunters had come back from roaming the region with tales of the rich flat land, the cane brakes extending for miles along the rivers, the buffalo and other game that made the region a paradise. Such descriptions drew a great press of people ahungering for new land. In October 1772, newspapers in Virginia and Pennsylvania advertised that all interested in marking bounty lands in Kentucky should meet at the mouth of the Great Kanawha the next spring. A large number gathered and worked their way down the Ohio, surveying the best tracts and marking them with slashes and initials on trees. Virginia had no satisfactory plan for granting land and conflict over such haphazard grabbing was inevitable. It came the next year with such violence that forever after Kentucky suffered the name and reputation inherited from warring Indians, the "Dark and Bloody Ground," a violence that embroiled whites against whites and Indians and whites against each other.

The grabbing was on a large scale. In January 1774, John Murray, earl of Dunmore, royal governor of Virginia, seized western Pennsylvania and claimed the territory under a new division of Virginia, which he called West Augusta. He appointed John Connolly governor of the new territory and made Pittsburgh the seat of government. Connolly promptly transferred the Augusta County government from Staunton to Pittsburgh and changed the name of Fort Pitt to Fort Dunmore.

In April, after minor attacks by Indians on settlers and surveying parties, Connolly, himself a speculator in Kentucky land, issued a proclamation urging the settlers to defend themselves. The settlers responded, and both organized and random attacks spread along the frontier. Indians retaliated. Soon the conflict grew into what came to be called "Lord Dunmore's War." A general alarm was sounded along the frontier, and people began building forts in which those from isolated cabins could take refuge.

At that time two forts were built in the upper part of Tygart's Valley: Westfall's, at the site of present Beverly; and Currence's, a short distance away. Danger became so great that settlers moved into the forts for extended stays, with short trips only back to their cabins to look after crops and livestock.

Lord Dunmore decided that the situation warranted calling out the militia in the frontier counties. Settlers from Tygart's Valley responded, among them Benjamin and Charles Cleaver, who joined a company commanded by their neighbor, Captain Jonas Friend. Other able-bodied men, William Cleaver among them, took up the duty of guarding forts and houses.

On June 10, 1774, believing the time had come to break Indian resistance in the Ohio Valley, Dunmore warned the settlers that the war had begun. He organized two expeditions against the Shawnee towns: one under his command that would descend the Ohio from Pittsburgh; the other under the command of Colonel Andrew Lewis and made up of militiamen from frontier settlements, chiefly in northwest Virginia, that would descend to the mouth of the Great Kanawha at the Ohio. The two commands would meet there and march up the Scioto River.

Colonel Lewis drew his soldiers chiefly from the New River,

Greenbrier, and upper Monongahela areas. From Tygart's Valley Captain Friend and his troops went by trail over the mountains to the Greenbrier, where they rendezvoused with Colonel Lewis and his troops, about a thousand strong all together, at the present site of Lewisburg. Troops they were, but hardly an army. Poorly trained, those who were trained at all, uniformed in the dress of the backwoodsman, armed with a long rifle, long knife, and here and there a tomahawk, they looked what they were—rough and ready. They were still about one hundred and sixty miles from the mouth of the Great Kanawha, and there were no well-traveled trails for them to follow. At the mouth of the Elk River they paused long enough to build canoes and barges to transport their supplies. Again they started out, with most of the men on foot working their way through the heavy growth.

While they were making their way toward the Ohio, Lord Dunmore decided to take the eleven hundred men in his command up the Hocking River to the Shawnee towns. He sent Simon Girty, a renegade white man sometimes called "the white Indian," to the mouth of the Great Kanawha to inform Colonel Lewis of a change of plans and to deliver an order for Lewis and his troops to join Dunmore and his troops. Colonel Lewis was still struggling down the Great Kanawha when Girty arrived. Unwilling to wait, Girty stuck the order in a hollow tree, where he thought it would be found, and returned to Dunmore's camp.

Soon after, Colonel Lewis arrived at the mouth of the Great Kanawha, his troops exhausted by the long march. Not seeing the order, not knowing to look for it, he went into camp on the narrow point of land between the Great Kanawha and the Ohio, the place called Point Pleasant.

Chief Cornstalk of the Shawnees, pleased to see the two armies divided, decided to conquer one and then the other. On October 9 he arrived on the opposite side of the Ohio with about a thousand warriors. In the night they crossed over on log rafts and set up camp about two miles from Colonel Lewis's camp. At daybreak they were discovered by two Virginia soldiers out hunting. One Virginian was killed. The other escaped and gave the warning.

Thus began the Battle of Point Pleasant, which for the Virginians could have been a disaster. Cornstalk had planned well. He stretched his line from river to river, closing the Virginians in. They had to come up against his line or escape by one of the rivers. To prevent the latter, he set up detachments to patrol and control the water. His intention was annihilation.

The battle began at sunrise and soon men were fighting along the entire line from river to river, often in close combat, close enough for the tomahawk to be used. Whites and warriors alike fought from behind trees, logs, embankments. For six hours the battle raged and then the Indians fell back to a strong position, still close enough for the Virginians to hear Cornstalk urging his warriors on. In the late afternoon Colonel Lewis decided to open a flanking movement with a small detachment of troops. When they attacked, the Indians, taken by surprise, retreated a short distance up the Ohio and then, taking what dead and wounded they could, crossed over on logs and barges. The Virginians were then ordered to "return in slow pace to our Camp carefully searching for the dead & wounded & bring them in, as also the Scalps of the Enemy."

The official report of their search, with only slight emendation follows:

This day The Scalps of the Enemy were collected & found to be 17 they were dressed & hung upon a pole near the River Bank & the plunder was collected & found to be 23 Guns 80 Blankets 27 Tomahawks with match coats Skins Shout [shot] pouches pow[d]er horns Warclubs & c The Tomahawks Guns & Shout pouches were sold and amounted to near 100 L.

It was a victory for Colonel Lewis, but an expensive one. He lost sixty men killed, including his brother Charles. Ninety-six were wounded. The extent of Cornstalk's losses was never fully known. He left thirty-three dead on the battlefield, and others had been thrown into the river. The wounded they managed to take with them. The Virginians were left with no doubt of the Indians' bravery or of their determination to fight for their land.

Many years later Benjamin Cleaver was able to state simply, "They had a battle with the Indians." In a long affidavit he gave no hint of his part in the battle, only that he served about four months and marched about three hundred miles. Military records are as terse: on January 18, 1776, he was paid three pounds, twelve shillings, for forty-eight days of service in Captain Jonas Friend's Company of the Augusta County militia. His brother Charles, the records show, was paid the same amount for the same period of service.

Not all the people were as reticent about the battle. Ballads began to be written and sung. One chronicles the battle action with considerable accuracy:

> Brave Lewis our Colonel, an officer bold,
> At the mouth of Kanawha did the Shawnees behold.
> On the tenth of October, at the rising sun
> The armies did meet and the battle begun.
>
> One thousand, one hundred we had on Ohio,
> Two thirds of this number to the battle did go,
> The Shawnees nine hundred, some say many more,
> We formed our battle on the Ohio shore.
>
> Like thunder from heaven our rifles did roar,
> Till twelve of the clock, or perhaps something more,
> And during this time the Shawnees did fly,
> Whilst many a brave man on the ground there did lie.
>
> From twelve until sunset some shots there did fly,
> By this kind of fighting great numbers did die,
> But night coming on, the poor Shawnees did yield,
> Being no longer able to maintain the field.
>
> Forty brave men on the ground there did lie,
> Besides forty more of our wounded did die,
> Killed and wounded on the Ohio shore,
> Was one hundred and forty and perhaps something more.
>
> What the Shawnees did lose we never did hear,
> The bodies of twenty did only appear.
> Into the Ohio the rest they did throw,
> The just number of which we never did know. . . .

A similar ballad sets forth both the loyalties expected of a Colonial soldier and the motivation for the battle:

> Bold Virginians all, each cheer up your heart.
> We will see the Shawnees before that we part,
> We will never desert, nor will we retreat,
> Until that our Victory be quite compleat.

Ye offspring of Britain! Come stain not your name,
Nor forfeit your right to your forefathers' fame,
If the Shawnees will fight, we never will fly,
We'll fight & we'll conquer, or else we will die.

Great Dunmore our General valiant & Bold
Excels the great Heroes—the Heroes of old;
When he doth command we will always obey,
When he bids us fight we will not run away.

Good Lewis our Colonel courageous & Brave,
We wisht to command us—our wish let us have.
In Camp he is pleasant, in War he is bold
Appears like great Caesar—great Caesar of old.

Our Colonels & Captains commands we'll obey,
If the Shawnees should run we will bid them to stay.
Our Arms, they are Rifles, our men Volunteers
We'll fight & we'll conquer you need have no fears.

Come Gentlemen all, come strive to excel,
Strive not to shoot often, but strive to shoot well.
Each man like a Hero can make the woods ring,
And extend the Dominion of George our Great King.

Then to it, let's go with might & with main,
Tho' some that set forward return not again;
Let us quite lay aside all cowardly fear
In hopes of returning before the new year.

The land it is good, it is just to our mind,
Each will have his part if his Lordship be kind.
The Ohio once ours, we'll live at our ease,
With a Bottle & glass to drink when we please.

Here's a health to King George & Charlotte his mate
Wishing our Victory may soon be complete
And a kind female friend along by our Side
In riches & splendor till Death to abide.

Health to great Dunmore our general also,
Wishing he may conquer wherever he go.
Health to his Lady—may they long happy be
And a health, my good friend, to you & to me.

The battle over, the victory in hand, Dunmore decided to attack the Shawnee villages, without waiting for Colonel Lewis and his troops to join him. The Indians, divided in defeat, afraid of what might happen to their women and children, sued for peace. Dunmore drove a hard bargain and forced the Indians to sign the Treaty of Camp Charlotte, in which they agreed to give up their claim to Kentucky, to use it no longer as a hunting ground, and to permit the passage of boats on the Ohio. On paper at least the Ohio was won, Kentucky was open to the land speculators, and settlers could risk grabbing land for themselves.

Grab they did, and there was no way to stop them. Dunmore was already experienced in the independence of the frontier character as it had developed over the mountains. His had been the responsibility to enforce the Proclamation of 1763, to drive the settlers who had crossed the Alleghenies back east of the mountains. It was a frustrating experience. He explained why in a letter back to England, with considerable insight into the character that by now could be called fully American:

But My Lord I have learnt from experience that the established Authority of and government in America and the policy of Government at home, are both insufficient to restrain the Americans; and that they do and will remove as their avidity and restlessness incite them. They acquire no attachment to Place: But wandering about Seems engrafted in their Nature; and it is a weakness incident to it, that they Should forever immagine the Lands further off are Still better than those upon which they are already Settled. But to be more particular: I have had, My Lord, frequent opportunities to reflect upon the emigrating Spirit of the Americans Since my Arrival to this Government. There are considerable bodies of Inhabitants Settled at greater and less Distances from the regular frontiers of, I believe, all the Colonies. In this Colony Proclamations have been published from time to time to restrain them. But impressed from their earliest infancy with Sentiments and habits, very different from those acquired by persons of a Similar condition in England, they do not conceive that Government has any right to forbid their taking possession of a Vast tract of Country, either uninhabited, or which serves only as a Shelter to a few Scattered Tribes of Indians. Nor can they be easily brought to entertain any belief of the permanent obligation of Treaties made with those People, whom they consider as but little removed from the brute Creation. These notions, My Lord, I beg it may be understood, I by no means pretend to Justify. I only think it my duty to State matters as they really are.

Lord Dunmore was accurate in his assessment of the feeling for independence, but less so in his assessment of how far the feeling had advanced. He saw the Battle of Point Pleasant as an ending. At least some of the frontiersmen saw it as the beginning of the struggle for independence. Many of the men who fought there had their first experience as American soldiers, and they had won. Friction was growing between the colonies and the mother country, a friction more pronounced in the older colonies, but rumblings of it had reached settlements all along the frontier. Even while Dunmore was gathering his army to put down the Shawnees, delegates from Virginia were on their way to Philadelphia to join delegates from the other colonies in the First Continental Congress. This Congress was still in session when the Battle of Point Pleasant was fought.

The Tygart's Valley that Benjamin and Charles Cleaver returned to when they were mustered out was quiet. Cornstalk lived up to his word. The Indians were peaceful. Settlers who had gone over the mountains for safety returned; new settlers came in. Clearing land went on.

The quiet lasted through the winter, but no longer. The shots fired at Lexington and Concord reverberated through backwoods settlements from Canada to Georgia. People took sides. Whigs and a small number of Tories—families, neighbors, friends—recruited men to fight, one against the other. The British, who had successfully driven the Indians back, now made friendly overtures to them and recruited them to fight the settlers, especially on the western frontier. The Indians, seeing a chance to drive the settlers back and regain their lands, joined the British and began a new reign of terror on people in remote settlements. For the settlers it was either fight or run, or both.

Tygart's Valley was much like any other remote part of the frontier. The people could have fled, as earlier settlers had been forced to do, back over the mountains to safety. But they were not Indians, nomads. They had their homes and crops, products of hardship and hard labor, and a love for river and valley and mountains and the land they had made their own. Grimly they prepared to defend themselves. There were already two forts: Westfall's and Currence's. Jonas Friend and his neighbors built a fort, called Friend's Fort, at Maxwell's Ferry on Leading Creek, only a short distance from William Cleaver's home. Two miles or so to the south Benjamin Wilson built his fort. Before the conflict was over two more forts had been built—Roney's and Hadden's—and Tygart's Valley had more forts than any other region of comparable size on the frontier.

Word of Indians on the prowl went rapidly from settlement to settlement, and from cabin to cabin, sending the people to a fort, where they remained "forted," as they called it, till signs of danger had passed. Not all the families made it to the fort. White scouts brought back stories of homes burned, of tomahawked and scalped bodies, of women and children taken into captivity. Nearly every family was touched by Indian warfare, but this time few fled back over the mountains. They had come to stay.

The forts they went to were built of hewn logs, thick enough to stop a bullet, more than enough to stop an arrow, with the chimneys built inside to keep Indians from climbing up and down them, and with loopholes for watching and shooting. Larger forts had palisades of logs driven into the ground and extra cabins to accommodate forted families. Smaller forts had one building, one story or—like Westfall's—two stories high, large enough for people to crowd into during attack but not for living. "Forted" families had to camp in the open. At night they stayed near the fort. In the daytime they could work in their homes and fields, but always on the alert for signs of Indians—strange moccasin prints on a trail, the sound of a bird that was not exactly right.

During the summer months the fort became a center for the settlement, a center in which life went on. In their isolation the settlers had to deal with all of life, from birthings to sickness to deaths. They had to support each other in the sad times when they came together for prayers of deliverance, or in the times of innocent mirth when they could liven the night with a ballad or a fiddle tune —at times with dancing. In the extremes of sickness they tried herbs from hills and fields and, they failing, turned to rituals of reading from the Bible, or to incantations and practices never learned from the Bible. Superstitious cures could be dredged from memory. So could old songs and old stories belonging to a dim past across the waters.

Fear of Indians became a major part of their lives, Indians and Indian warriors like Killbuck and now Cornstalk. Indians were treacherous: stories were told of Indians who had come feigning friendship and, after they had been let in, had tomahawked the men, knocked the brains of babies out against a tree, and taken the women off to become squaws or slaves. Indians were cunning: they had been known to disguise themselves as bushes and to creep up in a clump on unsuspecting white men. Indians were dumb: settlers laughed at the Indians' sign of rain—"Cloudy all around and pouring down in the middle." Most important, Indians were savage: border warfare was daily adding stories and rumors of Indian atrocities. These feelings were so pervasive that even the most humane settler might eventually come to the almost universal belief: the only good Indian is a dead Indian.

So the children of the frontier were taught, Stephen Cleaver among them and an apt pupil. He was nine years old when he was "forted" at Friend's Fort in the summer of 1775. He had watched his brothers go off to fight at Point Pleasant; he had seen them return and had listened to their stories of battle. He had been trained to watch for Indian signs. By this time he knew how to use the rifle, knife, and tomahawk—how to be an Indian fighter.

Not all colonials shared such intense feelings against the Indians. On October 5, 1760, Governor Francis Fauquier of Virginia wrote to the commanding general of British forces in America, "I most sincerely wish it had been the policy of these Colonies to treat Indians with that justice and humanity you show to them. This and this alone, if any thing can do it, must make them our friends. White, Red, or Black; polished or unpolished men are men." Such noble sentiments, however, would have been scoffed at on the edge of the frontier.

Captain Jonas Friend built his fort in the spring of 1775 under orders from the colonial government. Also under orders, he organized a company of volunteers to assist in guarding the forts and frontiers of Tygart's Valley. Benjamin Cleaver entered the service under Captain Friend again, apparently as a sergeant, and was stationed in Tygart's Valley. He built another fort under orders from the government and remained in service during the spring and summer. Apparently Captain Friend's company was casually organized, and as casually disbanded when he judged danger had passed. He knew there was no danger of attack by the British from east of the mountains. He knew also that Indians were unwilling to attack in winter because they could not cover their tracks in the snow. He was right on both counts. Tygart's Valley remained peaceful that winter.

Benjamin Cleaver was again ordered out in the summer of 1776 by the government of the United States or by Virginia—he could not remember which—guarding the forts and frontiers of Tygart's Valley. On one occasion he went to guard beef cattle from Tygart's Valley "on towards Pittsburgh." The cattle were intended for the army of the revolution and the journey took about a month. Though he did not state so in his affidavit, it is quite likely that troops who drove cattle to Pennsylvania brought back arms and ammunition to the settlements. Oley Valley had by now become one of the chief arsenals for Washington's army.

William Cleaver, Junior, swore as follows in an affidavit:

> That in the year 1776 he lived in Tiger's Valey in Virginia on the Monongahala river and the Indians being very troublesome the people were "forted." He volunteered for service guarding the forts and frontiers of Tiger's Valey, that he served under Capt Smith for the purpose aforesaid upward of three months. . . .

He was then fifteen or sixteen years old.

Then came the "Year of the Three Sevens," perhaps the bloodiest in Indian warfare on the whole Virginia frontier. After the outbreak of fighting between Britain and the colonies, most of the northern and western tribes joined with the British. Only the persuasion of Cornstalk kept the Shawnees from joining also. The settlers forted, unable to protect themselves, the colonial government decided to establish a chain of forts, including one at Wheeling and one at Point Pleasant. Then the Shawnees decided to go over to the British. Cornstalk, still trying to keep the peace, decided to go to Point Pleasant and wield any influence he could. He managed to convey information that the Shawnees were ready to join the other tribes in an attack, but the whites decided to take him hostage and hold him while an attack could be organized against the Indians.

Blunders ensued. Not enough volunteers could be found. Supplies that were supposed to arrive by water from Pittsburgh did not come. Cornstalk's son, worried over his long absence, came to the Ohio and was allowed to cross over to his father. The next day two whites crossed the Great Kanawha hunting and were attacked by two Indians. One was killed and scalped. Whites who had gone to bring back the bloody body took up a cry to kill the Indians in the fort. Cornstalk, facing death with his son, said, "My son, the Great Spirit has seen fit that we should die together, and has sent you here to that end. It is his will and let us submit;—it is all for the best." Cornstalk turned and fell, his body pierced by seven bullets.

The march against the Indians across the Ohio was never mounted. Indians retaliated with attacks on forts and lonely cabins. Tygart's Valley was one of the places attacked, in the first serious raid on that part of the frontier in the war. In early December a party of twenty Indians came within ten miles of the settlements, but snow having fallen, they were afraid to come closer because they could not cover their tracks. On December 15 they attacked Darby Connolly's house in the upper end of the valley, murdered him and his wife and several of their children, and took the rest prisoner. Then they went to the house of John Stewart and killed him, his wife, and child, and took his sister-in-law prisoner. A man discovered the murders and sent word down to Benjamin Wilson's Fort.

The next morning Colonel Wilson, then a commissioned officer in the Revolutionary army, took thirty men to the scene of the murders. They trailed the Indians five days through rain and snow, at times wading water up to the waist, in weather so cold that icicles formed on their clothing. When they saw that they could not overtake the Indians, they returned to Tygart's Valley. William Cleaver, Junior, was a member of Colonel Wilson's party.

In spite of raids and rumors of raids settlers continued to cross the mountains and hack out places for themselves in the wilderness. By the beginning of the Revolution most of the tillable land along Tygart's Valley River—the rich bottom land—had been taken up. Soon there were settlements on all the waters of the Monongahela, in some places up to the mountain slopes. Government became increasingly difficult, at times unmanageable. Renegades had to be dealt with, controversies settled. Augusta County was large; Staunton, the county seat, was far away, on the other side of the mountains. Recording a routine land transaction took days of travel. Transporting a person accused of crime required as much time or more, and guards as well. Settlers could justify themselves if they sometimes took the law into their own hands and meted out punishment as they saw fit.

The law of Augusta County, of the Commonwealth of Virginia,

was based on English law and any changes were subject to veto by the king. Punishment for crimes was harsh. Thieves got thirty-nine lashes on the bare back. So did runaway slaves, Negro or Indian. Men and women were pilloried in Staunton for minor disturbances. A long list of crimes required capital punishment. A gallows was built outside Staunton, ironically, across the road from the slaughterhouse.

Settlers in Tygart's Valley deemed themselves capable of managing their own affairs and setting up their own government. They had seen new counties formed east of the mountains and decided the time had come for new counties west of the mountains. Following the custom of the times, they joined with neighbors at Buckhannon's Creek and on the west fork of the Monongahela in a petition dated November 6, 1777, and addressed to the Speaker and the Gentlemen of the House of Delegates of Virginia:

The petition of a number of the inhabitants of Tiger's Valley settlement and the west fork of the Monongalia River and Buckhannan's Creek settlement Humbly sheweth that your petitioners labours under great hardships from their being obliged to tend court in Staunton(?) in order to have their necessary business done, at the distance of one hundred and eight miles from the nearest inhabitants in the Tiger's Valley, one hundred fifty from the nearest settlement on the west fork of Monongalia and two hundred miles from the last inhabited part of our settlement, which great distance and exceeding badness of the roads, and the difficulty of crossing eight large mountains, forty miles of which is uninhabited, vis, from the Tiger's Valley water to Powtomack waters. We are informed that the old part of Augusta are petitioning to have the same divided into towns or counties for the conveniency of the people; we your petitioners humbly pray we may not be joined to any county that lies to the east of the Allegania Mountains, nor included in any county on the waters of James River or the south branch of the Potowmack, nor Monongalia County, for we flatter ourselves we are able to build and support all publick buildings necessary for a county town—Therefore we your petitioners humbly request your Honourable House would take their case under consideration and grant them a new county including Tiger's Valley Settlement and the settlement on the west fork of the Monongalia and also Buckannon's Creek settlement, which will greatly ease your petitioners and they as in duty shall ever pray.

Among the signers of this petition were William Cleaver, Senior, Joshua Cleaver, Benjamin Cleaver, Charles Clever, and William Clever, Junior. As one hand wrote all the names, it appears to be more nearly a census of the men and older boys of the settlements. William Cleaver, Junior, for instance, was sixteen when the petition was signed.

This petition was rejected by the Assembly on November 25, 1778. Then, in opposition to the settlers' wishes, the Assembly included Tygart's Valley in the newly formed Monongalia County. The county seat was at Morgantown, still a considerable distance away over routes dangerous to travel. In 1784, Harrison County, including Tygart's Valley, was formed from Monongalia, and Clarksburg became the county seat. Then, in 1786 land was taken from Harrison to form Randolph County, with Beverly, where Files had his cabin and Westfall his fort, named the county seat.

As long as they were in Augusta County the settlers had to transact their affairs in Staunton, no matter the distance, the hazards of travel. In turn, county orders had to go out from Staunton. Much of the early history of Tygart's Valley is in those order books. For instance, William Cleaver, Daniel Westfall, Francis Wire, and John Warrick were ordered to locate a road from Jonas Friend's place to the plantation of Darby Connolly, deceased. This would have been from the mouth of Leading Creek up the valley to Connolly's Run, a distance of some thirty miles. Locating meant marking out a trail with slashes on trees. No need to build a wagon road at the time. There was still not a wagon in Tygart's Valley.

Early surveyors usually followed the easiest grades when locating a road, but not always, especially when the road crossed good land. Farmers were known to have said, "I don't mind you laying out a road on my land but keep it along the hills. Don't let it cross my meadow."

Augusta County records show orders for both William and Benjamin Cleaver as surveyors, and of William as appraiser. On July 2, 1778, he appraised the estate of Moses Thompson, the land lying on Cherry Tree Fork, Thompson's Meadows, and Big Lick.

Settlers of Tygart's Valley left few records of their own of their way of life. A few accounts, however, do exist. The great Methodist missionary, Francis Asbury, who once called Tygart's Valley "the valley of desperation," wrote in his diary in 1784:

At Cheat River we had a mixed congregation of sinners, Presbyterians, Baptists, and it may be, of saints: I had liberty and gave it to them as the lord gave it to me—plain enough. Three thick—on the floor—such is our lodging —but no matter: God is with us.

In July 1788 he was there again, and the hardships he reported must have been the hardships of all:

Thursday 10. We had to cross the Alleghany mountain again, at a bad passage. Our course lay over mountains and through valleys, and the mud and mire was such as might scarcely be expected in December. We came to an old, forsaken habitation in Tygart's Valley. Here our horses grazed about, while we boiled our meat. Midnight brought us up at Jones's, after riding forty, or perhaps fifty miles. The old man, our host, was kind enough to wake us up at four o'clock in the morning. We journeyed on through devious lonely wilds, where no food might be found, except what grew in the woods, or was carried with us. We met with two women who were going to see their friends, and to attend the quarterly meeting at Clarksburg. Near midnight we stopped at A———'s, who hissed his dogs at us: but the women were determined to get to quarterly meeting, so we went in. Our supper was tea. Brothers Phoebus and Cook took to the woods; old———gave up his bed to the women. I lay along the floor on a few deerskins with the fleas. That night our poor horses got no corn; and next morning they had to swim across the Monongahela. After a twenty miles' ride we came to Clarksburg, and man and beast so outdone that it took us ten hours to accomplish it. I lodged with Col. Jackson. Our meeting was held in a long, close room belonging to the Baptists. Our use of the house it seems gave offense. There attended about seven hundred people, to whom I preached with freedom; and I believe the Lord's power reached the hearts of some. After administering the sacrament, I was well satisfied to take my leave. We rode thirty miles to Father Haymond's [at Fairmont] after three o'clock, Sunday afternoon, and made it nearly eleven before we came in. About midnight we went to rest, and rose at five o'clock, next morning. My mind has been severely tried under the great fatigue endured both by myself and my horse. O, how glad should I be of a plain, clean plank to lie on, as preferable to most of the beds; and where the beds are in a bad state, the floors are worse. The gnats are almost as troublesome here, as the mosquitoes in the lowlands of the seaboard. This country will require much work to make it tolerable. The people are, many of them, of the boldest cast of adventurers, and with some the decencies of civilized society are scarcely regarded, two instances of which I myself witnessed. The great landholders who are industrious will soon show the effects of the aristocracy of wealth, by lording it over their poorer neighbours, and by securing to themselves all the offices of profit and honour. On the one hand savage warfare teaches them to be cruel; and on the other, the preaching of Antinomians poisons them with error in doctrine; Good moralists they are not, and good Christians they cannot be, unless they are better taught.

Tuesday, 15. I had a lifeless, disorderly people to hear me at Morgantown, to whom I preached on "I will hear what the Lord will Speak." It is a matter of grief to behold the excesses, particularly in drinking, which abound here. I preached at a new chapel near Colonel Martin's, and felt much life, love, and power. Rode to the widow R———'s, and refreshed with a morsel to eat; thence to M. Harden's, where, though we had an earth floor, we had good beds and table entertainment.

Sunday, 18. We had a warm sermon at M'Neal's, at which many were highly offended; but I trust their false peace is broken. There are many bears in this part of the country; not long since, a child in this neighbourhood was killed by one.

Monday, 19. Rode to Drinnon's, whose wife was killed, and his son taken prisoner by the Indians.

Tuesday, 20. I believe I never before travelled such a path as I this day rode over the mountains to reach Mr. Nelson's in Tyger-Valley.

Wednesday, 21. I preached at Wilson's. Here many careless people do not hear a sermon more than once in one or two years.

Antinomianism, the belief that not moral law but faith alone is necessary to salvation, could have been a comfortable doctrine and a pragmatic one in the presence of greed and violence on the frontier.

William Cleaver and his family prospered in Tygart's Valley but the promise of better land, better crops, better living in Kentucky drew him. Five years before Bishop Asbury made his first visit, William Cleaver with some of his neighbors, Daniel Westfall and Edward Skidmore among them, had set out to find a new home in the wilderness.

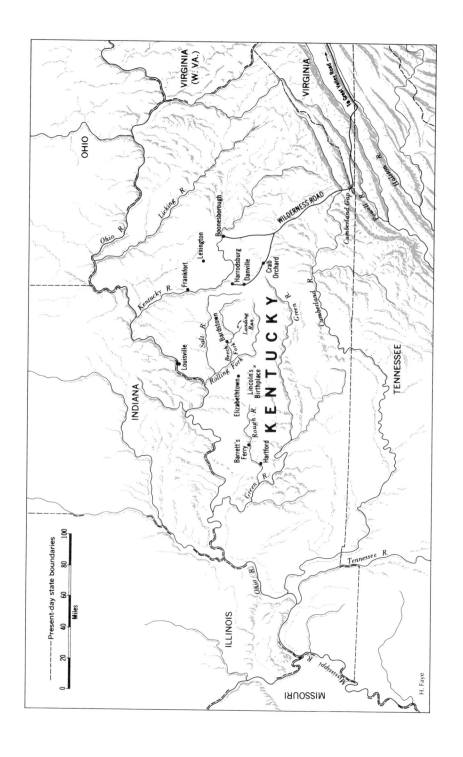

OHIO

VIRGINIA
(W. VA.)

Ohio R.

Licking R.

Lexington

Boonesborough

VIRGINIA

WILDERNESS ROAD

To Great Valley Road

Cumberland Gap

Holston R.

Clinch R.

Powell R.

Frankfort

Harrodsburg

Danville

Crab
Orchard

Kentucky R.

K E N T U C K Y

Green R.

Cumberland R.

Louisville

Salt R.

Bardstown

Beech Fork

Landing
Run

Rolling Fork

Lincoln's ×
Birthplace

Elizabethtown

Rough R.

Barrett's
Ferry

Hartford

Green R.

INDIANA

TENNESSEE

Ohio R.

Tennessee R.

ILLINOIS

Mississippi R.

MISSOURI

H. Faye

- - - - - Present-day state boundaries

Miles

0   20   40   60   80   100

Kentucky

Dᴜʀɪɴɢ ᴛʜᴇ ꜰɪᴠᴇ ʏᴇᴀʀs ᴛʜᴀᴛ ᴡɪʟʟɪᴀᴍ ᴄʟᴇᴀᴠᴇʀ ᴡᴀs ᴄʟᴇᴀʀ-
ɪɴɢ ᴀɴᴅ ʙᴜɪʟᴅɪɴɢ ᴀɴᴅ ᴘʟᴀɴᴛɪɴɢ ɪɴ ᴛʏɢᴀʀᴛ's ᴠᴀʟʟᴇʏ ᴛʜᴇ ᴍᴀɪɴ-
sᴛʀᴇᴀᴍ ᴏꜰ sᴇᴛᴛʟᴇᴍᴇɴᴛ ʜᴀᴅ ᴛᴜʀɴᴇᴅ ᴛᴏᴡᴀʀᴅ ᴋᴇɴᴛᴜᴄᴋʏ, ᴅʀᴀᴡɴ
there by accounts of rich land and good hunting reported by various
white hunters and explorers: Dr. Thomas Walker, perhaps as early
as 1747; Christopher Gist and George Croghan in 1751; John Findlay
and Daniel Boone in 1769; George Washington as surveyor for John
Fry in the period between 1770 and 1772; and numerous others,
including English traders and long hunters. In October 1774, in the
Treaty of Camp Charlotte, made with Lord Dunmore, the Shawnees
yielded hunting rights in the part of Virginia called Kaintuck, and at
the same time agreed to let white men go up and down the Ohio
River unmolested. Thus the way was opened for settlers to press on
to the lush meadows of the blue grass. The risks, in spite of Indian
agreements, were greater than any before encountered by western
pioneers; so were the potential rewards, especially for the land
speculators. Even before Dunmore's war began, the speculators
were at work—chief among them Judge Richard Henderson, a North
Carolina lawyer.

For some ten years, with Daniel Boone as his spotter and surveyor, Henderson had speculated in frontier lands, but in a comparatively modest way. Then Kentucky, with its broad sweep to the Ohio,
became known. It was enough to make a land speculator dream of
empire, and Henderson did. In August 1774, he organized the Louisa
Company, based on a proposal to lease from the Cherokees twenty
million acres of land south of the Ohio and west of the Great Kanawha, with an access route through the Cumberland Gap. He and his

[97]

associates found the Cherokees quite willing to negotiate, and able to do so because the treaties with the Iroquois at Fort Stanwyx and with the Shawnees at Camp Charlotte had left them in control. In December 1774, Henderson advertised in Virginia and North Carolina newspapers for settlers to take up Louisa Company land in five-hundred-acre plots at twenty shillings a hundred acres and a yearly quitrent of two shillings.

Then, imbued with prospects of owning a vast proprietary domain, even of founding a fourteenth colony, to be called Transylvania, Henderson decided to buy rather than lease. Again the Cherokees—most of them—were willing. In January 1775, Henderson reorganized the Louisa Company as the Transylvania Company and arranged a meeting with the Cherokee chiefs at Sycamore Shoals on the Watauga River. In exchange for ten thousand pounds in trading goods the chiefs, over the objections of a few of their number, ceded all of Kentucky lying between the Ohio River and the Kentucky and Cumberland rivers, and east to the Cumberland Mountains.

This purchase, entered into by private citizens without government sanction, had dubious legality, but that did not deter Henderson. A week before the treaty was signed he sent Daniel Boone with thirty axmen to blaze a track through Cumberland Gap to the Kentucky River, a track soon to be known as the Wilderness Road. Boone knew this country well. As early as 1769 he had entered through the Gap and followed the Warriors' Path deep into the wilderness. He had first seen the Ohio in 1770. In May 1773, he had made his first attempt to settle his family in Kentucky, an attempt in which he lost his son James, who was tortured to death by Indians. Boone had been forced to turn back then but he was willing to try again. Three days after the purchase was signed Henderson, with some thirty men and a train of wagons and packhorses, set out on the trail Boone had blazed. They had to give up the wagons but eventually they arrived at the Kentucky River, where they found that Boone and his men had built some cabins but had spent most of their time laying off choice tracts of land for themselves.

Though the Indians had not been troublesome on a broad front up to this time, Henderson started building a fort, which he completed in June and called Boonesborough as a compliment to Daniel Boone. It was not the first in Kentucky. Benjamin Logan had already established Logan's Station, also called St. Asaph's, and James Harrod had built what was first called Harrod's Town, then Old Town, and finally Harrodsburg. Both built their forts in defiance of Henderson's claim of ownership. They were not the only defiant ones. Settlers singly and in groups had tomahawked claims for themselves secure in the knowledge that Kentucky was a territory of Fincastle County, Virginia, where their allegiance lay rather than with the proprietors of the Colony of Transylvania. Henderson himself was doing a land-office business at Boonesborough: deeds to five hundred and sixty thousand acres had soon been entered.

Recognizing the threat posed to his proprietary control, the lawlessness inherent where there was no law, Henderson invited the other stations to send delegates to a meeting at Boonesborough on May 23, 1775, the purpose being to establish proprietary laws. This congress, held one month after the Battle of Lexington and Concord, was the first legislative body west of the Allegheny Mountains. Eighteen delegates gathered under an elm at Boonesborough and heard Henderson proclaim in oratory as unrestrained as the wilderness itself, "You, perhaps, are fixing the palladium, or placing the first cornerstone of an edifice, the height and magnificence of whose superstructure is now in the womb of futurity, and can only become great and glorious in proportion to the excellence of its foundation."

Under his direction the delegates proceeded to set up a system of courts and militia, provisions for the punishment of criminals, the preservation of game and range, the latter presented by Daniel Boone and his brother Squire, and, perhaps as significant for Kentucky as any act of the day, controls for the proper breeding of horses, a measure also presented by Daniel Boone.

Whatever else might have been inferred at the end of their deliberations, this was still a proprietary government. The Transylvania Company still owned the land and the disposal of it, so long as the original terms of sale were adhered to. The proprietors could still expect to collect a quitrent of two shillings per hundred acres to the end of time—this when residents of the thirteen colonies were in the process of breaking away from a government that was in many respects proprietary, though the men at Boonesborough did not know the battle had been joined. It did not take into full account the character of frontiersmen, as succinctly described by Lord Dunmore: ". . . They do not conceive that Government has any right to forbid their taking possession of a Vast tract of Country. . . ."

Such men would not look long with favor on paying quitrents to Richard Henderson. During the summer of 1775 new settlers crowded into Kentucky, squatting on land that pleased them, ignoring the claims of the Transylvania Company. These were tough, rugged men, in search of independence, in search of land. Unable to cope with the squatters, Henderson raised the price from twenty shillings to two pounds and ten shillings per hundred acres, to squeeze out what profits they could while they could. Dissatisfaction increased. Soon the Transylvania Company proprietors were in Philadelphia appealing to the Continental Congress, then in session, to make Transylvania the fourteenth colony.

In 1776 George Rogers Clark, a young Virginian who had visited Boonesborough the year before, returned to Kentucky as a permanent settler. Seeing the extent of dissatisfaction over the land deals, he called for a convention to meet at Harrodsburg on June 6. Delegates from all the stations attended and after due deliberation took two important actions: they denounced the operations of the Transylvania Company, and they drew up a petition asking that Kentucky be made a county of Virginia. Early in 1777 the House of Burgesses in Williamsburg took the desired action and established Kentucky County. Henderson, for compensation, received from Virginia two hundred thousand acres lying between the Ohio and Green rivers. Later North Carolina yielded to him the same amount.

Thus Virginia came into control of the frontier west of the Allegheny Mountains northward to Pennsylvania and southward to the Tennessee territory—a ragged line several hundred miles long, with pockets of settlements, "little wests," all along it, where thousands of determined men and women fought on two fronts: the hostile Indians and the frightening wilderness. This in the midst of the Revolution, when war at hand engaged most of the energies of the colonies to the east, when people on the outer frontiers were left to carry their fight almost entirely alone.

Their numbers increased. In that lay their strength. Daily they were joined by settlers long experienced on other frontiers, and by newcomers getting their first taste of the wilderness—English, Welsh, Scotch, Scotch-Irish, Germans—in an ever-increasing stream. They came and no questions were asked, no lineage required. Cruelly they fought the Indians. Some of them feuded among themselves as cruelly. Kentucky became what the Indians called it: the dark and bloody ground.

Beech Fork

WILLIAM CLEAVER WAS among those who came. In the early spring of 1779 he was surveying land in Tygart's Valley. In the fall of the same year he was surveying land for himself on the Beech Fork of the Salt River in Kentucky County. Word of the Kentucky Canaan had been spread by Richard Henderson's newspaper notices. Long hunters and scouts told of broad expanses of level land, of rich blue grass far as the eye could see, of bottom land where cane grew dense and higher than a buffalo's back—of land untouched except by the buffalo trace and the Indian trail. True, there were also reports of troublesome Indians, of murders and scalpings and whites taken prisoner, but these were the same all along the frontier.

The will to move on out west grew strong in William Cleaver and in at least some of his neighbors and friends. Without having seen Kentucky, they sensed that it promised more than Tygart's Valley, which, squeezed as it was between mountains, had little more land to be cleared and farmed. William Cleaver had sons, seven of them. They would have to have land for themselves and their families. No doubt this need for land was the most compelling reason for moving on, but there were others, including the need for adventure, the need to see another part of the wilderness, the hope perhaps that by getting in early he might better establish himself and his sons.

William Cleaver had lived in Tygart's Valley five years or so— long enough for trees he had deadened to rot and fall, for houses and barns to be built, for orchards to grow out of seeds and cuttings carefully carried over the mountains, for him and his neighbors to overcome some of the worst trials of a first frontier. Because of the work done, the conflict in him, as well as in his neighbors, must have

[101]

been great: whether to go, whether to stay. No doubt the land was a deciding factor for him. There was just not enough. The original thousand-acre tract still had not been divided. When it was, at best he could not hope for more than a fifth. Better to leave behind the accumulations of five years of hard work, hard living when there was so much more to be had farther on. Among his neighbors there were others of like mind: Westfalls, Donohos, Skidmores. They had pioneered together in South Branch Valley and Tygart's Valley, both in Virginia. There was comfort, perhaps, in the knowledge that Kentucky, though far away, was still within the boundaries of Virginia.

The decision made, three routes to Kentucky were open to them: one by water, two by land. If they traveled at all by land they had to leave on foot or on horseback; there was still not a wagon rut in all of Tygart's Valley. By water, they had to go up toward Pittsburgh to Red Stone and then down the Monongahela and Ohio, or they had to go by land over to the Great Kanawha and down it to the Ohio. Because of hostile Indians, travel down the Ohio was thought more dangerous.

One land route would have taken them by trail to the Greenbrier River and then down the Hunter's Trail to Cumberland Gap and on into Kentucky by Boone's Wilderness Road. The other would have taken them back over the Alleghenies to Winchester or Staunton, more likely Staunton, and down the Philadelphia Road to a branch that led toward Cumberland Gap. By either of these routes they would have had to cross mountains incredibly rugged, where paths dark and narrow wound through long stretches of laurel. If they went by Staunton the journey could have been made on horseback; a part of it probably by wagon. This last was the main stream south to west at the time; occasionally there were taverns and houses along it where travelers could stop. By this route they would have gone down the Great Trading Path to where it intersected the Wilderness Road at the Long Island of Holston River, just south of the present Abington. Then, miles after they had passed through Cumberland Gap, they would have come to where the Wilderness Road forked—the right fork to Boonesborough, the left to Harrod's Town. Then they would have taken the left past Harrod's Town and St. Asaph's and come at last to a little settlement on Beech Fork called Salem.

The only clue to the route they took appears in an affidavit made by Benjamin Cleaver more than fifty years later in which he stated that they came to the falls of the Ohio, the site of Louisville. At the same time William Cleaver, Junior, stated that they had come to the country near the falls of the Ohio. Neither defined the route conclusively.

If their route was by water, it was not an easy one. First they had to get to the Monongahela or the Ohio. Then they had to cut logs and build flatboats or rafts big enough for their goods and some kind of shelter and sturdy enough to withstand currents and shoals. As they floated downstream they had to be constantly on the lookout for unfriendly Indians—or just for Indians. By now they had been through enough to make them regard all Indians as unfriendly, unreliable. Stories had circulated of settlers lured by land speculators with promises of supplies and safety, only to be set upon, scalped, taken prisoner. So they traveled in fear, with advance guards by day, sentinels at night. The Ohio was wide—wide enough for them to be out of danger from arrows if they stayed close to the middle. They could rest by day, travel by night. Still, around every river bend Indians might be lurking. Every night had its own nightmare of possible ambush. Every sound, every movement had to be suspected. A turkey gobbling on the river bank might be a good meal. It might also be an Indian sign, a lure to ambush.

The journey by water or by land might take six months, or in some cases as much as a year. Those who traveled by water often sent cattle and horses by land, guarded by a few men, moving slowly, as they had to graze on the way. Nights, the animals had to be hobbled to keep them from straying into the wilderness. Mornings, the hobbles had to be removed for another day of travel.

In the fall of 1779 William Cleaver and his family came to where Landing Run empties into Beech Fork, given the name because, running swift and deep, it made a natural boat landing. On one side of Landing Run the land was rich bottom land, covered with cane, good for farming. On the other it rose to a bluff where houses might be built. In the edge of a low range of hills called "The Knobs," it was remote from other settlers. John Ritchie was among the nearest, the John Ritchie who was reportedly the first distiller of corn whiskey in Kentucky. Salem was some six miles away and across Beech Fork, an older settlement though still made up of only a few scattered houses. As early as 1776 James Cox, Proctor Ballard, and others had explored this area on Beech Fork. Some of these explorers moved on. Enough remained to form a settlement.

Why William Cleaver came to Beech Fork is not known. He did have in his possession several treasury warrants and there was land on Beech Fork still to be taken up. It may have been that he had known some of the early explorers of the region, some of whom were from the Monongahela settlements. He may have had information from the men from whom he had purchased his Old Treasury Warrants: William Handold, John Madison, Moses Hunter, and William M. Williams.

In his long trek across the frontier he may have known some of the Linns of Red Stone in Pennsylvania and his neighbor John Ritchie, who is believed to have come to Kentucky with them. Whether he knew them or not, when he surveyed for himself the eight-hundred-and-eighteen-acre tract that he later called his plantation he began at John Ritchie's line, about two miles from Linn's Station, Benjamin Linn's home on Beech Fork. It is known that from the time of their settlement on Beech Fork the Cleaver and Linn families were closely intertwined.

Three of the Linn brothers—Benjamin, Nathan, and William— all typical of the Scotch-Irish settlers on the frontier, made Kentucky history. They were there earlier than the Cleavers, but not much. On December 28, 1778, Nathan and Hannah Linn sold their land near Red Stone and the next May settled on Hingston's Fork of Licking River in Kentucky. William was in Kentucky as early as 1775 and in 1779 made his home on Bear Grass Creek, near present Louisville. As early as 1767, when he was about seventeen, Benjamin crossed the Ohio and traveled among the Indians enough to become a trusted Indian scout and spy. In 1776 he visited Harrodsburg. On July 9, 1777, he married Hannah Sovereigns, or Severns, at Harrodsburg. George Rogers Clark noted in his diary, "Lieutenant Linn married. Great merriment." In the fall of 1778 Benjamin explored Pottinger's Creek near where it empties into Rolling Fork River and the next spring followed it up to its headwaters. He would then early in 1779 have come close to the spot on Beech Fork where William Cleaver took up his land.

On Beech Fork the Cleavers were on a different part of the frontier but their problems were much the same: the same wilderness, the same hostile Indians, the same struggle to claim and hold the land. As a surveyor and land appraiser, William Cleaver knew a good piece of real estate. He also had resources for acquiring it. Between 1779 and 1786 he took title to thirty-six hundred and eighteen acres, all within what was then Jefferson County, all within forty miles or so of the falls of the Ohio. It was at the outer edge of the blue grass, well watered, well timbered. In the bottoms there was a heavy growth of cane for grazing and large beech trees on which he and his sons carved "CLEAVER," a remembrance as well as a sign of ownership. This land would grow the corn and wheat and pumpkins they needed. Cattle could graze on the hillsides. Hogs could fatten in the fall on oak and beech and chestnut mast.

William Cleaver, the records show, acquired this land in the manner of the time. In Williamsburg he purchased Land Office Treasury Warrants. Then he located and marked out the land and showed some kind of improvement—a half-faced house or a cabin, a deadening of trees where he might put a field, perhaps some planting. After that, he could apply for official grants. Delays in this procedure account for the time lags between settling on a place and proving title. They were also a factor in the abuses that arose. A man could mark out a tract simply by putting slashes on trees along his boundary. Another man, and at times still another, could claim the same land or parts of it by putting slashes on different trees. This layering of grants, sometimes three deep, led to innumerable lawsuits and often to the loss of the land by the man who first proved it. Among those who sued and lost was Daniel Boone, who, when he was finally shorn of most of his vast holdings, left Kentucky in bitterness.

William Cleaver, perhaps because he surveyed his own land and lived on it or close to it, apparently avoided these conflicts over ownership. He acquired his land in at least seven different grants and pressed his case on each until it was signed by the governor of the Commonwealth of Virginia. The one for eight hundred and eighteen acres, the original homestead, which he surveyed for himself, was finally signed by Governor Edmund Randolph on January 17, 1788, close to nine years after it was first located. This warrant was numbered 1184 and dated August 30, 1780. As proof that Kentucky County was indeed doing a land-office business, the grant that was issued to him on May 8, 1783, was numbered 15813.

The survey of this plantation, which he dated March 2, 1785, is descriptive of the land and some of the timber on it. The survey locates it

. . . On the South Side of Beech Fork adjoining John Richie's survey on said Fork about two miles from Linns Station and bounded as followeth To

wit Beginning at two beech trees and an Ash said Richies corner on the
Beech Fork thence East one hundred and forty poles to two white oaks &
hickory corner of said Richie thence North forty poles to to a white oak ash
and buckeye thence North Seventy-eight Degrees East eighty poles to two
Ash trees thence South Fortyeight Degrees East fifty poles to two white oaks
near a Glade thence South twentyfive degrees—East seventytwo poles to
two Ash trees and an Ironwood thence South fortysix degrees West ninety
poles to three white oaks at the edge of a glade thence South three degrees
West two hundred and sixtyeight poles to three white oaks on the edge of
a glade thence South thirteen degrees East one hundred and forty poles to
two poplars at the foot of the knobs thence South seventyfive degrees West
two hundred and thirty poles to two white oak and poplar standing on a small
drain of bullrun thence North eight degrees West two hundred and forty
poles to two white oaks and Dogwood North fifty degrees West one hundred
and thirty poles to a sugar and honey locust in the glade North thirty Degrees
east fiftyfive poles to two box oaks on the River bank thence up the meanders
of said Fork to the beginning.

Countless surveys of the time used only trees as markers. In this and
other of his surveys William Cleaver anchored at least some of his
points on identifiable water courses.

This was apparently the last of his tracts to be proved up. Earlier,
deed records show, he had acquired these others:

400 acres	Cedar Creek	January 23, 1784
600 "	Beech Fork	March 16, 1784
1000 "	Harden's Creek	March 16, 1784
400 "	Harden's Creek	October 6, 1784
300 "	Benjamin Linn's Run	January 13, 1784
100 "	Beech Fork	January 13, 1784

By now he had what most pioneers went west for, land—land in his
own name that he could work or let lie fallow, keep or sell, hand
down to his children and their heirs and assigns forever.

Benjamin Cleaver, a surveyor in Augusta County, took up the
work again in Jefferson County. Thirty years old or past, with a family
of his own to look out for, he also acquired land:

100 acres	Beech Fork	October 6, 1784
100 "	Horse Run (Branch)	January 13, 1785
100 "	Poplar Neck	September 25, 1788

Tax lists for 1792 show two entries for William Cleaver, Junior—one for two hundred and fifty-nine acres, the other for two hundred and twelve acres.

William Cleaver's younger sons—Stephen, David, and James—do not appear in early land records. Neither do the other two—Joshua and Charles—whose names do not show in records after Tygart's Valley, though one of them may have been the Cleaver who died on a hunting trip in a cabin at the mouth of Blackford's Creek, where it flows into the Ohio. This would be suggested by the close association of the Cleavers and Blackfords.

At the same time they were acquiring land, building houses, and planting crops, William Cleaver and his older sons had to bear their share of guarding the settlements from Indian marauders from across the Ohio. Indian attacks had been, almost from the beginning, more frequent, more violent in Kentucky than they had been in Tygart's Valley, or in any other part of the frontier north or south. By December 1775, Indian leaders realized that they were losing this vast region that had traditionally been their hunting ground. Their scouts had seen surveying parties marking off the land, and white settlers—men, women, and children—clearing ground for cabins and fields, taking for their own the springs and streams, the woods and meadows, the best places for hunting bear and buffalo. Their only hope, the Indians thought, was to drive the settlers back—back across the mountains. They began their attack not as an organized drive but as a series of raids, by warriors aroused to fight as word against the whites passed from wigwam to wigwam, from village to village.

The first scalping raid at Boonesborough occurred on December 23, 1775, while William Cleaver and his family were still at Tygart's Valley. It left one white boy scalped and dead in a corn field, another missing, either dead or a prisoner. This raid came after a warning. Chief Cornstalk, who in October had signed treaties with the whites at Fort Pitt, had sent word that there were raiding parties over whom he had no control headed for Kentucky. At least some of these parties reached Kentucky and, for weeks after, raids were frequent and punishing. Whites fought back as well as they could—for their own safety and for the reward of five pounds that had been offered for every Indian scalp. For many it was a discouraging fight. They were cut off from the older settlements by hundreds of miles of wilderness through which Indians came and went, or waited in ambush for the moment to strike. To make matters worse, the settlers were short on ammunition and had to rely on what could be brought down the Ohio or over the Wilderness Road, both easy targets for Indians on the warpath.

There were no more warnings and raids were so frequent that by July 1, 1776, there were recommendations that the settlers, because they were unable to defend themselves, should give Kentucky up entirely. These recommendations did not come from Daniel Boone or the settlers at Boonesborough. In spite of intermittent scalping raids on less-protected stations, the settlers at Boonesborough felt comparatively safe, but not for long. On Sunday afternoon, July 7, three young girls, including Daniel Boone's daughter Jemima, went for a canoe ride on the river. Unable to manage the canoe, they let it drift toward a bluff on the opposite side of the fort where, unseen by them, a party of five warriors waited in the thick cane, spying on the settlers. After a brief struggle the girls were prisoners and on their way to the Shawnee towns.

The story of the chase and rescue, with Daniel Boone leading the rescue party, which included Captain Floyd, was one to be told over and over again in lonely cabins. With broken twigs and strips torn from their clothing the girls left whatever sign they could, but they were not missed at the fort till milking time. When the alarm was sounded the men took up the trail as fast as they could but night came before they could travel far. They rested that night and followed the trail all the next day. Again they rested and early in the morning came to a crossing where moccasin prints were still fresh and the water still muddy. A little farther on they came upon a freshly killed buffalo. About noon they found the raiders cooking buffalo meat, and the girls resting. Indians and whites saw each other at about the same time. The first shot hit the Indian sentry but did no more than knock him down. Then Boone took a shot. So did John Floyd. Both had to aim with care to keep from hitting the girls but they were still close to target. After a brief fight the Indians disappeared into the cane brake and the girls were at last safe. Boonesborough was spared but Indian troubles were not over. In fact, they were worsening.

In Kentucky, as on other parts of the frontier, 1777, "the year of the three sevens," began ominously, as the year 1776 had ended.

On December 29, 1776, Indian raiders under Chief Pluggy attacked McClelland's Station, near the site of the present George-town. Though they were fresh from a Christmas Day ambush in which they had killed several whites, they were not able to take the fort and Chief Pluggy himself was killed. The settlers, however, had seen enough. On New Year's Day they decided to abandon their station, though they had fortified it well, and seek safety at Boones-borough. Other stations also gave up. In a short time only three stations were left in all of Kentucky: Boonesborough, Harrodsburg, and St. Asaph's, or Logan's. This consolidation did not come too soon. Blackfish, whose curious friend-enemy relationship with Daniel Boone is one of the strangest in border warfare, was on the warpath. More ominous for the settlers, the Revolution had flared on the frontier and the Shawnees had joined the British. Knowing they could expect little help from outside, Kentucky men formed them-selves into companies and prepared to fight. They also appointed scouts, Benjamin Linn among them, to watch the movements of the Indians.

Early in March a large body of Indians moved toward Harrods-burg and cut off some whites who had gone out to learn what had happened to some abandoned cabins. Benjamin Linn was one of the men cut off. In a trick to decoy the whites, the Indians had left some new rifles stacked near one of the cabins. Linn, suspecting an am-bush, persuaded the others not to go for the rifles. When the Indians realized their trick had failed they began shooting. In the fight that followed Benjamin Linn killed and scalped the first Indian slain in what became the Siege of Harrodsburg, a siege that was to be kept up sporadically for about six months, at times in open fighting, at times in the kind of harassment Captain John Cowan described in his diary on April 25, 1777: "Fresh signs of Indians seen at 2 o'clock; they were heard imitating owls, turkies, &c. at 4; centry spied one at 7; centry shot at three at 10 o'clock."

While keeping the pressure on Harrodsburg, Blackfish, leading almost a hundred warriors, made an attack on Boonesborough. Boone had only twenty-two men. Of necessity he formed them into two reliefs, one for soldiering, one for farming. Though there were fresh Indian signs around the fort, two men went out one morning at sunrise. Within a short time Indians fired on them and chased them back toward the fort. Then, in plain sight of the people inside, they tomahawked and scalped one of the men. Then they attacked the fort. In the fight that followed Boone and others were wounded, but they managed to hold the fort. Frustrated, the Indians stole whatever they could and left. In May they again attacked Boonesborough and then Harrodsburg, only to be driven back. On July 4, Blackfish led still another attack on Boonesborough. Then white reenforcements arrived from North Carolina and the worst fighting was over for the year.

But not the other problems. In the winter of 1777 Benjamin Linn carried a letter from Colonel John Bowman, Kentucky County lieutenant, to Fort Pitt. The letter sets forth the desperate situation:

> . . . The poor Kentucky people who have these twelve months past been confined to three forts on which the Indians have made several fruitless attempts. They have left us almost without horses sufficient to supply the stations, and we are obliged to get all our provisions out of the woods. Our corn the Indians have burned . . . at this time we have not more than two months bread—near 200 women and children . . . many of these families are left desolate widows with small children destitute of necessary clothing.

News of Burgoyne's defeat at Saratoga in October reached the Kentucky frontier in the winter, but it offered small comfort to settlers who had just come through "the year of the three sevens" and could see no end to the Indian depredations.

On February 8, 1778, Daniel Boone and twenty-eight of his men were captured while making salt at the Salt Licks on Licking River. Elated that they had at last taken the big one, Blackfish and his warriors took their prisoners on the long march to Chillicothe and then on to Detroit, where they received a reward from the British. Then, back in the Shawnee towns, Blackfish adopted Boone into the tribe in a long and at times painful ritual. Meanwhile, word of their capture got back to Boonesborough and so discouraged the settlers that some of them, including Rebecca Boone, who thought her husband dead, had retreated all the way back to North Carolina. On June 16 Boone managed to escape and to make his way back to Boonesborough, where he found ruin and desolation. He was not a minute too soon. The largest Indian attack on the settlements was in the making and defenses had been neglected. Blackfish, still angered at Boone's defection from the tribe, laid siege to the fort for more than a week. The defenses held and Blackfish finally withdrew. In the lull that followed, Daniel Boone rejoined Rebecca in North Carolina and remained there until October 1779. During his absence John Bowman led about two hundred men against the Shawnee villages. In an attack they made on Little Chillicothe, Blackfish was wounded by a rifle ball in the thigh, a wound from which he died a few weeks later. The whites destroyed some cabins and crops and withdrew back to Kentucky.

The Cleavers arrived on Beech Fork in the fall of 1779, probably about the time Daniel Boone returned to Boonesborough, certainly in time to know the anxiety and fear brought by Indian raids. They found themselves in a country broken by streams and hills, isolated by woods and rank growths of cane, the way in or out by buffalo trail or shallow water. They were thirty or forty miles from Harrodsburg, somewhat farther from Boonesborough and St. Asaph's. Now that these three had held through all the Indian troubles, other strongholds were coming into being. The Virginia legislature "founded" the town of Louisville at the Falls of the Ohio in 1779, but four years had to pass before it had enough settlers to support a store. In the same year a fort was built at Lexington, and there were others. At the time, however, there were no forts in the Beech Fork area and the settlers, widely scattered, were almost defenseless in the event of a surprise attack, the Cleavers among them.

People have a saying that three moves equal a fire. This was never truer than on the frontier, and must have been true of the Cleaver family. During their five years in Tygart's Valley they had made by hand most of the tools necessary for providing food and shelter, tools they had to leave behind when they moved to Kentucky. Here again, starting with only the few things they could carry into the wilderness, they went through the pioneer experience of building pole cabins, breaking new ground for planting corn, working from daylight till dark with their eyes and ears constantly alert for some Indian sign. While night came on there was anxious watching till the last one had returned from woods or fields and the cabins had been made as secure as they could for the night.

Darkness increased the sense of isolation. Daytime, there might be thin smoke rising from the three-quarters chimney of a distant cabin. Nighttime, there was nothing—not even a candle beam. Candles were scarce, when they had any at all, and their light might catch a lurking Indian's eye. So their light was from a dirt fireplace in a stick-and-dirt chimney rising from a dirt floor. At night they had to be inside, hugging the fire, at times hogging it as winter wind whistled and cold seeped through dirt and wood. On the same fire the women boiled the meat and in the ashes parched the corn or baked the bread, when they had corn or meal. Around it they ate with hunting knives and fingers—fingers were made before forks was a pioneer joke—and Hannah Cleaver, apparently at the "nussing" stage with Sarah, sat among them, and after the nursing she chewed meat and corn and, using her finger, passed it from her mouth to her child's.

Around the same fire they worked at night, cutting and thonging leggings and moccasins; hewing out and smoothing down wooden hoes and rakes and plows; hollowing out the end of a log for a mortar and rounding the end of a stick for a pestle to beat corn into coarse meal; shaping wooden wedges and mauls for riving out boards for roofs and oak and hickory withes for weaving baskets. Anything they bought had to be packed down from Philadelphia and over the Wilderness Road or brought by boat up from New Orleans—both routes hazardous and expensive. A man fortunate enough to bring in a broadax or a drawing knife could be expected to share them with his neighbors.

At night they talked, their talk mostly of the present—of the work done today, the work waiting to be done tomorrow—of hunting meat and vegetables in the woods, for they were living mostly on the range—of Indians, always of Indians, interspersing, sobering anything they had to say. They were more exposed than they had ever been in Tygart's Valley. They had to live daily with the fear of an attack on cabins when the men were away, of women and children tomahawked and scalped or taken away prisoner, of finding one of their number dead and scalped in a corn field, of a call for the able-bodied men to go out as soldiers in the never-ending struggle. Talk that hardened hearts and ossified minds until in them a belief was distilled: the only good Indian was a dead Indian.

There were at least a dozen members of the Cleaver household ranging in age from adults in their early fifties to children not yet able to talk. Inevitably they absorbed feelings against the Indians, "the yellow bellies"—against their cruelty first and then against their laziness, their slovenly way of life. If the question ever arose, they could easily justify taking the Indians' lands for themselves with two basic arguments: Indians never really used it; Indians did not understand the meaning of individual ownership. Children were taught fear and hatred—teaching they passed on to their children and their children's children for the next hundred years while the venom of one against the other made ever-suppurating sores.

There must have been talk of the past, but for the Cleavers on Beech Fork it was talk of an American past. Unlike the newly arrived settlers they frequently met on the frontier—Scotch-Irish from Northern Ireland, "Old Sod" Presbyterians from Scotland, Germans with an accent to be laughed at—the Cleavers were fourth-generation American. They could say they had "Dutch blood" or that their kinfolks were English but the European experience was no longer in their minds except for here and there a song or tune or story, and even these were undergoing Americanization—of changes to include American place names or to make the lords and ladies of balladry little different from somebody down the road a piece. Forgetfulness had to a large extent cleared the European past from their minds, and there were few books to refresh their memory. Had there been books, few could have read them. So their talk of the past was of the closer generations, parents and grandparents, and of their struggles for survival against hardship and danger. They had stories closer at home, of one or another among them who had become a hero, though the word was not used—for overcoming an Indian, for driving a panther away from a cabin in the middle of the night. These stories, told and retold, had their part in the creation of the frontier myth.

Talk must have turned at times to the American Revolution, of which they were a part but a part so remote that they felt left out, neglected. The fight with the now-hated Redcoats was a wilderness away and settlers on Beech Fork got little word of either victory or defeat. Their fight, they knew, was against the Indians—Indians fighting more for themselves than for the British—and they had little help. True, Virginia sometimes sent them powder and bullets and a few militia men but the supply was not enough or regular enough to be counted on. They had to depend upon themselves. This only increased their feeling of independence from Virginia or from anyone else.

In spite of dangers and hardships, settlers kept coming in, undeterred even by tales of horror and fear they heard from families on the Wilderness Road going out, retreating. They came in such numbers that in 1780 Kentucky County was divided into three counties: Jefferson, with John Floyd colonel; Lincoln, with Benjamin Logan colonel; Fayette, with John Todd colonel and Daniel Boone

lieutenant colonel. The Cleavers were in Jefferson County, on a part
of Beech Fork that was being settled rapidly. In Salem alone there
were thirty-three families. Defenses closer at hand were needed. In
1780 Isaac Cox and other settlers built a fort and stockade about five
miles north of Salem and called it Cox's Station. In the same year
James Rogers built a fort near Cedar Creek and to the west of Salem.
Benjamin Linn settled on Beech Fork and built Linn's Station two
miles from William Cleaver's land in 1783, or perhaps earlier. There
were soon others in the area: Pottinger's, Goodin's, Polk-Kincheloe's,
the latter called the Burnt Station because Indians killed or captured
a number of whites forted there and burned the buildings.

These forts were not built too soon. During the early part of 1780
there were a number of Indian attacks on isolated settlements and
the people spent much of their time forted, as soon as there were
forts to retreat to. These attacks left whites tomahawked and scalped,
their survivors afraid and angry and of a mind to perpetrate some
atrocities of their own. A few did, even on squaws, and proudly
displayed scalps as trophies.

In October 1780, Daniel Boone and his brother Edward went to
the Upper Blue Licks to boil salt. On their way home they stopped
to rest and graze their horses. Edward cracked hickory nuts with
stones. Daniel shot a bear, wounded it, and followed it into the
woods. Just as he came upon the carcass he heard shots and knew
Indians had attacked Edward. Knowing he was too late to be of any
help to his brother, he hid in the cane and waited till the Indians gave
up the hunt. Then he slipped away. The next day the whites found
Edward's body with the head cut off.

The whites had to fight back. The Cleaver men, like other able-
bodied men on the frontier, were expected to take part and were
subject to calling out at any time. There is no record of their having
served officially during 1779, when they were on the move from
Tygart's Valley, or in 1780, when they were getting settled on Beech
Fork. No doubt they—father and sons—were called on to guard
against Indians and to help build Linn's Station or Rogers' Station or
perhaps others.

Seventeen eighty-one was a bad year for the settlers, especially
in the rise of British influence among the Indians and in the deaths
of leading Indian fighters, among them William Linn. A man in his
late forties, William Linn had served as scout and Indian fighter in
both Braddock's and Dunmore's campaigns. In the latter, while on

a raid against Shawnee towns in Ohio, he was wounded in the shoulder seriously enough to be out of combat for a time. After the Battle of Point Pleasant he went to Kentucky, where he visited Boonesborough and tomahawked a claim for himself that included the Big Blue Lick. From then on his name was prominent in Kentucky Indian fighting, as second in command to George Rogers Clark, and as a spy in the territory west toward the Mississippi. On February 9, 1780, he secured a certificate to land on Bear Grass Creek, near the falls of the Ohio, where he built William Linn's Station. He was one of the petitioners for the founding of Louisville and became active in the affairs of Jefferson County. On March 5, 1781, he was shot by Indians, apparently from ambush, while riding alone to attend county court in Louisville. Others in his party, riding along behind him, heard some shots and went in search of him. They found his horse dead. The next day they found his body about a mile from the station. Ironically, in spite of all he had done for Kentucky, the station was lost to his heirs because the land legally granted to him was subject to a prior claim.

His brother Nathan suffered a similar fate on May 9, 1781. Indians attacked McAfee's Station, six miles from Harrodsburg, where Nathan lived with his family. Nathan responded to the call for help and was killed, leaving his wife, Hannah, and three young daughters, among them one named Hannah. Though not as well known as either his brother William or his brother Benjamin, he was a soldier in the Colonial Army and fought in a number of Indian skirmishes. In his will, probated in Lincoln County, he divided his property equally among his wife and three daughters and named his wife and Ozias Welch executors.

The situation had become so desperate that on April 16, 1781, John Floyd wrote a letter to Thomas Jefferson, governor of Virginia, in which he described conditions at the falls of the Ohio in the winter and spring of that year:

We are obliged to live in Forts in this County, and notwithstanding all the Caution that we use, forty seven of the Inhabitants have been killed & taken by the Savages. Besides a number wounded since Jany. last—Amongst the last is Major William Lyn.

Whole families are destroyed, without regard to Age or Sex—Infants are torn from their mothers Arms & their Brains dashed out against Trees, as they are necessarily removing from one Fort to another for safety or Convenience—Not a week passes & some weeks scarcely a day without some of our distressed inhabitants feeling the fatal effects of the infernal rage and fury of those Execrable Hell Hounds.

Our garrisons are dispersed over an Extensive Country, and a large proportion of the Inhabitants, are helpless Widows & Orphans who have lost their Husbands and fathers by Savage Hands, and left among Strangers, without the most common necessities of life.

In 1781—the month or day not exact in their affidavits—Benjamin Cleaver, then thirty, and William Cleaver, Junior, twenty, were called out to service. No doubt they went garbed like the ordinary frontier soldier, wearing leather moccasins, leggings, pants, and belted jacket, with a tomahawk hung from the belt on one side, a scalping knife on the other, with a long rifle over the shoulder and shot pouch and powder horn in easy reach. They had been ordered out by George Rogers Clark to assist in building and guarding Fort Nelson at the falls of the Ohio and were under the immediate command of William Linn.

Clark, not to be confused with his brother William, the explorer, had been commissioned by Governor Thomas Jefferson on January 22, 1781, as "brigadier-general of the forces to be embodied in an expedition westward of the Ohio." It was a good choice. George Rogers Clark was already a frontier hero, and with reason. He had been a settler at Harrodsburg in its earliest days and had been fighting Indians since as early as 1777. In May 1778, as a lieutenant colonel he had sailed with a force of 175 men down the Ohio almost to the Mississippi, crossed over land, and in a daring raid on July 4 captured Kaskaskia. As a spoil of conquest he organized this new territory as a part of Virginia. In February 1779, he recaptured Vincennes from the British. In July 1780, with two regiments, one under Colonel Benjamin Logan, the other under Colonel William Linn, he crossed the Ohio and built a blockhouse where Cincinnati now stands. Then, in surprise attacks on the Indians, he destroyed their towns of Piqua and Chillicothe. Later in the year, under orders from Jefferson, he built Fort Jefferson on the Mississippi, five miles downstream from the mouth of the Ohio.

All of these activities, the settlers knew, were pressures to keep the Indians away from the settlements. Still, there were attacks and rumors of attacks, of tomahawkings and scalpings, of prisoners taken in settlements as far north as the Greenbrier, among them women and children.

The appointment of General Clark to head "an expedition west-ward of the Ohio" was timely but the early results were not spectacu-lar. As a matter of fact, an attack on Fort Jefferson itself was driven off only after five days of hard fighting and terrible carnage.

One attack came close to home, pioneer families intermingling as they did. In September 1781, Daniel Boone's brother Squire, then a Baptist preacher, hearing rumors of raids, decided to leave his own cabin and take refuge in the William Linn Station, nearby on Bear Grass. With his family and some neighbors he started, but before they could reach the fort they were attacked from ambush. They managed to fight off the first attack but lost several of their men. Outweaponed, perhaps outnumbered, they had to retreat as well as they could toward the fort. Squire's son Moses, ten years old at the time, ran with the others until he had to stop and defend himself with his gun. One of the men saw him and asked what he was doing. He answered that he was aiming at an Indian who was trying to kill him. At that moment an Indian raised his head into sight. Moses tried to shoot him but could not. His gun was wet. The white man shot the Indian and they headed for the safety of the fort. Safe inside, Moses was praised for his courage. He may also have been laughed at for failing to keep his powder dry.

According to their recollections fifty years later, each of the Cleaver brothers served about fifteen days on this call-up.

Seventeen eighty-two became known as Kentucky's "year of blood." Raids came one after the other in such number that settlers again began fleeing back over the Wilderness Road, while those who remained took to the forts, if they could, or, if they could not, worried out the days and nights under their own protection. In Detroit, British and Indians prepared together for a push designed to put an end to white settlements in Kentucky—this in spite of the fact that British effort on other fronts had begun to weaken. To make matters worse for the settlers, the British and Shawnees were joined in con-siderable numbers by the Wyandots, another warlike tribe. In March a band of Wyandot warriors passed by the well-fortified Boones-borough and went on to Estill's Station. There they caught a young girl outside the stockade and in plain sight of the people inside killed and scalped her. In retaliation, Captain Estill led a party of whites against the Indians. He found them but in the battle that followed —now called Estill's Defeat—he was killed and only a few of his men managed to escape.

Two events outside Kentucky had a profound effect on Kentuckians. In the first, a band of whites massacred ninety-six unarmed and unresisting Christian Indians in a Moravian mission. Word of the massacre traveled among the Indian villages and the Shawnees watched for a chance for revenge. It came in a battle on the Sandusky River in Ohio when the Indians defeated nearly five hundred soldiers from Virginia and Pennsylvania under the command of Colonel William Crawford. To complete their revenge, they burned Crawford at the stake. His was a long, slow death, two hours in the fire, hastened only when warriors scalped him alive and poured live coals on his head. His story became even more widely known than that of the Moravian Indians, but both continued to stir hatred and fear.

By August there were Indian raiding parties wherever there were white settlements in Kentucky. George Rogers Clark, in an attempt at keeping them from crossing the Ohio, built a galley with gunwales of thick wood, bullet proof, and additional four-foot gunwales hinged so that they could be raised during battle. This was the white man's first attempt at naval warfare on the western rivers, but it was not a success. In places the Ohio was narrow, easily crossed by a swift canoe, and there were two hundred miles to be patrolled. Indians had only to wait till the "Gallie" was out of sight and then cross over safely.

The Indians, knowing through their spies that numbers of settlers had taken refuge in Bryan's Station, decided on it as a major point of attack. As a diversionary move they lurked around Hoy's Station long enough to take two boys prisoner and create an alarm. Seventeen men under Captain Holder went in pursuit, only to be ambushed at the Upper Blue Licks and defeated. This was on August 12. Three days later six hundred Indians and a few British soldiers under the command of Major Caldwell and the renegade Simon Girty laid siege to Bryan's Station with its garrison of forty to fifty men. Deceived by the attack on Hoy's Station, the settlers inside the fort were not prepared, and their situation was soon desperate. When their water supply had run out the women and girls, in a show of bravery characteristic of pioneer women, went out under the gun barrels of the startled Indians, calmly but fearfully filled their buckets, and brought them back inside the fort. The Indians attacked but the fort held. Girty called on them to surrender but they refused. After two days of fighting the Indians silently disappeared.

The next day Daniel Boone went in pursuit with one hundred and eighty-two volunteers, all of them eager for revenge for depredations, for livestock killed, for fields and cabins burned. With Boone was his young son Israel, recently risen from a sick bed, and several other relatives. The first day they marched some thirty-five miles following trails clearly marked by Indian signs. The next day, on August 19, they let themselves be led into an ambush at the Lower Blue Licks—an ambush with more than four hundred Indians waiting, carefully hidden, with fewer than two hundred white men approaching in the open. The battle, less than an hour in length, left a scene of carnage and defeat for the whites: sixty killed, twelve wounded, seven taken prisoner. Among the dead was Israel Boone. His death as Daniel Boone described it remains vivid: Boone, seeing how fearfully the fight was going against them, seeing only one route of escape, gathered his men and started out through the woods. Israel paused for one more shot. There was the sound of a rifle and Boone turned to see his son with blood gushing from his mouth. Daniel took Israel in his arms and began carrying him away, but the Indians were close upon him, with one warrior advancing on him with a tomahawk. Seeing that the boy was either dying or dead he laid him on the ground and made his own escape. In the battle the Indians had lost sixty-four killed and had taken only sixty scalps. Apparently to even the score they butchered and scalped four of their prisoners.

The whites were defeated and humiliated but not willing to give up. Instead, they began organizing a force to punish the Indians and to persuade settlers not to run from the fight. At the end of September George Rogers Clark assembled a thousand men at the mouth of Licking River, on the Ohio, among them the best of Kentucky's fighting men. Daniel Boone had brought his men together at Bryan's Station, where he joined Benjamin Logan with his men. John Floyd brought his Jefferson County men up the Ohio. Benjamin and William Cleaver, Junior, were among John Floyd's men, under the direct command of Captain Davis.

To stop the flight of settlers back over the mountains, Clark closed the Wilderness Road and stationed guards along it. Then on November 3 or 4 with one thousand and fifty men he crossed the Ohio and started up the Big Miami toward Chillicothe and Piqua. They expected trouble at burned-out Chillicothe but encountered none until they reached Willstown, where they came upon some Indians cooking: bear meat on spits, beans in pots. The warriors fled. The whites captured some Indian women and took the food. Then, fearing that an alarm had gone ahead of them, they marched on to

Piqua. Apparently the Indians had no warning as John Floyd and his Jefferson County men reached the bottom surrounding Piqua without being discovered. The whites attacked and prevailed, but they had no great sense of either victory or revenge. The warriors simply withdrew without fighting, leaving only a few squaws and children to be captured. The whites remained in Piqua four days, during which Clark negotiated a treaty with the Indians, a treaty that was never adopted. Then he and his men set out for the Ohio with whatever loot they had been able to collect. In his official report of the campaign Clark stated that he had lost one man killed, one wounded.

Benjamin and William Cleaver, Junior, in affidavits made many years later, added a few details, but only in summary. According to them, they had had several skirmishes with the Indians, burned their towns, took fourteen prisoners, and returned home.

On July 22, 1783, the Auditors of Public Accounts for the Commonwealth of Virginia certified that "Benjamin Cleaver is entitled to the Sum of Twenty pounds 8/o Specie, for his service in the militia of this State, under Capt. Davis from Jefferson County."

No record has been found of payment to William Cleaver, Junior. In his affidavit, however there is a detail not mentioned in Benjamin's. A few days after they returned from this foray he and his brother had an encounter with a body of Indians. He wounded an Indian; his brother was wounded. Then they were both taken prisoner and remained with the Indians six months, during which they suffered much from cold and hunger. Frequently they had to eat dog meat without salt. As Benjamin made no mention of this capture, this brother must have been Stephen, who in later years stated that he had been a prisoner of the Indians. If it was and he remained a prisoner for six months, he would have celebrated his seventeenth birthday among them.

The Battle of Blue Licks was in many ways the closing battle of the American Revolution, as the Battle of Point Pleasant had in a way been the opening. Ironically, the whites won the first, the Indians the last. Also ironically, while Clark was taking his revenge against the Shawnee towns, formal negotiations for peace between England and the American colonies were under way in Paris, with Benjamin Franklin chief spokesman for the Americans. On November 30 the preliminary articles of peace were signed, but unfortunately the news took six months or so to reach Kentucky. By then it was all but over. Hostilities were ordered to cease in February; the final treaty was to be signed in April. On April 15 it was ratified by Congress.

John Floyd, like many other Indian fighters, never lived to see the peace for which he had fought. On April 12, while riding through the woods, dressed in his scarlet wedding coat, he was ambushed by Indians and wounded. He died only a few hours later.

Indian troubles in the years 1779 through 1783 could slow the settlers but not stop them. Though some gave up and retreated back over the mountains, there were more than enough newcomers to replace them. In the year 1780 alone some three hundred family-size flatboats arrived at the falls of the Ohio. By 1790, when the first United States census was taken, the population of Kentucky, exclusive of Indians, had reached 73,677: white, 61,133; slave, 12,430; and free colored, 114. In the face of almost constant harassment the settlers went ahead clearing land and planting crops, replacing leantos and pole cabins with houses made of hewed logs, opening up stores and mills and blacksmith shops, laying foundations for two of Kentucky's most notable enterprises: raising racing horses and distilling corn whiskey. At the same time there were beginning organizations of churches, schools, and government.

As has been said before, freedom of worship had been one of the compelling forces that drove thousands of people from Europe to America, where they thought they could be free of the established church, whether Roman or Anglican or any other state-controlled religious institution. In America, they found the reality far short of the dream. In New England they found the Puritans, who persecuted Baptists and other non-Puritans. In Maryland they found the Roman church to be very similar to the Roman church as they had known it in Europe. In Virginia they found that the Anglicans persecuted Baptists and other dissenters and exacted a head tax on all non-Anglicans, a tax that extended to settlers in Kentucky. Only in Pennsylvania did they have a taste of religious freedom until they crossed the Allegheny Mountains, and even there restrictions laid down by the Quakers caused some chafing. Across the mountains, far beyond the reach of denominational control, they were able to search for and, in many cases, find forms of worship and congregational governance that met their needs.

Finding the right religion was of paramount importance. There were few preachers among them and no organized congregations to perpetuate in its entirety any particular doctrine. Unlettered themselves, led by preachers who often could not read or write, these pioneers in great numbers turned to the only source they had—the Bible. They accepted it as the one perfect book, the fundamental statement of the relationship between God and man—perfect, inviolable, not to be altered by one jot or tittle. Any doctrine, any form of worship not found in the Bible had to be false, especially any liturgical form suspected of having originated in Rome. Any preacher who in any way veered from a literal explanation of the Bible had to be a false prophet. A true preacher, for the multitude, was one who had been converted and had received the call. Beyond that, it was enough if he preached Christ and Christ crucified.

Of these, Benjamin Linn was typical. An Indian scout and fighter who could hang at least one scalp on his belt, he was converted to the Baptist faith somewhere along the frontier and perhaps as early as 1780 answered the call to preach. An uneducated man, he read his Bible as well as he could between scouting and exploring expeditions and preached in lonely cabins wherever people gathered. On one of his expeditions he and his brother-in-law, John Severns, also spelled "Sovereigns," explored what came to be called Severns Valley, the present site of Elizabethtown. Here with others they organized the Severns Valley Baptist Church, the first Baptist church in Kentucky and perhaps the first church of any kind organized west of the Alleghenies.

This church was organized on June 18, 1781, under the shade of a big sugar tree, with eighteen members, including three Negro servants, slaves. They had no pastor and no meetinghouse other than the half-faced or log houses of their members. They set John Gerrard aside as pastor but his services ended eleven months later when he was taken by the Indians, never to be heard of again.

Church meetings at Severns Valley became typical of those on the frontier. A description by an early member survives:

... The male members, partly in Indian costume, leather leggins, breech cloths, and moccasins, with hats made of buffalo wool rolled around whiteoak splints, and sewed together, and the females in the simple costume of bed gown and petticoat, all of buffalo wool, underwear of dressed deer skin, for as yet no flax, cotton, or sheep's wool was to be found in their wilderness home. The males sat with rifles in hand, and tomahawks at their sides, with sentry at the door. . . .

The women wore moccasins or went barefoot.

Crowded into a small cabin they stood or sat or knelt on a dirt floor singing and praying and listening to the preaching, their minds ever divided between duty to God and duty to protect themselves from an Indian attack. Even Benjamin Linn carried a gun when he went to preach. Crowded together, body touching body, warmth flowing to warmth, they prayed, listened, testified to God's eternal goodness to them, and sang of happy meetings in a better life:

> Say, brother, will you meet me?
> Say, brother, will you meet me?
> Say, brother, will you meet me
> On Canaan's happy shore?

It was a song they could repeat over and over by substituting father, mother, sister, preacher, and so on, with the refrain repeated each time:

> Glory, glory hallelujah,
> Glory, glory hallelujah,
> Glory, glory hallelujah,
> We are marching on.

At times the emotion became so great that people wept in lamentation or shouted and danced together to the glory of God.

The second Baptist church in Kentucky was organized on July 4, 1781, across Beech Fork from William Cleaver's home and near his Cedar Creek land. One of the men prominent in the organization was James Rogers, a Baptist preacher from Virginia, who had established Rogers' Station nearby the year before. He became prominent in the development of legislation that eventually separated Kentucky from Virginia. He was also the author of a pamphlet that defended Restricted Communion on the grounds that the ordinance had to be preceded by public repentance, faith, and baptism, the latter, called "dipping" on the frontier, by total immersion only. This was a chief doctrine separating Baptists from other denominations. Benjamin Linn, whose station was across Beech Fork from Cedar Creek, was probably among the founders. The first pastor they called was Joseph Barnett, one of the neighbors.

Whether the Cleavers were members of the Cedar Creek Baptist Church is not known, the minutes of meetings in the early years having been lost. However, it seems likely, as they were connected with Benjamin Linn by marriage and with James Rogers and Joseph Barnett in other ways, and there was no other church near them at the time.

These two churches were organized in Kentucky. There were others, called traveling churches, that were organized in Virginia and moved as a church body to Kentucky. Still others were organized by preachers who felt a call to this work. For instance, in 1785 Benjamin Linn founded the Pottinger's Creek Baptist Church and became its first pastor. He also assisted in founding Level Wood Church and served as pastor there. He also served as pastor at South Fork Church —in all these churches regarded as a good preacher, a pious man, and a devout Christian. Like many others of his time, he was deeply concerned with doctrinal differences—differences which, whether great or minute, led to divisions within his own denomination with names such as Regular Baptists, Separate Baptists, Presbyterian Baptists, Pedobaptists, and so on. His pursuit of truth brought him at last to the New Lights, an outgrowth of the revivalism of George Whitefield, which encouraged people to throw aside all tradition and accept the word of God as the only guide in all matters of faith and practice.

Baptists were afraid of any ecclesiastical authority other than that voted by the members of an individual congregation in a called business session. They did, however, see the value of association as a means of fellowship and a forum for resolving doctrinal differences. On Saturday, October 29, 1785, messengers, as delegates were called, from four churches—Severn's Valley, Cedar Creek, Bear Grass, and Cox's Creek—met at Cox's Creek Church to explore the possibility of organizing. Joseph Barnett preached the opening sermon and was elected moderator. Out of this meeting came the Salem Association of Regular Baptists, the first Baptist association west of the Alleghenies.

The belief in a right religion assumed the existence of a wrong religion and the presence of error that had to be put down. There were disputes among Baptists over various points in doctrine but these were not as divisive in the early days in Kentucky as those they had with other denominations: Methodist, Presbyterian, and some that could be identified only by the names of the preachers who founded them. Taken all together, the Baptists had the greatest number, but the Methodists were increasing. As early as April 1790, Bishop Francis Asbury was in Tennessee on his way to Kentucky, "groping through the woods . . . depending on the fidelity of the Kentucky people, hastening them, and being unwilling they should wait a moment for me."

But the Methodists had to wait a full month because their bishop's horse, turned out to graze, strayed away and the bishop and his party were forced to stay "in a house in which a man was killed by the savages; and O, poor creatures! they are but one remove from savages themselves."

Unable to find the horses they turned back on foot ten miles and the Bishop made another entry in his diary:

> We came back to Amis's—poor sinner. He was highly offended that we prayed so loud in his house. He is a distiller of whisky, and boasts of gaining L 300 per annum by the brewing of his poison. We talked very plainly; and I told him that it was of necessity, and not of choice, we were there; that I feared the face of no man. He said, he did not desire me to trouble myself about his soul. Perhaps the greatest offense was given by my speaking against distilling and slave holding.

When he finally reached Kentucky he entered his discouragement in his diary: "The Methodists do but little here—others lead the way."

In spite of the bishop's feeling of discouragement, the Methodists increased and prospered. His counterpart, John Taylor, a Baptist who had preached in various churches on the frontier, wrote, ". . . The Methodists have also gotten a foot hold in Frankfort."

There was religious rivalry, proselytizing, caviling. Two significant denominational splits occurred: the Cumberland Presbyterian Church withdrew from the parent body; the Christian Church, their members later called Campbellites for Alexander Campbell, from the Baptist church. These splits worked numerically to the benefit of the Methodists, but as late as October 6, 1814, Bishop Asbury wrote the following:

> We have lost members from the society, and gained, perhaps, one preacher in the itinerancy in two years; the local ministry is enriched; may we expect more help? Ah! the labour is too hard, and the wages too low. We cannot, like the Quakers, *take abroad* when we get tired of home, and go

feasting from one rich friend's table to another's, and *bark* or be *dumb*, as the fit may take us. Our discipline is too strict; we cannot leave four or five thousand congregations unsought, like the Church of England, the Presbyterian, Independent, and Baptist Churches. *Go*, says the command; go into all the world—go to the highway and hedges. *Go out*—seek them. Christ came *seeking* the lost sheep. *Seek me out*, says the parson; or advertise and offer a church and a good salary, and I will *seek* you. And is this all these pretenders can do?

But criticism alone, no matter how extensive or bitter, or seeking out with missionary zeal, did not lead to control of one denomination over another, even of Protestants over Roman Catholics, who began coming in from Maryland in 1785. Some of them settled on the Poplar Neck of Beech Fork, where Benjamin Cleaver had his land, and built St. Thomas Catholic Church no more than a few miles from the Cedar Creek Baptist Church. Nor did it lead to control of the Shakers, of whom a preacher said when they first came to Kentucky, "They are a set of worldly minded, cunning deceivers whose religion is earthy, sensual and devilish."

Given the zeal, at times fanatic, to stamp out error in others, the various religious bodies enjoyed their freedom, a critic might have said, not so much because they believed in it but because one denomination never had enough numbers to enforce its will on another. For whatever reason, in Kentucky religious freedom was a fact, a way of life, beyond the control of any established church.

Religious groups did speak their concern over moral issues. One of these, as Bishop Asbury said, was the distilling of corn whiskey. In spite of his speaking against it, and that of others, it was not stopped or slowed. Distilling corn whiskey had been a frontier enterprise from the beginning. Farmers with surplus corn found that twenty-four bushels of corn could be reduced to the equivalent weight of four bushels by the process of distilling. Transportation by packhorse thus became easier and less expensive. Untaxed in the early days of the Republic, whiskey yielded a good profit—so much so that distillers on the South Branch of the Potomac were willing to enter into what became called the Whiskey Rebellion to protect their profits. It is believed that the first distillery in Kentucky was set up by John Ritchie, next to William Cleaver's plantation. If so, it is likely that some Cleaver corn ended up in a Ritchie jug. Preaching or not, bourbon was on the way to becoming one of Kentucky's leading products.

Slavery, the other moral problem raised by Bishop Asbury, was equally untouchable, an issue of deep import for many, a system too deeply ingrained to be easily dislodged. Negro slaves had been brought to Virginia in 1619. Slaveholders moving west from Virginia and Maryland took their slaves with them. Slavery became a way of life in Kentucky, especially in the good farming areas. Slaves were bought and sold, hired or leased out, hunted when they ran away, as they had been in the older settlements. Any real change was religious, in acceptance of the belief that a slave had a soul to be saved.

Baptist church records, and probably some others, reflect that change. Again and again persons designated as slaves, after going through the steps of repentance, public confession, and baptism, were accepted into full membership in the church, except that they could not vote. Their vote, some argued, might be too much influenced by opinion of their masters. Minutes of the Long Run Baptist Church, where Abraham Lincoln (the President's grandfather) had his membership, was assasinated by the Indians, and was buried, contain interesting proof: "June 27, 1807. Black Sisters, Betsey and Darkus (belonging to Mr. Frasure) living in the bounds of South Long Run solicits the church for letters of dismission, which the church grants."

Except for the vote, slave and master were equal in the eyes of the church. They went down together into the baptismal waters of pond or stream to be spiritually washed white as snow. Sometimes they rose from the water shouting and singing together.

Indoors or out, singing was a part of the worship, singing of hymns remembered from the past or created out of the emotion of the moment. In Virginia, slaves had sat in balconies of Anglican churches enough to learn the English liturgy and the sound of plainsong. Farther out on the frontier, where liturgy rarely reached, Baptists and others taught the slaves revivalist songs. To these, and to whatever they remembered of plainsong, the slaves supplied their own rhythmic and tonal enrichment, remembered or handed down from Africa. John Taylor described some of the results:

The poor blacks, whose voices generally exceed the whites, have learned many of those precious songs; they are now abundantly stirred up to devotional spirit; they flock together, and in the dead of night, you may hear them at a distance praying to, and praising God with charming sound, and as you travel the road in day time, at their business, you hear them singing such heavenly melody, that your heart melts into heavenly sweetness

—while you may in solemn pause say, "O happy days long looked for, the Comforter is come.

Some of those "precious songs," according to the Reverend Samuel Davies, a Presbyterian minister, were from the *Psalms and Hymns* by Isaac Watts. Of their singing Davies said, "I cannot but observe that the Negroes, above all the human species I ever knew, have an ear for music, and a kind of ecstatic delight in Psalmody; and there are no books they learn so soon, or take so much pleasure in, as those used in that heavenly part of divine worship."

Consciously or not, these ministers were reporting early manifestations of a peculiarly American body of religious music, the Negro spiritual, which was made through the hybridizing of the white hymn, with its deep religious feeling, and the African rhythm, born of the syncopated drum beat; the African sense of harmony, which allows gliding up and down the scale until a tone is reached; the African timbre, which finds the sound not so much in pitch as in emotional intensity. On the other hand, it shows an attitude of whites toward blacks, a romantic attitude built up through listening to such moments, the whites not close enough to get all the words, especially when blacks increased enough in number to organize their own churches and meetings—not close enough to hear or understand the angry complaint, the bitter irony that often imbued what on the surface seemed only a religious song. Thus masters passed down to their children knowledge they thought they had gained from observation: Happy people sing. Negroes sing. Therefore, Negroes are happy people.

There is no doubting the religious fervor among both whites and blacks, a fervor easily traced to "the New Light Stir," which grew out of George Whitefield's preaching a generation or so earlier, as easily traced to the impact of danger and fear and hardship—the short life, the sudden death—on men and women who had to find physically and spiritually the means to survive. The power of this fervor shows through a statement by John Taylor:

I once baptized 26 myself, on a cold freezing day, the ice about 6 inches thich where the people stood, close to the edge of the icy grave. And though my clothes froze before I got dry over—I know I speak safely when I say I suffered no inconvenience, and tho' this may be attributed to enthusiasm, I know not why enthusiasm may not be used in religion, as in any other laudable work.

Not all was enthusiasm and brotherhood in the frontier church, especially in those frontier churches separated from the benefits of civil law. Though under the nominal jurisdiction of Virginia, settlers in Kentucky were so far from the seats of government that law could only rarely be enforced. Then the church often judged in matters that seem more civil than religious. An example in the minutes of the Long Run Baptist Association is mildly to the point: "Fourth Sunday, February, 1808: The church took up the grevance against George, a black man for his disorder in swearing and secludes him from her fellowship." Later minutes from the same association seem even more to the point: "December 24, 1808. A greviance laid in to the Church by Brother Woodworth against Brother Isham Bridges for attempting to choake a man or acting unchristianly to said man."

Preachers were looked to as authorities in matters of dress and behavior as well as sin. In matters of dress they were explicit: clothing was to be plain, with not even a border on cap or garment. In matters of behavior they were equally explicit, though lines between behavior and sin were not so clearly drawn. Church members, the preachers said, should constantly demonstrate zeal against even the appearance of sin, especially of dancing, drinking, or looseness between the sexes. For some, fiddling and dancing were cardinal sins. John Taylor could write in all seriousness, "It may be taken for granted, that what is called a good fiddler, is the Devil's right hand man."

Church members, the records show, were often brought before the congregation for violations. The discipline was severe and swift. If a member found guilty did not repent with acceptable humility, or if there was a question of the sincerity of his repentance, fellowship was withdrawn—a harsh punishment if his neighbors and friends were in the church.

Some there were hardy enough or irreverent enough to withstand such pressures. Fiddles and fiddlers could be found—fiddles carried across the Atlantic or fashioned from gourd and stick and animal gut in the wilderness, fiddlers playing tunes by ear, tunes brought across the water or made up as the urge arose. Wherever fiddlers played there were some ready to dance to the tune, and callers to guide them through square dance steps like "Swing Your Partner" and "Do C Do." Some found a way to have both church fellowship and dancing. They put the dance calls in a song and did without the fiddle. One of these, handed down in the Cleaver family, may have been made up on the Kentucky frontier:

Rise you up, my dearest dear, and present to me your hand,
And we'll all run away
To some far and distant land
Where the women weave and sew,
And the men they plow and hoe,
And we'll ramble through the canebrake
And shoot the buffalo.

While Mozart was composing music for the drawing rooms of Europe the play-party game was being created for the log cabins of frontier America.

Frontiersmen were often caught between the desire for the independence that comes with more elbow room and the need for protection afforded by law and government. A man might say, "If you can see smoke from another man's chimney, it's time to move on." The same man might complain that the government had failed to protect him in his person and property, especially when Indians were prowling near, or when squatters set up camp on his land and refused to leave. Kentucky, from the days of the Transylvania Company on, proceeded with all due, if somewhat irregular, speed to set up government, with smaller, more clearly defined divisions at each step, from a territory of Virginia to Fincastle County in Virginia to Kentucky as a separate county of Virginia and then, in 1780, to three counties: Jefferson, Lincoln, and Lafayette.

Soon, as more and more new settlers arrived, it was apparent that the areas embraced by these counties were too large for effective government. In the following manner residents of the Beech Fork area petitioned the House of Burgesses in Williamsburg to establish a new county: "Whereas appears an advertisement: Salem, Feb. 11, 1782—Whereas it appears to the inhabitants that Jefferson County requires to be divided, and that the new town of Salem is central for a Court House."

The creating law, signed by Governor Patrick Henry, was passed on November 27, 1784, and became effective on January 1, 1785. Thus Nelson County, named for Thomas Nelson, former governor of Virginia, came into being, and steps had to be taken to form a county government and establish a county seat.

The name Salem had by this time been largely superseded by the name Bard's Town, according to tradition, for David Biard of

Pennsylvania, who, also according to tradition, never saw the place. The name was apparently given by his brother William, who preferred the "Bard" spelling. Of the original one-thousand-acre tract granted to David Biard and John C. Owings, one hundred acres were set aside as a town site and, with the approval of the House of Burgesses in 1788, Bardstown came into being as the county seat of Nelson County.

The tentacles of law now stretched from Williamsburg through hundreds of miles of wilderness to the new county of Nelson, as they had previously stretched from London to Williamsburg. Those from London to Williamsburg were drawn thin and eventually snapped, but those from Williamsburg to Nelson County never snapped, though they were often drawn thin. They continued to exist for many reasons, not the least of which was the desire of the settlers themselves to live under orderly government. They were drawn thin because the settlers were independent enough to want government on their own terms. They were living through a time of remarkable change in government—from monarchy to democracy. Men charged with setting up government in Nelson County, Kentucky, had to erase from their minds such writs as the following recorded in Pennsylvania:

George the Third by the Grace of God of Great Britain, France and Ireland King, Defender of the Faith & c. To the Sheriff of the County of Berks GREETING. We command you, as heretofore we commanded you, that you take John Cleaver late of your County Yeoman if he be found in your Bailiwick and safely keep so that you have his Body before our Justices at Reading at Our County Court of Common Pleas there to be held for the County of Berks the thirteenth Day of August next to answer Samuel Boone of a plea of Trespass on the Case & c. And have you there then this Writ WITNESS James Seely Esquire at Reading the Seventeenth Day of May in the fifth Year of Our Reign.

Samuel was probably Daniel's uncle; John was probably the son of Derrick Cleaver. No matter how their conflict was settled, what was important in Nelson County was that authority was now vested not in George the Third but in the people, and the people had in them the element of rebellion. They had thrown off the Crown by force. They now had a stronger though less than perfect weapon—the vote.

As in many other frontier counties, the history of Nelson County is best preserved in order books where minutes of actions of the county justices were recorded. In Nelson County there were eighteen justices drawn from various parts of the county. Among them were men who had some familiarity with the law. There were also two Baptist preachers: Joseph Barnett and James Rogers. They met first in the log cabins of members and then in a log courthouse.

Among their first concerns were public roads and public buildings. In order after order men were appointed to view the best way for a road from one point in the county to another. William Cleaver was among those appointed surveyor. So was his son Benjamin. Sometimes the "viewer" was also ordered to cut the road, using men from the tithables list; that is, able-bodied men, residents, all of whom were required by law to contribute time and labor to building and maintaining public roads.

A minute for the court meeting on July 28, 1785, states, "The Court are of opinion that two prisons be built for those of this County." Specifications were carefully drawn:

That for debtors to be fifteen feet square clear in the inside; to be built with square loggs a foot thick with floors above and below of the same thickness and to have a good stone chimney well barred at a proper distance from the hearth in which prison there are to be two windows each eighteen inches square, both of which are to be secured with strong iron barrs crossing each other and not more than five inches apart. The doors of which to be made of two inch oak plank and doubled. To be well spiked within and without with strong barrs, bolts and locks, the whole prison to be lined with plank four inches thick and to be let into the floors above and below at least five inches and to be pinned with two pinns in the end of each plank and also through each logg they cross.

The prison for criminals was to be constructed in much the same way except that it was to be ten feet square, and to have two windows twelve inches square. No specification for a chimney was included. Both prisons were to be raised one foot above the surface and to be supported on stone platforms. Obviously debtors had better accommodations, perhaps indicating this early the sentiment that would soon abolish debtors' prisons.

A minute of the same court points to other punishments:

James Morrison and Thomas Morton gent are appointed to contract with a workman for erecting stocks, pillory and whipping posts for the use of this

County. And it is ordered that Benjamin Pope and James Rogers gent are appointed to fix on the place where such erections ought to be placed.

The stocks was a simple arrangement for exposing a culprit on a public bench, where he was confined by having his ankles made fast in holes under a movable board. The pillory, an instrument of torture going back at least to the Middle Ages, consisted of a wooden frame erected on a stool with holes for neck and wrists, and was commonly called a stretch-neck. The whipping post was a straight post high as a man and furnished with clasps at the top for the wrists.

Cases coming before the justice court often had to do with debt, trespass, and eviction. The minutes kept, summaries of actions though they are, often give rewarding insight into the characters and customs of the people. For instance, instead of using John Doe to conceal a name either real or fictitious, they entered such curious appelations as those that appear in the following: "Solomon Saveall, Plaintiff, against Simpleton Spendall, Defendant, in Ejectment"; and "Solomon Stronghead Plaintiff against Simeon Wronghead Defendant in Ejectment." More important cases were reserved for Chancery Court, where lengthy affidavits reveal bitter legal battles over title to land.

Much has been said of the tendency toward lawlessness and violence on the frontier, and with justification, though often without information. For a hundred years or so England had made the colonies, especially the Southern colonies, a dumping ground for convicts from debtor prisons and criminal jails. Many of these, when their sentences had been served, fled to the frontier, some to become solid citizens, some to pursue the criminality that had put them in jail in the first place, and to pursue it where law had little force. Indians called Kentucky "the dark and bloody ground" because of tribal wars over it as a hunting ground. Whites found the image apt, partly because of Indian depredation against the settlements, partly because of the duels and feuds characteristic of the time and the people. The code of honor that required duels for satisfaction affected a comparatively small part of the population, but like the few that involved residents of Bardstown, they were given wide publicity. The feuds, on the other hand, could easily embroil whole families and at times communities. Some of these feuds, it is true, were older than Kentucky, having had their origin in older settlements and been carried across the mountains. Others were Kentucky born and bred, and frequent enough to give rise to the saying "jest a-fussin' and a-feudin'."

Much can be said of the tendency toward lawfulness on the frontier and of the impact of the frontier on all the institutions of law. The frontier did offer a window of escape for anyone in trouble, a place to maintain old ways of lawlessness. Some of this lawlessness came from attempts to enforce bad laws. The frontier became a place for ignoring some old laws and for molding some new ones in freer, more open circumstances. In Kentucky, as in other parts of the frontier, institutions of law that reached far back into English parentage moved with the frontier and began functioning in some form wherever there were enough people, and with the consent of the people. In Kentucky, lawyers, as well as planters, doctors, and teachers, moved with the front edge of the frontier, and in the long development more than counterbalanced the people of violence in "bloody Breathitt" and similar well-advertised areas.

Early arrival of professional men on the Kentucky frontier assured early attention to education. Some kind of school was kept in some of the forts from the earliest days. Some families taught their children at least the simplest steps in reading, writing, and ciphering at home. The Cleavers must have been among the latter, for the Salem Academy, the nearest they could attend, was not opened until 1788, when most of William Cleaver's children were beyond school age. It is possible that the youngest rode horseback the six miles to Bardstown and sat at the feet of the founder of the Academy, the Reverend James Priestly, but there are no records. The Cleaver name does appear on many land and other records signed. It may appear as "X his mark" but not often.

County organizations well under way, Kentucky advanced toward statehood. New settlers came down the Ohio or over the Wilderness Road, the wealthy with their trains of packhorses driven by slaves, the poor on foot. As late as 1797 Moses Austin, who had come through the Cumberland Gap on his trek from Virginia to Missouri, described people he passed on the Wilderness Road:

> I cannot omitt Noticeing the many Distress'd families I pass'd in the Wilderness nor can any thing be more distressing to a man of feeling to see women and Children in the Month of Decemb'r Travelling a Wilderness Through Ice and Snow passing large rivers and Creeks with out Shoe or Stocking, and barely as maney raggs as covers their Nakedness, with out

money or provisions except what the Wilderness affords, the Situation of such can better be Imagined then discribed. to say they are poor is but faintly express'g theyre Situation—life *What is it, Or What can it give,* to make Compensation for such accumulated Misery. Ask these Pilgrims what they expect when they git to Kentucky the Answer is Land. have you any. No, but I expect I can git it. have you any thing to pay for land, No. did you Ever see the Country. No but Every Body says its good land. can anything be more Absurd than the Conduct of man, here is hundreds Travelling hundreds of Miles, they Know not for what Nor Whither, except its to Kentucky, passing land almost as good and easy obtain'd, the Proprietors of which would gladly give on any terms, but it will not do its not Kentuckey its not the Promis'd land its not the goodly inheratence the Land of Milk and Honey, and when arriv'd at this Heaven in Idea what do they find? a goodly land I will allow but to them forbidden Land. exausted and worn down with distress and disappointment they are at last Oblig'd to become hewers of wood and Drawers of water.

Austin's parallel of these people in their wanderings with those of the Israelites as they marched through the wilderness in search of the promised land of Canaan is not lost. Neither is the irony of his comparison. Led neither by God nor man these people straggled on and on, in religious fervor singing of a new Canaan, a promised land, only to find that the land had been taken up, not through the drawing of lots as in Israel of old but through power of money in the hands of speculators, the goodly inheritance lost to them, their fate to work on land owned by others or to keep moving deeper into the wilderness.

But this was not the fate of all. Some, perhaps wiser, perhaps more industrious, paid the price for level land and prospered. Others, perhaps more independent, went up some lonely "holler" in the hills, built cabins which, even if never improved, could last a century, and fathered generations who subsisted in isolation on little patches of ground and what they could get by rifle and range—generation after generation killing off the game, wearing out the land in what some called the Scotch-Irish way.

Thus early in her history, Kentucky was a land of contrasts. A decade or more before Moses Austin saw the people traveling in their rags there were towns with fine houses and stores that sold, in addition to guns and bullets and scalping knives, a variety of tools and goods, including fine linens and laces from Europe, brought by boat from New Orleans or by packhorse from Philadelphia, which was still the chief center of trade. There was also a newspaper, *The Kentucky Gazette*, a weekly published at Lexington, which except for the *Pittsburgh Gazette* was the first newspaper in the West. The first issue appeared on August 18, 1787, with an editorial policy apparently designed to inform Kentuckians not so much about Kentucky as about the world. The advertisements, closer to home, let readers know about livestock strayed or stolen, stallions at stud, runaway slaves, and goods to be bought and sold.

The end of the Revolution brought peace to the eastern states but not to the Kentucky frontier. The British still held the northwestern territory and hostile Indians could still raid from their villages across the Ohio. In the spring of 1783 Kentucky was made a separate district and in the following summer a log courthouse and jail were built on the site of the present Danville. During the summer of 1784 Indian raids spurred leaders from the settlements to meet at Danville to develop means of self-protection. What they found was that they had no means—no way to call up troops, no way to command their few scattered resources. All legislation had to come from Richmond, hundreds of miles away, over rugged mountains, through wildernesses in which Indian raiders lurked. A government separate from that of Virginia, they saw, was imperative.

Movement toward separation, which required approval of both the Virginia legislature and the Congress of the United States, was slow and tedious, and involved calling one convention after another at Danville, eight in all. The eighth convention met in Danville in July 1790, and accepted the Virginia act of separation, to become effective on June 1, 1792. On February 4, 1791, an act passed both houses of Congress for the admission of Kentucky as a state. The ninth and last convention met at Danville on April 3, 1792, and drew up a constitution that embodied at least some of the progressive liberalism of the frontier, a constitution that granted suffrage to all male citizens over twenty-one and that guaranteed religious freedom in unequivocal terms:

That all men have a natural and indefeasible right to worship Almighty God according to the dictates of their own conscience; that no man can of right be compelled to attend, erect, or support any place of worship, or to maintain any ministry against his consent; that no human authority can, in any case whatever, control or interfere with the rights of conscience, and that no preference shall ever be given by law to any religious societies or modes of worship.

Thus in a decade or less the Americans struck down the authority of two institutions imported from Europe: the Crown and the established church. A third, the most inimical—slavery—remained. Antislavery members argued vigorously for abolition but lost to those who put property above principle. Another chance to undermine this institution was lost. The Cleavers supported slavery at least by owning slaves.

Though the main sentiment among Kentuckians was for statehood within the Union, frustrations over the long delays aroused some feeling for declaring Kentucky an independent nation. This feeling was strengthened as Kentuckians looked to the West and to the Mississippi River as an outlet for their produce. In both the second and third conventions strong resolutions in favor of separation were addressed to the Assembly and to the people of Kentucky. Spain then entered on the side of separation, with the proposition that it would grant Kentucky navigation of the Mississippi and the export of produce to New Orleans provided Kentuckians would become a separate state; it could not grant these privileges as long as Kentucky was a part of the United States. During 1788 Spaniards carried on various intrigues in Kentucky. In 1793, after statehood was achieved, the French minister to the United States, known as Citizen Genêt, sent four agents to Kentucky to engage men in an expedition against New Orleans and the Spanish possessions, and with some success. George Rogers Clark accepted a commission as major general in the armies of France for the purpose of recruiting volunteers to reduce Spanish power on the Mississippi, to open trade on the river, and to give freedom to its inhabitants. This and other activities caused President Washington to demand his recall. Genêt's scheme failed but looking to the West continued. In 1804, after his fatal duel with Alexander Hamilton, Aaron Burr asked the British minister for funds to be used supposedly for separating the western states from the Union. The British refused, but the Spaniards gave him a small sum. During 1805 he toured United States army posts in the Mississippi Valley. In 1806 he organized a small military expedition and started it down the Mississippi toward New Orleans. Above Natchez he was arrested on February 19, 1807, and brought to trial in Richmond, Virginia. He was indicted for treason but acquitted.

These incidents show how tenuous were western ties with the Union, how deep the feeling for independence.

Indian depredations during this time remained a constant threat. Raids were frequent on boats on the Ohio and on lonely cabins and settlements. Reports of whites left dead and scalped sent terror through all Kentucky. Among those massacred was Abraham Lincoln, President Lincoln's grandfather. Defenses were weakened. Travel was limited. Periodically *The Kentucky Gazette* announced a date when travelers bound out over the Wilderness Road would assemble at the Crab Orchard, provisioned for the long journey, prepared to fight if they encountered Indians. The Kentucky militia had no legal power and the men considered themselves settlers, not soldiers. They were willing to go out when Indian raids threatened but not to maintain organized defense. It was as difficult a time for the regular army. Soldiers were disaffected and desertions high. Almost every issue of *The Kentucky Gazette* carried notices of rewards for the apprehension of deserters. A serious malady called "Shawnee fever" became widespread. This malady became especially virulent during an ill-fated expedition of a thousand volunteers under General Clark, who went out to punish the Indians along the Wabash. Frustrated with disorganization and inaction, three hundred volunteers gave up and went home to Kentucky. Clark had no choice but to follow.

White failures and Indian successes made the Indians more daring, more arrogant. On the night of November 3, 1791, the whites under General Arthur St. Clair suffered a defeat that turned into a rout. Reports of the defeat and the part Kentuckians played in the fight, to appear later in this account, reached Kentucky. Kentuckians immediately volunteered to fight the Indians. At the same time they became more eager for statehood and a chance to take matters into their own hands.

The process toward statehood was already in motion. In May 1792, General Isaac Shelby was elected first governor of Kentucky, the first state to be formed west of the Applachians, the first on the west-flowing waters. Other state officers were appointed and the celebration of statehood was set for June 1 at Lexington.

All these steps were taken in a time when there were almost incessant raids from the Indians. Even the celebration at Lexington was marred by the appearance of Indian warriors in full battle dress.

When Kentucky became a state William Cleaver, Senior, had been on Beech Fork thirteen years. He had settled there when he was in his fifties. He had followed the frontier at least two-thirds of his life and had prospered, more in Nelson County than in earlier times. He owned close to four thousand acres of land, with sturdy buildings, with fields cleared and well planted. He probably owned slaves. As surveyor and appraiser of estates he had sources of income other than from farming. On May 28, 1791, he was given permission to erect a mill, probably on Landing Run. The water mill was a third development in the technique of grinding grain. The first was with wooden mortar and pestle. The second consisted of a nether stone, round and cut with sharp edges like a sunburst, and an upper stone, also cut and set with spokes for hand-turning. His was apparently the second water mill in Nelson County, and the first to serve the people in his part of Beech Fork.

Sons and daughters shared the bounty of the frontier with him. His sons, ranging widely in search of land for themselves, had carved the name "CLEAVER" on beech trees along numerous streams. Through deeds of purchase they were also marking the name on the land, so that every time it was bought or sold the name came fresh to the fore, leaving for themselves the kind of monument, the kind of history left by countless thousands who held the land for a time and then relinquished it to go on to some new promised land.

The history of William Cleaver's sons and daughters is irregularly recorded and incomplete.

Of Joshua there is no record after they left Tygart's Valley. Charles appeared at the Falls of the Ohio at least once in 1779. One may have been the Cleaver who died on a hunting trip where Blackford Creek empties into the Ohio.

Benjamin was twenty-eight years old and a family man when he came to Kentucky. His wife's name is not known. There is record of three of his children: Charles Cadle; Nancy, who married Joseph Reddish on August 9, 1802; and Martha, who married John Henry on February 4, 1806. Benjamin took up three tracts of land of one hundred acres each, all in the part of Jefferson County that became Nelson, and also served as a county surveyor. According to family tradition he also prospered. There is a tradition that he objected to his daughter Nancy's marriage because Joseph Reddish had long been a captive of the Indians and still carried certain Indian ways. When time for the wedding came, however, he provided her with a wedding dress of such rich silk and full cut that it would stand alone.

William Cleaver, Junior, married Susannah Westfall, daughter of Daniel, in Jefferson County on June 30, 1790. As late as 1788 Daniel Westfall's name appeared in Randolph County orders in Tygart's

Valley. He must have migrated to Kentucky between then and 1790. Nelson County tax lists for 1792 show that William Cleaver, Junior, owned two tracts of land, one for two hundred and fifty-nine acres, the other for two hundred and twelve acres. He and Susannah had eleven children: Hannah, Mary, Stephen, Judah, Anna, Phebe, Rebeckah, Sarah, Elizabeth, Ester, and Susannah.

Stephen, the next in order of birth, the one who traveled farthermost into new frontiers, requires a fuller account.

David was born apparently after 1766 and before 1768, probably in Virginia, though family tradition has New Jersey as his birthplace. He was about twelve years old when he came to Kentucky. His name appears in official records as of September 8, 1789, when he was recommended for lieutenant in the Nelson County Militia. On November 17, 1793, he married Letitia Griffey, daughter of Elizabeth Timrel, with the consent of Francis Timrel, and with Samuel and Hannah Griffey as witnesses. Letitia, according to family tradition, was born near what is now La Grange, Kentucky, on March 21 or 24, 1775. The place of birth is probably an error. White women, including Rebecca Boone, were not in Kentucky as early as the date given for her birth.

David was granted two hundred and five acres of land on Little Cane Creek in Washington County on February 26, 1795. He was appointed lieutenant colonel in the Washington County militia on February 10, 1809.

James remains an enigma among William and Hannah's sons. He was born about 1771, apparently in Virginia. He was about eight when he was taken to Kentucky, about twelve at the end of the American Revolution. Still at a young age, he married Hannah Linn on December 26, 1789, in Nelson County. She was a daughter of Nathan Linn, who was killed by Indians, and Hannah Welch, whose second husband was Ozias. The ceremony was performed by B. Linn, her uncle and a Baptist preacher, and James Adams of Nelson County signed for security. According to family tradition he migrated to Alabama in 1792, but records show a much later date.

Sarah married William Blackford on September 13, 1802, in Nelson County, thus joining the Cleavers to the Blackfords, who had been among the earliest settlers at Harrodsburg. She stated that she was past twenty years of age. Her father signed the marriage bond.

Hannah was named in her father's will but the record ends there.

Rough River

STEPHEN CLEAVER, in turn Indian fighter, judge, politician—to single out his major activities—lived the kind of life that was possible, at times imperative, among the second generation west of the mountains. His life spanned eighty years of the western frontiers, during which he lived in parts of what are now four states: Virginia, West Virginia, Kentucky, and Missouri. He also visited frontiers in Alabama and Arkansas. For more than half his lifetime he was in danger from the Indians, at times from random raids, at times from what amounted to siege. Born on May 20, 1766, in a part of Virginia where the Indians were already troublesome, he was no more than eight years old when his family took him over the mountains to Tygart's Valley. There for about five years he shared the fear of Indian raids. At any time of day or night he had to be ready for flight to Jonas Friend's fort. There at night, "forted" for days at a time, he listened to talk about Indians: the way they lived, their sneak attacks, their victims dead and scalped in lonely cabins. He also learned defense: the use of rifle and knife, the sign that said Indians were lurking, the knowledge that at times running might be the only way out. Ways of frontier warfare became deeply ingrained in him.

The move to Kentucky, when Stephen was thirteen, had to be a journey of fear, with the last thing at night a search for Indian signs, the first in the morning the same. By then he would have had his own knife and tomahawk, and probably his own rifle, shot pouch, and powder horn. In the isolation of their home on Beech Fork the danger continued. So did the harsh education of the frontier, especially the lore of Indian fighters. He would have known Daniel Boone by sight at an early age. During raids he was forted at Benjamin

[141]

Linn's fort, in the presence of a man who had killed and scalped Indians. He heard stories of battles and of men killed by Indians: William and Nathan Linn, John Floyd, others. No more than fifteen when Indians raided Polke's and Kincheloe's stations, he heard in detail the tragedy of stations burned, of men and women and children butchered or taken away prisoners. He watched his older brothers shoulder their rifles and go off to fight, with no way of knowing whether they would return. If, as accounts indicate, he was himself wounded by the Indians and taken prisoner, he had his own baptism of fire at a very early age.

Somewhere along the way he must have gone to school, but where and under whom is not known. Perhaps it was to his father at home, at night in the light of an open fireplace. Perhaps it was in the Bardstown Grammar School, which was open as early as 1782, when he was sixteen. He learned to read, and to write a fair hand. He also learned enough arithmetic, in school or out, to qualify as an official surveyor.

Stephen Cleaver's early military record is sketchy, a usual circumstance on the frontier, when enlistments were brief, when most men had to be summer soldiers, Indian raids being somewhat seasonal, and usually after crops were planted. Men planted their crops, enlisted for short terms, and returned home in time to gather their crops. In 1790, in the earliest military record available on him, he was a private in the Kentucky militia, and probably saw some action against the Indians. Somewhat later, the date is not definite, he became an ensign in John Caldwell's Battalion of the Kentucky Mounted Volunteers.

Meanwhile, Indian depredations and massacres of small groups of whites increased in number. As early as 1788 the whites sent raiding parties against the Indians. The Indians struck back and by 1789 the United States was again at war with the Indians. In the fall of 1790 General Josiah Harmar led an expedition against the Indians along the Maumee. The whites were maneuvered into an ambush that cost them one hundred and eighty-three dead. More successful expeditions were sent out under General Charles Scott and Colonel James Wilkinson, but they failed to subdue the Indians. As a matter of fact, they only served to strengthen the determination of the Shawnee warrior, Tecumseh. Stephen Cleaver was born in 1766, Tecumseh in 1768. For twenty years, during the peak of manhood, they were by the chances of war thrown together, on opposite sides.

Tecumseh's father died in a battle during Dunmore's campaign against the Shawnees. From an early age Tecumseh was trained in warfare and in the art of leadership, and conditioned against the presence of white men. He had seen whites kill and take scalps. When he was only seventeen he knew the story of the Indian warrior who, being burned alive by whites in revenge for torture of whites, laughed and asked for his pipe and tobacco so that he could have one last smoke. Through his youthful years he watched the seesaw conflict of Indians and whites back and forth across the Ohio, the destruction of white stations, the burning of Shawnee towns. Out of these conflicts he developed a guiding principle: Indian lands were held in common and neither chief nor tribe had the right or the power to sell or cede any part, a principle he held through twenty years more of Indian warfare.

General Arthur St. Clair mounted his expedition against the Indians in 1791, an expedition that from the beginning seemed doomed to disaster. St. Clair, the governor of the Northwest Territory, a soldier in the Revolutionary War, was by then old and infirm and unpopular. He was so unpopular in Kentucky that volunteers could not be persuaded to serve under him. One thousand Kentuckians were drafted and placed under the command of Colonel Oldham. They with two thousand regular soldiers made up St. Clair's force. Serving under Colonel Oldham were Major Patrick Brown, Stephen Cleaver, probably a very junior officer at the time, and John Helm, a soldier without rank. The forces assembled at Fort Washington, the site of Cincinnati, where they remained the latter part of the summer. Morale sagged; numbers deserted because they were restless and bored with waiting.

About the first of October General St. Clair moved toward the Maumee villages, with pauses along the way to build three log forts: Hamilton, St. Clair, and Jefferson. St. Clair was ill and had to depend on his second in command, General Richard Butler. Under way again, the march was slow, geared to the pace of wagons and artillery. The Indians had plenty of time to spy out their movements and spread the alarm. On November 3, by now greatly reduced in number, they camped south of the Maumee. St. Clair allowed his men to pitch their tents haphazardly on a rise and to go to bed almost without guard. Oldham tried to convince him of the danger but to no avail, and parted from him with the warning that history would record the tale of sorrow that would come out of such blundering.

Oldham rejoined his own division, which was camped on another rise about half a mile in advance of the main army and across a small stream. Aware of the danger, neither he nor his principal officers slept that night. Not since the days of Pontiac had the Indians been guided by such leaders, among them Tecumseh. Nor had they been able to assemble such strength, a strength Butler failed to report to St. Clair.

All night long the Indians crept in around the whites. A little before daylight John Helm went scouting beyond the lines of the army. While he was out the Indians began their attack with a rush on Oldham's division. About twelve hundred in number, the Indians surrounded the whites and under cover of woods poured in a fire more destructive than any before felt in Indian warfare. The Kentuckians fought but the fight was so fierce they had to begin a retreat. John Helm got back to his division, in time to see Colonel Oldham fall, from a ball that passed through his body. Then Helm received a bullet that shattered a bone in his left arm from wrist to elbow. Helpless, he watched the Kentuckians fight back, bayonet charge after bayonet charge, with some success at first, but the Indians kept up their fire until scores were dead or wounded and they had to retreat.

"Kentuckians! Let's go home!"

The order, according to Helm, came from Stephen Cleaver. As Helm reported long after the battle:

That word home had a talismanic effect. Their young wives and little children shot up before the mind's eye and nerved them for the struggle, and with a desperate shout they charged the Indians without firing a gun. The Indians for a moment seemed panic stricken, yielded for them to pass, whilst the balance of the shattered army, as if by one impulse, followed after.

The retreat turned into a rout. Never before had Indians defeated white men so completely. All day long the soldiers retreated, leaving behind six hundred dead, taking with them those of the two hundred and eighty-three wounded who could travel. At night they came to Fort Jefferson, some thirty miles from the scene of battle. There they reorganized and, with Butler dead, St. Clair in command, they retreated on to Fort Washington.

St. Clair's defeat gave a charge of confidence to the Indians and their British supporters, with the result that through the remainder of that winter the Indians carried on attacks against white settlements north of the Ohio and into Kentucky. They decided that they now had enough strength to push the settlers back across the Ohio and to force the United States to accept the Ohio as the permanent western boundary. If the United States refused, the Indians, with the aid of the British, would go to war.

News of the defeat carried terror to Kentucky settlements almost beyond imagination, a terror inflamed by stories of Kentucky dead and Kentucky valor. Oldham's prediction was right. Soon a history in ballad form, appropriately titled "St. Clair's Defeat," told the story and detailed reasons for the terror:

November the fourth in the year of ninety one
We had a sore engagement near to front Jefferson
St. Clair was our commander which may remembered be
For he then left nine hundred men in the Western Territory.

Our militia was attacked just as day did break
And soon we're overpowered and forced to retreat
They killed Colonel Oldham, Lemon and Briggs likewise
And the horrid yells of savages resounded through the skies.

He [General Butler] leaned his back against a tree and there
    resigned he lay
He like a noble soldier sunk in the arms of death to stay
And crowded Cherubs did await his spirit to convey
And unto the Elysian Fields they swiftly bent their way.

Cries Major Clark, "My heroes bold we can no longer stand
We'll strive to form in order and retreat the best we can
The word retreat it passed all round which raised the hue and cry
And helter skelter through the woods like lost sheep they did fly.

We left our wounded on the field O! Heavens! what a stroke
Some their thighs were shattered and some their arms had broke
The scalping knives and tomahawks soon robbed them of their
    breath
And with fiery flames of torment they tortured them to death.

St. Clair resigned his commission. Stephen Cleaver, on report of Colonel Brown, was elected lieutenant of the Second Regiment of the Kentucky state militia.

In the face of the Indian demands President Washington had no recourse but to attempt some conciliation with the Indians on the one hand, and to prepare a stronger military defense on the other. For the former, the Americans scheduled a meeting with the Indians at Sandusky in the spring of 1793, a meeting that never took place. For the latter, President Washington, on hearing that the Indians would insist on the Ohio as the boundary, ordered General Anthony Wayne, the new military commander in the West, to begin preparations for an attack.

In the summer of 1793 Wayne gathered a large force of regulars at Cincinnati and made a requisition to Governor Shelby of Kentucky for one thousand mounted riflemen. When no volunteers came forth, a thousand were drafted. They reached Wayne in October at Fort Greenville, a new fort he had built six miles beyond Fort Jefferson. Unwilling to risk a fall campaign, Wayne continued a regimen of training and discipline, and the Kentuckians now merged with the regular troops. Then the Kentuckians were allowed to go home to await recall in the spring. So great was their admiration for General Wayne that when the recall came, fifteen hundred answered and reported under the command of General Charles Scott, who had whetted his military skills at both Braddock's Defeat and St. Clair's Defeat.

In February 1794, the British told the Indians that war with the United States was inevitable and that when it came the British would fight on the side of the Indians. They also built Fort Miami on the Maumee River as a bulwark between Detroit and Wayne's army. By June two thousand Indian warriors had gathered at Fort Miami and had selected the place to make their stand—a place where fallen trees afforded good protection. Wayne, moving slowly, paused at the site of St. Clair's defeat long enough to build Fort Recovery and to fight off an Indian attack.

On August 8 Wayne reached the Maumee, and using information brought in by his scouts, put out word that he would attack the place of the fallen timbers on August 17. It was a deception, designed to take advantage of the Indians' habit of fasting before battle. He moved forward on schedule but stopped ten miles from the fallen timbers. There he waited three days. Then, when the hungry Indians were out gathering food, the Americans attacked. In less than two hours the Battle of Fallen Timbers was over, because the Indians fought for a few minutes and then ran. Fifty Indians were killed, and twenty-six whites. The Kentucky Mounted Volunteers got into the fight and lost seven men, all privates. Stephen Cleaver, by report, was there, serving under the command of John Caldwell. If so, he obviously saw little action.

After their defeat the Indians fled to the British forts but were denied entry. They realized then that the British had no intention of helping them; that if they were to continue the fight they would have to fight alone. Early in 1795 General Wayne called the chiefs together at Fort Greenville and dictated to them a harsh treaty in which the Indians gave up their claim to the major portions of the Ohio territory.

On February 22, 1795, General Wayne was able to proclaim an end to the Indian hostilities, twenty-one years after the first permanent settlement at Boonesborough.

By the time Stephen Cleaver returned after the Battle of Fallen Timbers he was firmly established in a military career, not in the regular army but in the Kentucky militia. His duties, however, were not enough to absorb the energies of a vigorous and enterprising man, especially in times of peace when the requirements were reduced to occasional meetings or uniformed parades. Like his father and brothers, he turned to the land. Land had drawn his father to Kentucky, and land had yielded rewards. As early as the Kentucky tax lists of 1792 Stephen had appeared as a landowner. The Indian troubles over, he could devote himself to two of the most important concerns of the frontiersman: acquiring land and raising sons.

On April 8, 1795, toward the end of his twenty-eighth year, Stephen Cleaver posted a bond in Nelson County as security for his marriage to Rebecka Smith, the bond binding only on condition that there be no legal obstruction to the marriage. The bond was also signed by R. Walker in the presence of John Grayson, county clerk. On the same day Lawrence Smith appeared in the Nelson County Court House and certified that Stephen Cleaver had his permission to marry his daughter Rebecka. John Houston witnessed his signature. They were married on April 13, 1795, by James Rogers, the Baptist preacher of Rogers' Station.

The young couple started their marriage at a strategic time in a strategic place. Settlers had come into Nelson County in such numbers and over such a wide territory that splitting off new counties became necessary. The first was Hardin, established in 1793, with the first term of the county court on July 22, 1793. Among the justices presiding was Stephen Cleaver's commanding officer and friend, Patrick Brown. After two years of meeting in log cabins of the justices, the court decided on Elizabethtown as the county seat, in what had been called Severn's Valley, the site of the Severn's Valley Baptist Church. It was about ten miles from Beech Fork, and about twenty miles from William Cleaver's plantation. The division put a part of Stephen Cleaver's land, including the place where he lived, in Hardin County.

For Stephen Cleaver another career was opened. On November 16, 1796, when he was thirty, he was appointed a justice of the peace of Hardin County. At a court held for Hardin County on Tuesday, December 27, 1796, a minute was entered: "Stephen Cleaver gent produced commission under the hand of his Excellency James Garrard Governor appointing him a Justice of the peace which was read in Court whereupon he took the Oath of a Justice and took his seat accordingly." The other two "Gent Justices" present were Robert Mosley and Stephen Rawlings.

Whatever other qualifications Stephen had for justice of the peace, he had "to take the oath prescribed by the Constitution; and should he presume to execute such office without first so qualifying, he shall forfeit and pay fifty pounds."

As for his duties, they were carefully detailed in the constitution:

> The justice so appointed and qualified shall be conservators of the peace within their respective counties, and shall have cognizance of all causes of less value than five pounds current money, or one thousand pounds of tobacco; in which causes they may give judgment and thereupon award execution. All judgments given by any such justice or justices, when the amount therof shall not exceed twenty-five shillings, shall be final; but when the amount shall exceed twenty-five shillings, the party against whom such judgments shall be given, shall have the right to appeal from the same to the next county court. No execution against the body of the defendant, unless the judgment exceed the sum of twenty-five shillings.

Execution against the body of the defendant apparently refers to a common punishment of so many lashes on the bare back well laid on.

In a new county a man might hold several offices. A minute in the records of the county court for the July term, 1797, follows:

Stephen Cleaver produced a nomination from Charles Helm Gentleman Surveyor appointing him his Deputy Ordered that Benjamin Helm & Robert Barret be appointed to Examine into his Capacity a report being made and returned and the Said Cleaver found duly Qualified took the Oath of a Surveyor.

Thus, like his father and his brother Benjamin, he qualified for the profession of surveyor, a profession that from George Washington on had eased the way for appraising and acquiring land. Stephen Cleaver must have had his eye open for opportunities. On September 25, 1797, with Harrison Taylor and Henry Rhodes, he took up a grant of one thousand acres on Long Fall Creek in Hardin County.

Hardin County was new; Elizabethtown, the county seat, a scattering of houses in the wilderness. Many of the men who carried on business for the county or for themselves rode long distances through the woods. Stephen Cleaver was among them. So was Thomas Lincoln, who came in from his farm on Mill Creek, five miles north of town. A cabinetmaker by trade, he at times served the county court as juror, at times as employee.

Meanwhile Stephen Cleaver was not neglecting his military career. On October 10, 1797, Governor Garrard appointed him major of the Second Battalion of the Third Regiment of the Kentucky Militia, Hardin County.

Though there is no record that he studied law, he began to assume responsibilities that required a knowledge of the law, or in an older settlement would have. The Kentucky state legislature passed an act vesting the estate of Joseph Barnett, deceased, in three trustees or commissioners: Stephen Cleaver, Harrison Taylor, and Henry Rhoads. Barnett, a Baptist preacher, was one of the earliest settlers in the area. As a deputy surveyor he made early entries and surveys of some of the best land in the vicinity of what became Hartford. He then sold a number of the tracts, but instead of making deeds he only executed bonds for their conveyance. He died without a will and leaving only minor heirs; hence the appointment of the trustees with authority to sell and convey and settle his estate.

The case, like many land cases in Kentucky, was complicated and long drawn out. Begun in Hardin County, it was carried over to Ohio County when the latter was carved out of Hardin. The new county was established in 1798, to become effective on January 1, 1799, with Hartford as the county seat. By this time Stephen Cleaver was living in Ohio County, probably on a bluff overlooking Rough River. Apparently he appeared last as a justice of the Hardin County Court on May 1, 1798. On December 22, 1798, he was appointed justice of the Court of Quarter Sessions of Ohio County.

With this appointment he entered fully into the work of organizing and administering the affairs of a new county. Other appointments were to follow: justice of the peace in Ohio County on July 2, 1799; county surveyor; trustee of an academy still in the organizational stage.

The Ohio County Court held its first session on July 2, 1799, at the home of Robert Mosely in Hartford, with justices Harrison Taylor, Robert Barnett, Jesse Cravens, Stephen Cleaver, Christopher Jackson, and David Glenn present. Their first order of business was to organize themselves into a court, the second to appoint Stephen Stateler sheriff and William Rowan county clerk, their qualifications for the positions having been duly examined and approved. Other business included appointing James Baird as coroner and recording the Reverend Ignatius Pigman's stock mark.

Jesse Cravens and Stephen Cleaver were appointed commissioners to contract for building a jail, on the general order:

The Court of every County within this Commonwealth, shall at the charge of such County, cause to be erected and kept in good repair, within the same, one common jail and county prison, well secured with iron bars, bolts and locks; and also one pillory, whipping post and stocks.

The sheriff of each county had the responsibility to provide a jury of "twenty-four of the most discreet house-keepers, residing within the limits of the jurisdiction of the said court." There were further instructions:

For the trial of all causes in the several courts where a jury may be necessary, the sheriff, or other officer attending the Court, shall, every day the court sits, summon a sufficient number of the by-standers, to attend the court that day as jurors: and if any person so summoned shall fail to attend, he shall be fined eight dollars.

Prospective jurors soon learned that, whether they found for or against a defendant, they might provoke enough wrath to be subject to angry words or even physical danger. Many preferred to pay the eight-dollar fine; others found it cheaper to stay away on court days.

This gave rise to a story on the Indiana frontier of a judge, who, ready to try a case, called to the sheriff, "You got your jury ready?" The sheriff replied, "We've got eleven tied and're running down the twelfth."

Laws the justices had sworn to enforce were harsh and the penalties severe, even for what might be regarded a minor offense:

The penalties for profane swearing, or getting drunk, are five shillings, or fifty pounds of tobacco, for every offence, recoverable before a justice of the peace. And if the offender be unable to pay the fine, he, she, or they, shall receive ten lashes on his or her bare back, well laid on for each offence.

Laws set forth clear distinctions for punishment for white, Indian, or black, as well as for free man or slave, as the following shows:

Every person convicted of horse stealing, or as accessory thereto, before the fact, shall restore the horse, mare, or gelding stolen to the owner therof, or the full value, and shall be punished by confinement and hard labor in the jail or penitentiary house.

If any person not being a slave, shall steal any hog, shoat or pig, he or she shall, for the first offence receive on his or her bare back, twenty-five lashes well laid on, at the public whipping post, or pay down ten pounds current money, to the use of the County; and shall moreover pay four hundred pounds of tobacco for every hog, shoat or pig, one half to the owner, the other half to the informer, to be recovered with costs, by the informer.

A white man convicted of perjury lost his privilege to vote or to hold office, a punishment more severe than that meted out to the others:

Negroes, mulattoes, or Indians, bond or free may give testimony against negroes, mulattoes, or Indians; but before they are examined (not being Christian) the court shall charge them to declare the truth, in the following words: You are brought hither as a witness, and by direction of the law I am to tell you, before you give your evidence, that you must tell the truth, the whole truth, and nothing but the truth, and that if it be found hereafter, that you tell a lie, and give false testimony in this matter, you must for so doing receive thirty-nine lashes on your bare back, well laid on, at the common whipping post.

Stephen Cleaver was dividing his time between the affairs of Ohio County and his own. The clerk of the July 1799 Term of the

Court of Ohio County entered the following minute: "Upon the application of Stephen Cleaver Esq the marks of his cattle which is a crop & hole in the right ear and a swallow fork in the left ear, is admitted to record. Fee paid." Registering this mark was important in an open-range country, where cattle were free to roam, where farmers fenced out rather than in, where rustling was already becoming a mark of the West.

With all this, Stephen Cleaver had time to begin yet another enterprise, as shown by a minute in the December Term, 1800: "Stephen Cleaver having given bond and security allowed to keep ferry at or near place where road leading from Hartford to Breckinridge crosses Rough creek." A ferry could be run by slaves, and require little of his time.

His land dealings became extensive. On January 12, 1799, for one hundred and seventy pounds he bought two hundred acres from Robert and Anna Baird, they being a part of the three-hundred-acre tract where the Bairds then lived. On the same day, as required by laws of the time, Anna Baird came before Gent justices Stephen Rawlings and Samuel Rice and "being examined apart from her husband freely relinquishes her right of Dower to the within tract of land." Such was the status of women.

On August 6, 1799, Stephen and Rebeckah Cleaver sold Massey Thomas a tract of one hundred acres on Rough Creek. On the same day they sold John Peak a tract of one hundred and forty-nine acres on Rough Creek "about forty poles from Sulphur Lick in the lower line of the six hundred acre survey where Cleaver now lives." That would place his house on Rough River, probably on the bluff above where the Great Road from Hartford to Breckinridge Court House crossed the river.

Perhaps a score or more of his other land dealings are recorded in the deed books of Ohio County—not an excessive number given the methods of assigning land grants practiced by Virginia on the frontier, methods so inexact that two, sometimes more, people could locate their grants on the same tract and establish claims. This process, called layering and shingling after a time, brought on much litigations and disillusionment. Countless settlers lost their land, including Daniel Boone, who, stripped by tax collectors and shrewd lawyers of the last of the thousands of acres he had patented, packed up and went to Missouri in September 1799.

Though Stephen Cleaver was involved in some minor litigation, he seems to have avoided the land losses suffered by other Kentucky pioneers. His work in the Joseph Barnett case, however, brought a heavy burden of criticism. Acting as they thought they had been directed, the trustees sold the land through a sheriff's sale and settled the estate. When the heirs reached their majority they entered suit against the trustees for recovery of the land. Joseph Barnett, Junior, petitioned the state legislature to set aside the actions of the trustees and claimed that his father had died "possessed of an estate in lands sufficient to set two tyrants at war and his children all of tender years." He complained that the legislature had appointed commissioners to settle the estate who, while not dishonest, were too ignorant to be honest, with this result:

> ... The harpies, taking advantage of their want of business capacity, had hovered around, feasted, gorged and fattened themselves on the spoil, and that the bungling of the commissioners had frittered the estate away. That he wanted no more Legislature enactments on the subject, but just to stand out of his moonshine while he carried into Grant the numerous entries and surveys of land made by Joseph, Barnett, now deceased.

The legislature stood "out of his moonshine" and he took the case to court. The judge of the circuit court under whom the suit was entered—a judge who, according to Harrison D. Taylor, "thought it his duty to guard well our sacred charter of rights against legislative encroachments"—declared the legislative act unconstitutional. All deeds of sale made by the trustees thus became void, leaving the purchasers with no recourse but to sue for their rights. Harrison Taylor summed up some of the results:

> The legal proceedings in these cases are a fit illustration of what a farce we make in our mode of dispensing justice of that provision of our constitution copied from the great Magna Charta of England which declares that justice shall be administered without sale, delay, or denial. Those poor men had bought and paid for these lands, and had spent the best periods of their lives in hard labor in improving them. After being kept in court term after term, spending every dollar that they could raise in paying fee bills, expenses, and lawfees, they were literally overwhelmed when the sheriff visited them to turn them out of doors, seizing most of their property to pay plaintiff's execution for cost, and yet denied justice because they had not the means to buy it by taking their cases to the Court of Appeals.

The commissioners obviously lacked both business sense and legal knowledge. One of them, Harrison Taylor, had a certain originality in spelling. On one occasion he reportedly wrote *kaughphy* for *coffee*. Once, needing an order to compel the production of a paper he applied for a writ of *axim stickma*. A less original speller, or one better versed in legal Latin might more correctly have applied for a writ of *subpoena duces tecum*. Frontier lawyers, like frontier preachers, were given to the florid oratory that appears in this case.

Stephen Cleaver became involved to a lesser degree in the land dealings of another speculator, Ignatius Pigman, a Methodist preacher and one of the earliest settlers of Ohio County. Originally from Maryland, he had begun circuit riding in Maryland and Virginia in 1780 and was ordained in Baltimore in 1785. Bishop Asbury wrote in his diary Thursday, June 5, 1781, "Here brother Pigman met me, and gave an agreeable account of the work on the South Branch of the Potomac."

Pigman arrived in Ohio County soon after the Revolution and obtained title to considerable tracts of land for speculation. Then he returned to Maryland, where he sold the land to neighbors and friends in exchange for their homes or for money from the sale of their homes. Arriving in Kentucky in the fall, these settlers found the rich bottom lands covered with heavy growths of cane and wild peavines. They rushed to take title to bottom lands and began building cabins and clearing for crops, only to find that in winter and spring their land was flooded. Many abandoned their first Kentucky homes and purchased land on higher ground. After raising a few crops they found that this land had washed away. At least some of them sued to recover their bottom land.

By now Pigman had fallen in esteem with some of his religious brethren. On September 1, 1800, Bishop Asbury wrote in his diary, "On the way dined at Joshua Pigman's. Here I once more saw his brother Ignatius. Art thou he? Ah! But O! how fallen! How changed from what I knew thee once! Lord, what is man, if left to himself!"

Pigman, like many another speculator, had been left to himself in Kentucky, where land was rich and cheap, and where no foolproof system of surveying and conveying existed. Many thought he was acting in good faith and to the good of the county when he brought the settlers from Maryland. Others, who found their titles complicated by layering, brought suit and he was convicted of breach of promise on July 3, 1805.

His property in Ohio County was sold at a sheriff's sale by Harrison Taylor, sheriff. Stephen Cleaver bought a tract of four hundred and ten acres in this sale, for sixty-five dollars. Apparently title to this land was not clear, for when Cleaver sold it he had the following inserted in the indenture: "And be it clearly understood that the said Cleaver is not to be lyable for any money or property in consequence of this Contract in Case the whole or any part of the land should be lost." He sold it for fifteen dollars, and lost fifty dollars on the deal.

In the meantime Ignatius Pigman went to New Orleans, where reportedly he lost any money he had left speculating in the sugar market.

Stephen Cleaver apparently had greater success in numerous other land deals. Grantor records in the Ohio County Court House show the following sales made by Stephen Cleaver and Rebeckah his wife: on January 4, 1800, a tract on Rough Creek on the bank of Cane Run to Elijah Craven; on August 2, 1802, a tract of ninety-two acres between Sulphur Lick Run and Hall's Creek to George Jackson; on July 5, 1804 a tract of two hundred acres to George Bell; on April 1, 1805, a tract of fifty acres on Upper Sulphur Lick, on the Great Road leading from Hartford to Breckinridge Court House, to Richard Lanham.

He was prospering. His family was growing. Rebeckah bore him four sons: William, born on May 27, 1796; Henry, in 1805; Thomas, in 1807, and Jacob; and a daughter, Charlotte. His career as a public servant was advancing. On December 18, 1804, Governor Christopher Greenup replaced himself on the circuit court by appointing Stephen Cleaver: "Know you, That reposing special trust and confidence in the integrity, diligence and ability of Stephen Cleaver Esquire, I do, with the approbation of the Senate, appoint him an assistant Judge in the Ohio Circuit." On February 11, 1805, he presented this certificate to Christopher Jackson, a justice of the peace, and took the several oaths required by law.

A case that came before the court, possibly before him—two cases, in fact—involved his brother James. Two grand-jury presentments were read, one after the other. The first:

Tuesday April 9 1805
They also produced a presentment against James Cleaver in the words and of the tenor following (to wit) the Commonwealth of Kentucky Ohio Circuit Ct (?) April term one thousand eight hundred & five the Grand Jury for the Circuit aforesaid—on their oath—present James Cleaver late of the

said Circuit for Drunkeness in this that the said James Cleaver, on the eighth day of April eighteen hundred & five in the house of Joshua Crow in the Town of Hartford and County of Ohio then and there being was then and there drunk, and deprived of the use of his mental powers with or by Spiritous Liquors, to the evil examples of all others, and contrary to the statute in that case made and provided and against the peace and dignity of the Commonwealth of Kentucky—Information given by Solomon Davis and James Jordan both of the Jury and Circuit aforesaid, John Stevens foreman.

The second:

The Commonwealth of Kentucky Ohio Circuit to wit April Term one thousand eight hundred and five—the Grand Jury for the body of the Circuit aforesaid on their Oath do present James Cleaver for profanely swearing three times, by profanely uttering these words to wit "By Good," "By God," and "Godalmighty damn your soul" at the house of Major Joshua Crow in the Town of Hartford and County of Ohio on the eighth day of April eighteen hundred and five, Contrary to the statute in that case made and provided, and against the peace and dignity of the Commonwealth of Kentucky— Information given by Solomon Davis and James Jordan both of the Jury and County aforesaid John Stevens foreman.

At the trial, held in the July term, on Monday 8, 1805, an attorney represented "James Cleaver late of the said Circuit" and heard the verdict read:

Commonwealth plaintiff v James Cleaver Defendant on a Presentment for profane Swearing This day, came as mete the attorney for the Commonwealth, & the defendant by his attorney—and the said James Cleaver, because he will not contend with the Commonwealth, saith, that he is guilty in manner and form, as in the presentment against him, is alleged—Therefore it is Considered by the Court that he forfeit and pay ten Shillings currency to the use of the said Commonwealth—and pay the cost of this presentment.

James Cleaver had left Ohio County. He may have left Kentucky as well, for his name appears on early records in Missouri Territory.

Stephen Cleaver's reputation seems not to have been impaired by his brother's troubles. In 1806 his house was designated as the upper place of voting in Ohio County, with him as clerk. On February 20, 1808, he was listed as a member of the 12th Brigade, Hardin County. On the same date he was commissioned brigadier general, two months or so before his forty-second birthday.

On September 23, 1799, William Cleaver, Senior, separated himself finally from Tygart's Valley. Through his attorney, John Wilson,
he sold his share of the thousand-acre tract he had purchased with
Jonas Friend, Joseph Donoho, Jesse Hamilton, and Edward Skidmore. The tract, on both sides of Tygart's Valley River and by the
mouth of Leading Creek, contained one hundred and seventy-five
acres and sold for five hundred dollars, including improvements of
houses, buildings, and orchards. He had been away from Tygart's
Valley twenty years. There is no indication that he ever went back.

By 1800 his name had dropped out of Nelson County orders. On
August 28, 1805, he made his will, beginning it in the oft-repeated
form:

In the name of God Amen I William Cleaver Senior of Nelson County
and State of Kentucky being of sound mind and disposing memory and
weighing only the uncertainty of life's continuing in a frail body have
thought proper and do hereby make and ordain this instrument of writing
under my hand and seal my last Will and Testament in manner and form
following to wit Imprimis It is my Will and Desire that my body be buried
in a Christian like Decent manner at the Discretion of my Executors hereafter named in sure & certain Hopes of a blessed Ressurection and the full
enjoyment of the peace happyness and Tranquility of the Life to Come—
And as to the Worldly Goods it has pleased an Alwise Creator has favored
me with the privilege of acquiring it is My Desire Should be Disposed of as
herein Devised and bequeathed. . . .

In the first item he stated the following:

I give and bequeath to my loving wife Hannah Cleaver the one third
part of all my personal Estate without Discriminating Together with any
Grain & wheat that may be on hand at my death. . . .

He also desired that

My Wife shall have free and peaceable possession of the one Third of My
Plantation whereon I now live to include my houses & During her natural
life.

At the settlement of the estate the remainder was to be equally
divided amongst his children: Benjamin, William, Stephen, David,
James, and Hannah. He appointed his son Stephen and his neighbor
Michael Campbell as executors. Ben Edwards, Ben Harrison, Cyrus

Talbot, and James Smiley signed as witnesses. The will was probated on December 11, 1807, probably within a short time after his death. There is no record of when or where he was buried. It is likely that he was buried in a family graveyard on his plantation and that his gravestone, if one was set up, has long since weathered away.

The will does not mention slaves or lands other than the plantation on which William Cleaver, Senior, lived. The slaves had probably been sold or given to his children. At least some of his land was later sold by his heirs. On December 15, 1807, Stephen Cleaver presented an inventory of the notes and cash belonging to the estate of William Cleaver and the inventory, totaling fifty-four pounds, six pence, was ordered by Ben Grayson, county clerk, to be recorded, as of January 11, 1808. On December 31, 1807, the appraisers presented a list of his property with the appraised value of each item. Then the three of them—Joshua Hobbs, John Lemon, and Cornelius King—took the oath as the law directed, before Charles Morehead, Justice of the Peace.

William Cleaver's personal property was sold at public vendue on January 1, 1808, and the buyer, the item, and the price paid were entered in court records. Among the buyers there were two of his sons—Benjamin and David—his son-in-law, William Blackford, and Benjamin's son-in-law, Joseph Reddish. As he did not mention his daughter Sarah Blackford in his will, it is likely that she preceded him in death. Also among the buyers there was a Wilson, a Westfall, and a Donoho—names he had been associated with in Tygart's Valley and earlier. In two days of sale his property was scattered among thirty-one buyers.

The items sold reveal both how they lived and how they earned a living. They lived very well for their time and place. In the bedrooms they had two bedsteads, beds, with sheets and furniture, and chests of poplar and walnut. In the dining room they had table and chairs, pewter dishes and plates, teapots, knives and forks, candlesticks and snuffers, and three tablecloths. In the kitchen they had a frying pan, teakettle, spice mill, tubs for milk and cream and butter, earthen plates, tubs and washtubs.

For weaving, they had four sets of cards and a loom. At the sale there were two lots of flax still in preparation, one unbroken, one unrolled.

For their work the men had knives of various kinds and whetstones and grindstones for sharpening them. There were also augers, a froe, ax, broadax, lathe, whipsaw, gouge, chisel, plane, handsaw, and gimlets. One mare was offered at the sale, and a saddle, collar, and traces. Also sold were a brown cow, a brindle cow, four hogs, and a sow and pigs.

Perhaps the most remarkable item sold was a looking glass, still a very rare item in Kentucky. The one whiskey barrel sold is not proof that William Cleaver was in the business of making whiskey.

The income from these items, plus several dozen others, was six pounds, three shillings, seven pence, as attested to by Stephen Cleaver, executor, and duly recorded in the county court in Bardstown.

While Stephen Cleaver was disposing of his father's property on Beech Fork, Thomas Lincoln was building a log cabin on the South Fork of Nolin, a dozen or so miles to the southwest, the cabin in which Abraham Lincoln was born a year later.

How some Kentuckians lived and thought at the time became a part of the story "Early Experiences of Ralph Ringwood" by Washington Irving—the part that describes a frolic at the home of "old Bob Mosely" on the Pigeon Roost Fork of the Muddy, possibly the same house where Stephen Cleaver met with the other justices to organize Ohio County. The name Ralph Ringwood was a disguise used by Irving to conceal the identity of the man who told him the story: William Pope Duvall, later governor of Florida, who came from Virginia to Kentucky and spent the time from 1799 to 1801 in the Green River country, hunting. Irving presents Duvall's words as his own:

It was on our return from a winter's hunting in the neighborhood of Green River, when we received notice that there was to be a grand frolic at Bob Mosely's, to greet the hunters. This Bob Mosely was a prime fellow throughout the country. He was an indifferent hunter, it is true, and rather lazy to boot; but then he could play the fiddle, so there was no having a regular frolic without Bob Mosely. . . .

In the words of the frontier it was a time for putting the big pot in the little one:

It was no small occasion, either, let me tell you. Bob Mosely's house was a tolerably large bark shanty, with clapboard roof; and there were assembled at the frolic young hunters and pretty girls of the country, for many miles around. The young men were in their best hunting-dresses, but not one could compare with mine; and my raccoon-cap, with its flowing tail, was the admiration of everybody. The girls were mostly in doeskin dresses; for there was no spinning and weaving as yet in the woods; nor any need of it. I never saw girls that seemed to me better dressed; and I was somewhat of a judge, having seen fashions at Richmond. We had a hearty dinner, and a merry one; for there was Jemmy Kiel, famous for raccoon-hunting, and Bob Tarleton, and Wesley Pigman, and Joe Taylor, and several other prime fellows for a frolic, that made all ring again, and laughed, that you might have heard them a mile.

Irving disguised Duvall's name but not the names of those at the frolic, not even those of the Schultz sisters. The young men and women began dancing after dinner and were hard at it when about three o'clock in the afternoon the Schultz sisters arrived with little looking glasses hung around their necks on red ribbons. Irving described the stir they caused:

By the powers, but it was an event! Such a thing had never before been seen in Kentucky. Bob Tarleton, a strapping fellow, with a head like a chest-nut burr, and a look like a boar in an apple orchard, stepped up, caught hold of the looking-glass of one of the girls, and gazing at it for a moment cried out: "Joe Taylor, come here! come here! I'll be darned if Patty Schultz ain't got a locket that you can see your face in, as clear as in a spring of water."

The young men gathered around, causing Peggy Pugh to say to Sally Pigman, "Goodness knows, it's well Schultz's daughters is got them things round their necks, for it's the first time the young men crowded round them!"

Irving concludes the incident with the statement, "This was the first time that looking-glasses were ever seen in the Green River part of Kentucky."

The young people named in the story were well known to Stephen Cleaver, who lived only a few miles from Bob Mosely. Wesley and Sally Pigman were the children of Ignatius Pigman, the Methodist preacher. A deed of land to Jemmy Kiel was the first recorded in Ohio County. William Pope Duvall went on to Bardstown, where he studied law and established himself as a lawyer.

Shortly before or after the frolic at Bob Mosely's the Reverend Barton W. Stone was preaching at Cane Ridge, Bourbon County, in a revival that swept through Kentucky. Manifestations were described by Mr. Stone: "In less than twenty minutes, scores had fallen to the ground—paleness, trembling, and anxiety appeared in all— some attempted to fly from the scene panic stricken, but they either fell, or returned immediately to the crowd, as unable to get away."

A camp meeting began at the Cane Ridge Church on August 6, 1801, and people from all parts of the country came. According to one report, "It was estimated by some that not less than five hundred were at one time lying on the ground in the deepest agonies of distress, and every few minutes rising in shouts of triumph. . . ."

Out of this revivalism evolved a new sect, the first to be developed on the frontier, called the Christian Church or the Church of Christ and, after Stone joined forces with Alexander Campbell, the Campbellite Church. At this time, or soon after, Stephen Cleaver became an admirer of Alexander Campbell and a follower, if not a member, of the Christian Church.

The Battle of Fallen Timbers brought a lull in Indian fighting but not the end. By 1806 two forces were developing that inevitably led to an intensification of the conflict: the forming of a new Indian confederation by the Shawnee chieftain Tecumseh, and his brother, called The Prophet; and a two-pronged confrontation with England. Land was at the bottom of both. Expansionists in both West Florida and the Northwest Territory were grabbing or waiting to grab land controlled by the British. Others, led by William Henry Harrison, governor of Indiana Territory, were taking land by treaty, by purchase, or by force from the Indians. Tecumseh, and The Prophet, seeing that it was impossible for the smaller tribes to resist the forces led by Harrison, decided that the Indians' only hope was through uniting. Like missionaries they traveled from village to village spreading their doctrine and bringing tribe after tribe into the confederation.

Harrison, learning of their success, decided to counter with an attack on The Prophet, a one-eyed epileptic medicine man who was believed by the Indians to have supernatural powers. He began with a letter to the Delawares: "If he is really a prophet ask him to cause the sun to stand still, the moon to alter its course, the rivers to cease to flow."

Both his tactic and timing were bad. The Prophet knew from the whites that there was to be a total eclipse of the sun on June 16, 1806. Confidently, he predicted it, and from then on he and Tecumseh were accepted by the Indians as law. As a result, other tribes came into the confederation. Tecumseh and The Prophet established a village, which they called Prophetstown, where the Tippecanoe Creek emptied into the Wabash River. From this he would extend his influence over the other tribes. At about the same time Tecumseh visited Fort Malden, the British post on the north side of the Detroit River, to enlist British aid. In the minds of many Englishmen the American Revolution had not been won and the United States had no bona-fide reason for being. Many also expected war to break out over the impressment of Americans into British service. Captain Mathew Elliott, in command at Fort Malden, welcomed Tecumseh and, without actually promising aid, encouraged him in his efforts to regain Indian lands.

Encouraged by British friendship, incensed at still another land grab—the forming of Illinois Territory in 1809—Tecumseh and his followers took to the warpath. Attacks on isolated white settlements began in the spring of 1810, and by the fall of that year they were widespread. Tecumseh appealed to Harrison to end the land-grabbing; Harrison remained adamant. In the summer of 1811 Tecumseh and twenty-four of his warriors went south to confer with chiefs of the Creeks, Cherokees, and Choctaws at a council meeting on the Tallapoosa River in Alabama Territory. They appeared at the meeting with their faces painted red and black to signify that no decision had been made between war and peace. Each carried a rifle, a tomahawk, and a war club. Of their appearance a white frontiersman said, "They were the most athletic body of men I ever saw. . . . Tecumseh was about six feet high, well put together, not so stout as some of his followers, but of an austere countenance and imperial mien. He was in the prime of life."

At night the warriors danced. Each day they put off conferring, apparently waiting for the government agent to depart. At noon the day the agent left, Tecumseh and his men appeared, weaponless, painted black, naked except for a loin clout. They went to the pole at the center of the council square. Without a word Shawnees and Creeks exchanged gifts and smoked the peace pipe. Then Tecumseh spoke:

In defiance of the white warriors of Ohio and Kentucky, I have traveled through their settlements, once our favorite hunting grounds. No war whoop was sounded, but there is blood on our knives. The palefaces felt the blow, but knew not whence it came.

Accursed be the race that has seized our country, and made women of our warriors! Our fathers, from their tombs, reproach us as slaves and cowards; I hear them now in the wailing winds.

The Muskogee was once a mighty people. The Georgians trembled at your war whoops. Now your very blood is white; your tomahawks have no edge; your bows and arrows were buried with your fathers. Oh, Muskogees, brush from your eyelids the sleep of slavery! Once more strike for vengeance! . . . Let the white race perish. They seize your land; they corrupt your women; they trample on the ashes of your dead. Back whence they came, upon a trail of blood, they must be driven. Back, aye, into the great water. . . . Burn their dwellings! Destroy their stock! Slay their wives and children! The red people own the country. . . . War now! War forever! War upon the living! War upon the dead; dig their very corpses from the grave; our country must give no rest to a white man's bones!

The speech over, the Shawnees danced a war dance in which they represented scouts on the trail and an ambush, and ended with brandished war clubs and blood-chilling war whoops.

Harrison, taking advantage of Tecumseh's absence, began a drive against Prophetstown with regular troops and Kentucky militia —together a thousand strong. On November 6, 1810, they camped outside the town. In the early morning of November 7, after some magic incantations from The Prophet, the Indians moved through darkness and rain and attacked the whites in their sleep. After the first confusion of a surprise attack the white soldiers held their ground and then drove the Indians back. By the end of the second day of fighting the Indians had deserted the village and the whites had destroyed it.

The Battle of Tippecanoe, as it came to be called, cost each side thirty-eight dead and one hundred and fifty wounded, an especially heavy loss for the whites, as they outnumbered the Indians by three hundred. More important, it was not conclusive and only opened up more hostilities. Tecumseh returned and sent his warriors against white settlements with tomahawk to kill, fire to burn. The length of the frontier was made unsafe for settlers, and the more isolated began fleeing to the safety of forts. Blame was on the British, with bitterness toward them for supplying the arms and ammunition by which white men were killed.

Frontiersmen, with dreams of driving the Indians on west, of conquering Canada, of putting to an end forever the British-Indian alliance, demanded a declaration of war. Their demands mattered little in the East; fear of subservience to British colonial and commercial dominance mattered a great deal. President Madison yielded to the stronger voices and sent a message to Congress. On June 18, 1812, Congress declared war on England.

At first the war went against the people on the western frontier. Then, realizing that control of Lake Erie was essential to the success of a western campaign, officials in Washington ordered Oliver Hazard Perry to build a fleet of attack boats. They were built at Erie and transported west by wagon train. On September 10, 1813, they met the fleet of British gunboats and defeated them. Perry was able to send a terse message to Harrison: "We have met the enemy and they are ours."

News of Perry's victory took some time to get back to Hartford, Kentucky, but it was still taken as occasion for a celebration. Inspired by the victory, men of Ohio County, probably inspired as well by a product of their own corn fields, burned the abandoned courthouse and jail. An apologist wrote, "In early times—when they used the pure essence of corn, which did not make men mad and vicious, but inspired them with unbounded patriotism and benevolence—it was not uncommon for the best of men to become a little fuddled on an extraordinary occasion."

Perry had furnished them one.

The Battle of the Thames was an even more extraordinary occasion. Perry's victory had opened the way for attacks on Detroit and Fort Malden and made possible the ferrying of troops to the Canadian side. Work began at once to move the United States regulars plus thirty-five hundred Kentucky militia under the command of Colonel R. M. Johnson. A landing was made on September 27, 1813, and the British started withdrawing along the Thames River. The Americans pursued, moving at a faster pace. On October 5 the British, with four hundred regulars and six hundred Indians under Tecumseh, made a stand on a plain between the Thames River and a swamp. In the afternoon General Harrison's troops attacked, with the Kentuckians yelling their own battle cry as they advanced. The battle, which lasted only a few minutes, left all the British troops killed or captured. The Indians disappeared in the swamp, pursued futilely by the Kentuckians. Tecumseh was killed; the British commander fled. This was a great victory, one of the most important of the War of 1812. Without Tecumseh, the Indian confederation fell apart. Without British support the Indians could not carry on the fight.

The manner in which Tecumseh met his death has long been disputed. Colonel Johnson's mounted regiment was ordered to make the first rush. He sent his brother James against the British and turned the remainder against the Indians in the swamp. He heard Tecumseh giving commands to the Indians. Obeying him, they held their fire until the Kentuckians were close. In the first volley Johnson was wounded in the hand. In the twenty minutes of fighting that followed, Tecumseh was killed, credit for his death going to Colonel Johnson.

Not all were willing to allow him that credit. Several made statements to the contrary, including Stephen Cleaver:

It will be recollected by those who knew Col. Cleaver that he was a great friend of Col. Johnson, but denied him the credit of killing Tecumseh. He said Tecumseh was killed some time after Col. Johnson was wounded and disabled; that he was killed at least three hundred yards from where the Colonel was shot. And while I am at it, I will go into a minute detail of Col. Cleaver's statement, as it corroborates the statement made by Doyle and Walton. He said, from the way the Indians rallied and fought around a certain Indian until he was killed, and a small trinket found on his person, that he was supposed to be a Chief. And there being but few if any among the whites that had known Tecumseh, except Gen. Harrison, it was some time after the close of the fight before it was ascertained that the dead Chief was Tecumseh; and it was only ascertained through the General. The circumstance of the bold stand made by the supposed Chief being communicated to G. Harrison, he visited the spot where the dead Indian lay; the body was much mangled, and as the General approached the spot a soldier was in the act of taking off a piece of skin from the Indian's thigh. The General ordered the soldier to stop, and said he regretted to know that he had such a man in his camp, and reprimanded him severely. He had some water brought, had the Indian washed and stretched his full length, examined his teeth and pronounced it to be Tecumseh. One of Tecumseh's legs was a little shorter than the other, and the foot on the short leg a little smaller, and he had a halt in his walk that was perceptible, and he had a tooth, though not decayed, of a bluish cast.

Another witness may have been Stephen's son William, who saw action as a private in Charles Wickliffe's Company.

Unfortunately, General Harrison, in his official reports, failed to mention Tecumseh or the circumstances of his death. Johnson himself did not claim to have killed Tecumseh, though later his political enemies circulated a rhyme calculated to ridicule him:

> Humpsy Dumsy
> Colonel Johnson killed Tecumseh.

No doubt General Harrison was justified in reprimanding the soldier for taking the piece of skin. It was not unusual for a white man to take a piece of Indian skin, tan it, and make it into a razor strop.

News of the victory eventually reached Hartford, Kentucky, and the men went on such a burning spree that soon there were no more vacant buildings to be burned. It may have been at this time that the following incident occurred. An old house had all disappeared except the frame of the roof, which rested on the ground, leaving the A-shaped garret intact. The celebrators selected this building for their bonfire and it was soon in flames. The men were patriotic and courageous. They were also increasingly under the effect of corn whiskey. Soon they were daring each other to run through the flaming roof. Several did so. Then a Major James Johnston started through and fell. He managed to get up and make his way on through, though exhausted and somewhat singed, and stayed for the rest of the celebration, adding his part to frontier myth and legend.

While General Harrison was marching toward the Battle of the Thames, Indian troubles were breaking out along the frontier in Georgia and Alabama, in what came to be called the Creek War. On August 30, 1813, the Indians attacked Fort Mims on the Alabama River and massacred many of the whites. In response, two small armies set out from Georgia, and a third, made up of five thousand militiamen under the command of Andrew Jackson, marched from their place of assembly at Fayetteville, Tennessee. One by one the Indian villages were subdued by raiding parties sent out by Jackson, with the exception of the village at Horse Shoe Bend on the Tallapoosa, which withstood the first assault. On March 27, 1814, Jackson charged again, with the advantage of three thousand whites against one thousand Indians. He also had the advantage of cannon against rifle and tomahawk. The result was carnage. At the end, about nine hundred braves were dead and resistance had been temporarily broken. Jackson ordered the surviving leaders to a meeting, at which the Treaty of Fort Jackson was signed and the Creeks, among other harsh terms, had to cede about half their land to the whites.

The War of 1812 was not yet over. Word came that the British had sent fifty ships and ten thousand troops to attack New Orleans. Again Kentuckians were called on to fight, two generations of Cleavers among them. Feeling ran high, stirred in part by a song made for the moment:

> Come all ye brave Kentuckians,
>   I'd have you for to know,
> That for to fight the enemee
>   I'm going for to go.
>
> And if you're freezin' for a fight,
>   Come go along with me,
> We'll show them for a thing or two
>   In front the enemee.
>
> If you ask where we are goin'
>   I'll tell you what it means—
> We're going on a big flatboat
>   Way down to New Orleans.
>
> And there we'll meet proud red coats,
>   All heeled with golden spurs,
> Though they belch big guns and bombs,
>   We'll thrash the Britishers.

This was a considerable boast in view of the fact that British troops had invaded Washington and set fire to the Capitol and the White House.

Unaware of the impending attack, Jackson marched toward New Orleans and reached there on December 1, 1814. When he learned that the British were on their way from Jamaica, Jackson, expecting the attack to come from the Mississippi, set up his main defense at Baton Rouge, one hundred and twenty miles away. Then, learning that the British had come in to the east of New Orleans, he marched his troops to within five miles of the city and built a line of breastworks. There was an artillery battle on January 1, 1815, and then on the morning of January 8 the British attacked the breastworks, where Jackson had assembled about forty-five hundred men, many of them expert riflemen from Kentucky and Tennessee. When the battle was over the British commander and two thousand of his troops were dead. Jackson had lost six men killed. It was a great victory—a victory that helped to catapult Jackson into the Presidency and permanently ingrained a fiddle tune in the American mind: "The Eighth of January," or "The Battle of New Orleans." Ironically, the battle need never have been fought. A peace treaty had been signed at Ghent two weeks before.

In Hartford, Kentucky, when the news came back, the men burned their last vacant building, and their biggest.

General Stephen Cleaver was reportedly at the Battle of New Orleans, though his name does not appear on the muster rolls. Records do show that a William Cleaver, probably the son of Benjamin, served as a private from June 24 to July 25, 1813, in Captain Kincheloe's Company of a detachment of the Kentucky Mounted Volunteers. His pay was eight dollars a month, with an allowance of forty cents a day for his horse. He drew a total of twenty-one dollars and ninety-seven cents, including traveling time from Hardinsburg, Breckinridge County, the place of discharge, to his home twenty-two miles away. Stephen Cleaver, probably the son of William, Junior, served the same length of time in the same outfit for the same pay. The difference is that he was appointed captain of the spies on July 2 and was in that service the remainder of the time.

Whatever his service in the war of 1812, Stephen Cleaver was promoted to major general in Nelson County on January 26, 1816, at a time when he was hankering to move farther west.

In 1817 Stephen Cleaver joined a group of families bound for Missouri. The reason why is not entirely clear, though Jemmy Kiel's statement in "Early Experiences of Ralph Ringwood" may be taken as partial explanation:

. . . Game, however, began to grow scarce. The buffalo had gathered together, as if by universal understanding, and had crossed the Mississippi, never to return. Strangers kept pouring into the country, clearing away the forests, and building in all directions. The hunters began to grow restive. Jemmy Kiel, the same of whom I have already spoken for his skill in raccoon catching, came to me one day: "I can't stand this any longer," said he; "we're getting too thick here. . . ."

Being too thick created problems:

> I've no idea of living where another man's cattle can run mine. That's too close neighborhood; I want elbow-room. This country, too, is growing too poor to live in; there's no game; so two or three of us have made up our minds to follow the buffalo to the Missouri. . . .

Missouri was the magic word, as Kentucky had been earlier. Daniel Boone had gone earlier. So had Stephen Cleaver's brother James. Others were on the way. Westering was in the air, that strange malady that addled the mind and set men old or young to dreaming.

Stephen Cleaver had lived in Kentucky thirty-eight years, since the age of thirteen, and though his course had at times been zigzag, it had been generally forward and useful. He had served Kentucky well and might have, by living out his years there, been listed among her stalwarts.

He had lost Rebeckah to death about 1808. In April 1810, he had married Elenor Tapley, and she had borne him two daughters: Rebecca and Ellender. He owned large tracts of land unencumbered by lawsuit over deed or title. The 1810 tax lists show that he owned twenty-one slaves at the time.

Wealth and honors he had, yet he was willing to leave it all behind, perhaps only for the sake of pioneering on a new frontier.

Restlessness was widespread in Kentucky. As on earlier frontiers, some went, some stayed. James and Stephen Cleaver went. The other sons of William Cleaver, Senior, stayed: David in Washington County; William, Junior, and Benjamin in Grayson County. Some of Benjamin's sons and daughters took their families across Indiana to Illinois, where some settled near Springfield, some in the part of Greene County that is now Jersey County. From there great-grandsons went on west as new frontiers opened: the Reverend David Myers to found the first Baptist church in Dallas County, Texas; another Benjamin Cleaver to Oregon.

Restlessness also touched Thomas Lincoln. After three years in the cabin on the South Fork of Nolin he moved to Knob Creek. He was farming, cabinetmaking, working for the Hardin County Court. He was appointed surveyor, a kind of commissioner, of the road between "Bigg Hill and Rolling Fork." Later he was appointed surveyor of the road from Nolin to Bardstown, a road that crossed Cleaver land somewhere between Landing Run Creek and Sugar Camp Creek on Beech Fork. But he heard of richer corn land to the west and in 1816 he moved on, first to Little Pigeon Creek in Indiana and then, when Abe was just twenty-one, on to Illinois.

Present-day
state boundaries

0   25   50   75   100
Miles

IOWA

NEBR.

Salt R.

Palmyra

Hannibal

Saverton

New London

Louisiana

Frankford

Spencer
Creek

ILLINOIS

Missouri R.

St. Charles

St. Louis

KANSAS

MISSOURI

Mississippi R.

Springfield

New Madrid

KY.

OKLAHOMA

ARKANSAS

TENN.

H. Faye

Missouri

Earlier than the settlement of Kentucky, explorers—Spanish, French, English—had crisscrossed that part of Louisiana territory called Missouri: De Soto in 1541, Father Marquette in 1673, La Salle in 1682, a few English long hunters who took their furs to market down the Mississippi to New Orleans. La Salle reached the mouth of the Mississippi on April 9, 1682, claimed the whole of the Mississippi Valley for France, and called it Louisiana. French it remained until the contest for the control of North America came to the fore in the French and Indian War. By the treaty signed in Paris on February 10, 1763, France gave up all its holdings to England with the exception of the Louisiana territory, which it ceded to Spain, which had entered the conflict late on the side of the French. Spain was also forced to make concessions. To regain control of Havana, it had to yield both East and West Florida to the British.

The contest for the title to the Louisiana territory was not over, partly because the transfer was generally regarded as temporary—only an expedient to keep it from falling into the hands of the British. French settlers, mainly from Illinois Territory, continued to settle along the Mississippi and established St. Louis in 1764.

At the beginning of the American Revolution St. Louis was a thriving center in the fur trade. It was soon to become a desirable prize for the British and their Indian allies raiding out from Detroit. The British already maintained posts at three forts they had taken from the French: Cahokia, across the Mississippi from St. Louis; Kaskaskia, down the river at the mouth of the Kaskaskia; and Vincennes, on the Wabash. As the war progressed and raiding parties increased

[175]

their harassment of settlers on the western frontier, action against these forts became imperative. In June 1778, George Rogers Clark led an expedition of one hundred and seventy-five men overland from Louisville. On July 4 he surprised the British at Kaskaskia and they surrendered. Cahokia also surrendered and with little resistance. Vincennes surrendered to a Catholic priest, who brought word of Clark's successes.

Clark's victories brought the Indians to the American side for a time, but because he could not muster forces to continue the attacks the Indians gradually drifted back to the British. In 1780 a combined force of a thousand British and Indians launched an attack, first at Cahokia and then at St. Louis. Clark was waiting for them. After a few unsuccessful tries, the British and Indians gave up and moved on against St. Louis. Again they found the defenses stronger than they had expected. Their campaign a failure, they pillaged a few farms and withdrew.

The Revolution ended, the United States replaced England as neighbor to the Louisiana territory, and American settlers, attracted by the potential wealth of the land and by the fact that the Spanish did not rigidly enforce religious conformity, came from New England, Virginia, and the nearer frontiers.

Napoleon Bonaparte, his power firmly established, became interested in regaining the Louisiana territory as one part of a new and vast French empire. At first the Spanish were willing to sell, the French to buy. Then in a treaty signed on October 1, 1800, Spain agreed to transfer the territory to France for what proved to be no compensation at all. Settlers in the West saw a threat to their use of the Mississippi and of New Orleans as transport and market for their goods. President Jefferson saw the purchase of New Orleans as a way out. Napoleon was willing to sell—not only New Orleans but the whole of the Louisiana territory. In a treaty signed on April 30, 1803, Louisiana was ceded to the United States in exchange for eighty million francs, approximately $15,000,000.

Significantly, the treaty stipulated that all residents of Louisiana would be admitted

as soon as possible, according to the principles of the Federal Constitution, to the enjoyment of all the rights, advantages and immunities of the citizens of the United States; and in the meantime they shall be maintained and protected in the free enjoyment of their liberty, property, and the religion which they profess.

Transfer of the upper part of the territory took place at St. Louis on March 9, 1804, and was followed by a ceremony in which the Stars and Stripes were raised over a vast new region, and in which residents became citizens, not subjects.

On that same day the retiring French governor addressed a gathering of Delaware, Shawnee, and Sac Indians:

> Your old fathers, the Spaniards and the Frenchmen, who grasp by the hand your new father, the Chief of the United States, by an act of their Good Will, and in virtue of their last treaty, have delivered up all of these lands. The new father will keep and defend the land and protect all of the white and redskins who live thereon. You will live as happily as if the Spaniard was still here.

He did not make clear—for the Shawnees at least he did not need to make clear—the marked differences in methods of settling. The French and Spanish had for the most part stayed close to the rivers in small towns from which they could carry on their Indian trade. English settlers, as they had all across the frontier, wanted to turn hunting grounds into farms and meadows. Hatred of English settlers in Missouri was inevitable.

For the convenience of government the Spaniards had divided the Province of Louisiana into Upper Louisiana with the seat at St. Louis and Lower Louisiana with the seat at New Orleans. In a census taken in 1801 Upper Louisiana had a population of over nine thousand whites and one thousand slaves. Of the whites at the time of the purchase more than half were Anglo-American, and the majority of those were settlers from the United States.

Among these was Daniel Boone, who set out for Missouri in September 1799, disillusioned over loss of land, eager to find less crowded spaces, intent on owning land again. He was welcomed by the representatives of the Spanish government who in recognition of his distinction and his promise to bring in one hundred and fifty families from Virginia and Kentucky granted him ten thousand acres of land, to be located wherever he chose. His son Daniel Morgan had paved the way with Spanish officials for him and had explored some of the territory as early as 1795.

Boone chose a site sixty miles from the mouth of the Missouri River and twenty-five miles up from St. Charles. There, at age sixty-five, he would start all over again. It was not an easy journey. Boone himself traveled over land with a train of packhorses, accompanied by some of his neighbors and a few slaves, driving their stock before them. Rebecca traveled in a dugout canoe sixty feet long, and with her Daniel's brother Squire, their sons Daniel Morgan and Nathan, and their daughter Jemima probably in other canoes. The journey took them down the Big Sandy, down the Ohio, up the Mississippi, up the Missouri, to the Femme Osage settlement, which Daniel Morgan had settled two years earlier. There, as they had done so many times before, on so many frontiers, Daniel and Rebecca built a half-faced house for shelter while they built a rough log cabin.

Apparently James and Hannah Cleaver were among the settlers recruited by Daniel Boone. Records show that he served in Captain Daniel Morgan Boone's Company from June 13, 1813, to May 25, 1814. This was a territorial troop of rangers, sometimes called "the minutemen of the frontier." They patrolled settlements from the Salt River on the Mississippi to Loutre Island in the Missouri.

In any case, word of new territory opened, new land to be settled, spread fast in story and speculators' hand bills and song. A song known as early as 1820 is a kind of hymn of westering:

> To the west, to the land of the free,
> Where the mighty Missouri rolls down to the sea;
> Fruit of the soil,
> Where children are blessings, and he who has most
> Has aid for his fortunes and riches to boast;
> Where the young may exalt, and the aged may rest,
> Away, far away, to the land of the west.

Spencer Creek

IN 1817, Stephen Cleaver gave up all he had in Kentucky, his property, his accumulation of living from the time he was thirteen, and set out for Missouri. At the time he held high position in both the judiciary and the military. He owned slaves and land and had not been bedeviled by the kind of lawsuit that had stripped Daniel Boone. There are no apparent reasons for him to pull up stakes and go, but he did. According to family tradition "he went to Missouri with Daniel Boone"—not with him certainly but possibly recruited by him. Like Boone, he may have wanted more elbow room. He may have been bored with what he had in Kentucky and excited at the prospect of gaining more in Missouri.

Missouri was the only new territory open to him if he wanted to keep his slaves. Some, like Thomas Lincoln, his fellow resident in Hardin County, had gone to Indiana; some of his brother Benjamin's children had gone to Jersey County, Illinois. Indiana and Illinois were both part of the Northwest Territory, in which introduction of slavery had been abolished by Congress. He took his slaves with him.

They went in a wagon train, in covered wagons, hauling their household goods, driving their stock along with them, making only a few miles in a day, camping out at night. Stephen Cleaver had his wife and children, ranging in age from six to twenty-two, and at least several slaves. In the train there were other men, some with families: Dabney Jones, Harrison Jones, Richard Jones, William Jones, and a man named Keathley. Quite likely there were others. It was a slow journey but easier than any had been over the mountains. They had to stop in the middle of the day to cook for themselves and for the animals to graze; and for the night, when the animals could be hobbled to keep them from straying, when after supper the settlers could sit around a fire for talk and songs and sometimes prayers. Clear nights they could sleep under the stars; rainy nights they could crawl into wagons and be lulled to sleep by the sound of raindrops on stretched canvas.

At last the train came to the Mississippi, where there was ferry service across to Louisiana, Missouri. They crossed there into what was then St. Charles County and went on to their final destination on a hill overlooking Spencer Creek, not far from where it empties into the Salt River. This place is about five miles southeast of New London, where William Jamison had settled in 1800, and two miles or so from the present site of Frankford. It was a good place to settle. The hill commanded a good view of the fertile bottom land along Spencer Creek. There was a good spring, still called the Cleaver Spring. There was enough timber, especially along the creeks, for buildings and for fuel. Most important, it was west of the Mississippi. They had come out of the mountains, out of the heavily timbered land they had known in Virginia and Kentucky to a land that was gently rolling, open, with broad skies, horizons seldom broken.

Stephen Cleaver came to Missouri as farmer and land speculator. Getting a farm started was easier than it had been on Beech Fork. Large trees thinly scattered could be girdled and left standing to rot or they could be cut down and split into rails for fencing. There were no rocks to be dug out or plowed around. In the prairie spaces the sod could be broken with a team of six oxen to a plow. The land was not good for cotton or tobacco but especially suited to corn and wheat. A wise farmer could get ahead fast.

So could a wise speculator. In opening up Missouri lands the General Land Office in Washington had tried to avoid the problems that had arisen over land titles on earlier frontiers, especially in Kentucky. This time a general survey was ordered. Land was laid off in ranges and the ranges divided into sections of six hundred and forty acres each. Property lines followed straight section lines rather than the meanderings of streams. This squareness became a characteristic of western states, counties, and farms.

The method of granting land in Missouri is demonstrated in a grant dated August 9, 1820, and certified in the name of President James Monroe:

Know ye, That Stephen Cleaver of St. Charles County, Missouri, having deposited in the General Land Office a certificate of the Register at the Land

Office at St. Louis in Missouri, whereby it appears that full payment has been made for the Southeast quarter of Section Twenty. . . .

Stephen Cleaver was granted three quarter sections of one hundred and sixty acres each in his own name and six quarter sections as assignee of John Taylor—for a total of fourteen hundred and forty acres. He also began acquiring lots in nearby communities—New London, Saverton, and Palmyra—often at depressed prices in a sheriff's sale. Again, as a surveyor he had an advantage. He laid out the town of Frankford and assisted in laying out Palmyra. In 1820 the Missouri legislature created Ralls County, which was to embrace the whole of Northeast Missouri. Immediately there was rivalry over the location of the county seat, a rivalry won by New London over Hannibal and Saverton. William Jamison was awarded the contract to lay out the town of New London. Stephen Cleaver became his assistant.

Missouri was filling up fast. In 1810, the population was 20,845; by 1814 it was 26,000; in 1820 it was 70,000. In 1804 there had been four main towns with the following populations: Ste. Genevieve, 2,350 whites, 520 slaves; St. Louis, 2,280 whites, 500 slaves; St. Charles, 1,400 whites, 150 slaves; Cape Girardeau, 1,470 whites, 180 slaves. In addition there was New Madrid, which took in a part of what is now Arkansas, with 1,350 whites and 150 slaves. As the population increased so did the number of towns and the needs for services. Farms were being expanded. New markets needed to be opened. Government more suited to the needs of the settlers became obvious.

Steps toward statehood moved rapidly from talk to action, so rapidly that John Scott, the Missouri Territorial Delegate, was able to present a petition to Congress on March 16, 1818. Soon the question of Missouri became a political argument in Washington. Slavery was at the center of the argument. The petition ran head-on into the struggle for control of new territory: whether it would be slave or free. On March 2, 1807, Congress had passed a law that forbade the importation of slaves into the United States after January 1, 1808. Penalty for violation was the forfeiture of ship and cargo. Seized slaves were to be disposed of by the state in which the ship was condemned. The law was difficult to enforce; slaves seized in the ships could still end up in servitude. Admission of new states as slave or free was a prerogative of Congress. The Missouri petition was turned over to a committee, with Scott as chairman. It was duly reported out by the select committee but bottled up by the committee of the whole and not acted upon before the first session had adjourned.

Thus began a conflict that was to extend over a period of three years, during which sectional rivalry became increasingly dangerous. From the time of the establishment of the Constitution, Congress had been able to maintain a balance in the admission of free states and slave states. Incorporation of the vast Louisiana territory threatened to upset that balance. Missouri became a case in point. Along the Mississippi and Missouri rivers large landowners who had migrated from the older Southern states and had brought their slaves with them became active on the side of slavery. Stephen Cleaver was among them.

After a year of delay on the Missouri petition, Congress in February 1819 began considering enabling acts for the admission of Alabama and Missouri. James Tallmadge of New York offered an amendment:

> Provided, that the further introduction of involuntary servitude be prohibited, except for the punishment for crimes whereof the party shall have been duly convicted; and that all children born within the said state after the admission thereof into the Union shall be free, at the age of twenty-five years.

This amendment being unacceptable to Southern planters, Henry Clay took the floor against it. In spite of his argument that diffusion of slavery into the larger territory would lessen any bad effects of the system, the House passed the amendment. It was defeated, however, eleven days later and Henry Clay became a hero to most Southerners and a special hero to Stephen Cleaver.

In December 1819, Congress still had the application from Missouri for admission to statehood before it plus an application from Maine. Senator Jesse B. Thomas, during debate on the application from Maine, proposed a compromise: that Maine be admitted as a free state, Missouri as a slave state, and that slavery should be prohibited north of 36 degrees, 30 minutes, in the rest of the Louisiana Purchase. This compromise—known then as the Missouri Compromise but without the connotations history has given that name—passed the Senate on February 20, 1820, and the House on March 2, 1820. Missourians could at last elect delegates and get on with the business of organizing a state government.

The election of delegates to the Constitutional Convention was held on the first Monday and the two succeeding days of May 1820.

Stephen Cleaver was elected as the only delegate from Pike County, which at the time embraced the whole of northern Missouri. Nathan Boone, who was born in Kentucky in 1780 and who lived some sixty miles to the south of Stephen Cleaver, was a delegate from St. Charles County. The question of a candidate's attitude toward slavery was crucial, and those strongly proslavery won a majority. Of the forty-one delegates, thirty-three were born in slave states, six in nonslave states, and two in the British Isles. Ironically, the latter eight were all persuaded against putting restrictions on slavery.

Stephen Cleaver was no doubt typical of the delegates born in slave states. As a boy he must have seen slaves bought and sold on the stone slave block outside the courthouse in Bardstown, Kentucky; as a man he had bought and sold slaves. Around him slavery was not a moral issue. The Bible countenanced it. Preachers owned slaves. Slavery had been a way of life for him, and more important than ever on this Missouri frontier, where there was land to clear, ground to break, planting to be done before the promise of the land could become a reality. He also shared with his neighbors a feeling for independence—a feeling that made them resist anything that they considered interference in their affairs.

The delegates met on Monday, June 12, 1820, in St. Louis at "Mansion House," at the corner of Third and Vine—in a hall and two rooms provided for the convention for a rental of thirty dollars a week. They elected David Barton of St. Louis President and adopted a resolution: "That each member of this convention take an oath to support the Constitution of the United States, and also an oath for the faithful discharge of the duties of his office. . . ."

The oaths administered, they moved on to another resolution:

. . . That it is expedient now to form a Constitution and State Government for the people of said territory, included within the boundaries designated by an act of Congress, entitled "an Act, to authorize the people of Missouri territory to form a constitution and state government, and for the admission of such state into the Union on a equal footing with the original states, and to prohibit slavery in certain territories.

This resolution was adopted unanimously. Among those voting was Pierre Chouteau, Junior, a Frenchman, a resident of St. Louis. The Louisiana territory had been slave under both the French and the Spanish.

The constitution they wrote was based on Kentucky's second

constitution, which was framed in 1799 and had become effective on January 1, 1800, without submission to the people. Of the resolutions adopted, five deal with subjects of special significance to this narrative: suffrage, slavery, separation of church and state, education, and dueling.

Kentucky had been the first state to abolish ownership of property as a requirement for voting. Missouri followed this precedent with this article:

> Every free white male citizen of the United States who shall have attained to the age of twenty-one years, who shall have resided in this state one year before an election, the last three months whereof shall have been in the county or district in which he offers to vote, shall be deemed a qualified elector of all elective offices.

An amendment to strike out twenty-one and insert eighteen was voted down, thirty-one to six, one hundred and fifty years ahead of its time. Yet the liberalism of the frontier had exerted itself in an important area. By the same a new watchword entered the language: "Free, white, and twenty-one."

This liberalism did not apply to slaves. In an article remarkable for its fidelity to the Kentucky model the Convention resolved as follows:

> The general assembly shall have no power to pass laws for the emancipation of slaves, without the consent of their owners, or without paying their owners previous to such emancipation, a full equivalent in money for the slaves so emancipated; they shall have now power to prevent *bona fide* emigrants to, or actual settlers in this state from bringing with them such persons as are deemed slaves, by the laws of any one of the United States, so long as any persons of the same age and description shall be continued in slavery by the laws of this state; they shall have power to pass laws, to prohibit the introduction into this state of slaves who have committed high crimes in other states or territories; they shall have full power to pass laws, to prevent any slave or slaves, from being brought into this state for the purposes of speculation, or as articles of trade or merchandise; they may pass laws to permit the owners of slaves, to emancipate them, saving the rights of creditors, and preventing them from becoming a public charge, or provide in such case that the slaves so emancipated, remove and remain without the limits of this state, as the general assembly may from time to time deem expedient. They shall also have full power to prevent any slaves or their

offspring, from being brought into this state, who heretofore may have been, or hereafter may be imported into any of the United States, or the territories thereof, from a foreign country, in contravention of any of the laws of the United States; they shall have full power, and it shall be their duty to pass such laws, as may be necessary to prevent free negroes and mulattoes, from coming to and settling in this state, under any pretext whatever. And they shall have full power, and it shall be their duty to pass such laws, as may be necessary to oblige the owners of slaves, to treat them with humanity, and to abstain from all injuries to them, extending to life or limb, and in case of neglect or refusal to comply with the directions of such laws, to have such slave or slaves sold for benefit of their owner or owners.

This article was a kind of credo for slaveholders in frontier states, putting forth as it did the state's right to pass its own laws, to exclude those slaves with records of uprisings in states like Virginia and North Carolina, to set its own regulations for emancipation. At the same time it legislated for humane treatment of slaves. The vote was passed—thirty-eight for, one against.

In the Kentucky constitution of 1792 provision had been made for complete freedom of worship. In the next quarter of a century there was considerable agitation among some of the clergy, especially in the Baptist and Christian churches, for constitutional safeguards for insuring complete separation of church and state. In this frame of mind delegates to the Missouri Convention passed the following resolution:

No person while he continues to exercise the functions of a bishop, priest, clergy man or teacher of any religious persuasion, denomination, society or sect whatever, shall be eligible to a seat in either branch of the legislature, or to be elected or appointed to any office of profit within this state, the office of justice of the peace excepted.

A resolution that would have made void any gift, sale, or lease of land exceeding ten acres for a church and burying ground was voted down.

The section on education was read three times to the convention and was agreed upon:

. . . Schools and the means of education shall forever be encouraged in this state, and the general assembly shall take measures to preserve from unnecessary waste or damage, such lands as now or hereafter may be granted by the United States for the use of schools within each township in this state, and apply the funds which may be raised from such lands in strict conformity to the object of such grant. . . .

The resolution provided for public schools in each township. It also provided for the exclusive support of a state university, for the support of the arts, literature, and the sciences.

The delegates passed over to the general assembly the responsibility for making laws against dueling. The resolution reads, "The general assembly shall have power to pass such laws to suppress the evil practice of duelling, as they may deem expedient." The votes were twenty-one for, thirteen against.

The Missouri Constitutional Convention convened on June 12, 1820, and adjourned on July 19, after the delegates had affixed their signatures to the document. Stephen Cleaver was in regular attendance and voted regularly but he served on only one of the several committees. With only slight exception he voted with the majority, and in every case for the resolutions cited.

The constitution was put into effect without written approval from Congress or submission to a popular vote. The provision excluding free Negroes and mulattoes from the state created antislavery sentiment in Congress when the constitution was presented the following November. Again Henry Clay was involved in working out a compromise: that this provision would never, in effect, be used to abridge the rights of United States citizens. This compromise was accepted by Missouri on June 26, 1821. President Monroe, on August 10, 1821, proclaimed the admission of Missouri as the twenty-fourth state. Thus slavery was solidly entrenched in Missouri. The compromise, instead of easing tension, had opened the way for compromise after compromise till there could be no more.

In the same year that Stephen Cleaver's wagon train traveled overland from Kentucky to Missouri the first steamboat to reach St. Louis, *Zebulon M. Pike*, puffed its way upstream at the rate of three miles per hour from Louisville. Thus St. Louis became the new gateway to the West—a starting point for goods that eventually were hauled by wagon over the Santa Fe Trail. There were new people, new goods, new prosperity.

Stephen Cleaver shared in the prosperity, both on his farms and in his land speculation. Conveyances made by him and Ellender his wife are some indication: on April 15, 1823, fifteen lots in Palmyra for $55; June 2, 1828, five lots in Saverton for $15; August 23, 1828, two tracts of two hundred and twenty acres each in Ralls County for $480; September 9, 1829, fifteen acres in Ralls County for $30. These sums may seem small now but they did not at a time when money was scarce and most trade by barter.

Except for Thomas, who remained at home, Stephen Cleaver's children went their own ways during their first decade in Missouri: Charlotte, Jacob, Ellender, and Rebecca married and set up their first homes in northeast Missouri. In 1826, William and Henry caught the "Alabama fever" prevalent in Missouri and went south. The malady might as well have been called "cotton fever." The cure for it was reportedly a large plantation, plenty of slaves to cultivate it, and a steady market for cotton.

In the constitutional convention Stephen voted in favor of laws against dueling, and with good reason. Just as settlers from east of the Alleghenies brought their feuds to Kentucky, settlers from Kentucky brought their feuds to Missouri. For many the only way to end a feud was to fight to the death in a duel.

Ralls County had from the first been the scene of feud after feud. One of these involved on one side the Purdom, Boarman, Matson, Porter, Tracy, and other families; on the other the Caldwell, Gentry, Jones, Wright, Cleaver, and other families. Both sides represented wealth and social standing. Among the latter were men prominent in county and state politics: Dabney Jones was the first sheriff of the county; Caldwell and Cleaver had been influential in founding the county.

The feud came to a head over a lawsuit. Charles B. Rouse, a brilliant and accomplished young attorney, came to New London in 1828, at a time when litigation was widespread. Soon clients came to him in numbers. Among these was one who brought suit on an old account against John Alexander Boarman, William B. Purdom, and Colonel Dick Matson. The amount was trivial, only four dollars and eighty-six and one-half cents, but Rouse won the case and the debt was collected. For him it was not the amount but the principle that mattered. The judgment was a surprise for the debtors and they could only blame Rouse.

Later on the same day Purdom met Rouse's wife on the street. He spoke to her and began to abuse her husband. A young Kentucky woman, a recent bride, she turned on him with all the sarcasm she could command and gave him a frontier dressing down. In a rage he came close and spat in her face. He went on his way; she went and told her husband.

A few hours later Rouse was walking along the street when he heard footfalls behind him. Turning, he saw that Purdom was following him. Enraged, Rouse rushed upon him, jerked a pistol from his pocket, and shot him to the ground. Purdom fell on the same spot where he had insulted Rouse's wife. Rouse stood over Purdom while he was drawing his last breaths and said, "You dog! you will not spit in the face of another lady."

Rouse gave himself up and was indicted for murder in the first degree. At the trial he pleaded the unwritten law and was acquitted. The verdict only served to intensify the feud.

During the next few months feelings died down somewhat but did not disappear. Then a strange and mysterious man appeared in New London. All that could be learned from him was that his name was Sam Samuels.

On Sunday morning, December 6, 1829, at the Caldwell Tavern, Charles B. Rouse was mysteriously murdered. He had just finished eating breakfast and was standing in the front door. A shot was fired, Rouse sank to the floor, and died a few moments later without a word. The bullet went through his heart and broke the wrist of a man standing near. The shot was fired from an old warehouse diagonally across the street from the tavern and about fifty yards away. It was fired through a hole in the wall apparently made for that purpose.

Suspicion turned to "Old Sams," as Samuels was then called, but he had disappeared. Then a manhunt was on with Stephen Cleaver prominent among the posse. He turned the search toward Colonel Matson, who was no friend of his but had been a friend of Purdom's. He suspected that Matson was hiding Samuels in the most likely place, the old cave located a few hundred yards from Matson's mill. They set up a close watch over Matson's house and the cave but found no clues.

A week or so later Matson and his wife went to Hannibal for the day. Stephen Cleaver, who had been waiting for such a chance, got Dabney Jones, the sheriff, and David Rice, who was deputized, and the three went to the Matson place. Their plan was not so much to search for "Old Sams" but to get the confidence of Uncle Mose, a slave on the Matson place. When they arrived, however, they saw in the snow a woman's tracks going into the cave. They went in and made a thorough search but could not find "Old Sams."

They then found Uncle Mose and, to make him more talkative, persuaded him to partake liberally of the "credentials" they had brought. After a time he said what they wanted to hear: "Marse Cleaver, maybe you haint looked high enough in dat dare cave."

They found Samuels on a rock shelf under which they had passed in their earlier search.

After a legal battle lasting more than two years he was convicted in Boone County, on a change of venue, of murder in the first degree. He paid the penalty with his life on December 13, 1831. His real name was Samuel Earls. He was sixty years old and a homeless tramp.

Still the feud was not over. Apparently Richard Matson made remarks about the case and people involved, remarks that Stephen Cleaver thought scurrilous. The remarks are not recorded but he thought his honor grossly impugned by them. His response was to challenge Matson to a duel in the following letter:

7th Aug.
Sir you must understand that I am not to be imposed on by you—You may Chuse your arms & distance—We will fight in the State Illenois opposite the Town of Palmyra on the 10th of the Inst.

STEPHEN CLEAVER

Previous preparation will be made by my Second.

STEPHEN CLEAVER

Col. Dick Matson

Cleaver was then sixty-three years old, Matson probably in his thirties. Yet he wrote the challenge and signed it with a firm hand.

The duel was never fought. Matson apparently refused to fight and turned the matter over to the courts, from which the following indictment was issued in the October Term in 1829:

The grand jurors for the State of Missouri empannelled, sworn & charged to inquire in & for the body of the County of Ralls aforesaid upon their oath present—That Stephen Cleaver late of said County being an evil disposed person & a disturber of the peace of said State and intending to do great bodily harm and mischief to one Richard Matson late of the said County of Ralls and to provoke & excite him the said Richard unlawfully to fight a duel with & against him the said Stephen Cleaver . . . did unlawfully, wickedly & maliciously write & deliver . . . a certain paper writing in the form & manner of a Letter . . . to the great damage and terror of the said Richard Matson, to the evil example of all others in like cases offending. . . .

The trial was held on February 16, 1830. Richard Matson appeared as a witness against him. So did others from the opposing side of the feud. The letter was entered as evidence. Stephen Cleaver was found guilty and fined twenty dollars plus costs. He paid, but he maintained that if he had to he would do it all over again.

Such activities apparently did not lower Stephen Cleaver's standing in the community or curtail his business activities. The 1830 census shows that his household had dwindled to himself and his wife, and three young females who are unidentified. He also had four slaves: one female over thirty-six, one female under twenty-four, and two males under ten. He and Ellender continued to sell land: on December 17, 1830, two hundred acres for $400; April 6, 1834, a lot in New London for $55; July 30, 1836, a lot in New London for $100. In the latter, Ellender's name appears on a deed for the last time. On August 5, 1837, Stephen alone sold a lot in New London for $200.

Ellender Cleaver, it can be assumed, died between July 30, 1836, and August 5, 1837. On March 4, 1839, Stephen Cleaver made an indenture to his son Thomas "That the said Stephen Cleaver as well for and in Consideration of the natural love and affection which I have and bear for Thomas Cleaver as of one dollar lawfull money of the United States to me in hand paid" transferred to him more than four hundred acres of land with all its appurtenances. Three days later he married Mary Hays, widow, in Ralls County. The marriage certificate reads, "This is to certify, that I, A. Allison a preacher of the Gospel did on the 7 day of March solemnise the rite of matrimony between Stevin Clever and Mary Hase."

In the time immediately after Ellender's death Stephen Cleaver must have felt longings for new frontiers. He visited his sons in Alabama. He reportedly spent some time in Arkansas. By then Texas was independent and settlers were on the roads of Missouri headed in that direction. There was an optimism abroad strong enough to stir the heart of any old frontiersman. The expression "manifest destiny" would be coined within a decade but the feeling it distilled was in the hearts of people who wanted to annex Texas, people who feared that foreign powers would prevent "the fulfilment of our manifest destiny to overspread the continent allotted by Providence for the free development of our yearly multiplying millions." It was a slogan suited to a man who had crossed so many frontiers.

It was a time of optimism. It was also a time for humor. In church the people still sang their doleful hymns. Outside, they found that they could laugh at themselves in song and story. They could create anew, or they could take the old and change it to their use. "Come All You Virginny Girls" became "Come All You Missouri Girls" with a bit of Texas thrown in:

> Come all you Missouri girls and listen to my noise,
> Don't you marry those Texas boys;
> They'll take you out on a pine knot hill
> And that's going to be right against your will,
> And that's going to be right against your will.

They had learned to laugh at their pioneer ways of living and to put their laughter into a joking song. Another version of this song tells it as they saw it:

> I went out a-sparking, I didn't know where to go:
> I went to a man's house down here below;
> The children crying for bread and the old folks gone;
> The girls all mad and their heads not combed,
> The girls all mad and their heads not combed.

> I set and sparked till I got ashamed
> And every once in a while they'd ask me my name,
> And every once in a while they'd ask me my name.

> When they go to cook I'll tell you how they do;
> They build up a fire as high as your head;
> Scratch out the ashes and pile them on the bread,
> Scratch out the ashes and pile them on the bread.

> They called me to dinner and I thought for to eat;
> The first thing I saw was a big chunk of meat
> Cooked half done and tough as a maul,
> An old ash cake baked bran and all,
> An old ash cake baked bran and all.

One old knife and nary a fork;
I sawed for an hour and couldn't make a mark,
I sawed for an hour and couldn't make a mark.

Kept on sawing till I got it out of my plate.
One of the girls says, "You'd better wait."
Kept on sawing till I got it on the floor,
Up with my foot and kicked it out the door,
Up with my foot and kicked it out the door.

'Long came the old man with a double-barreled gun.
One of the girls says, "You'd better run."
Stood and fought him as brave as a bear,
Tangled my fingers in the old man's hair,
Tangled my fingers in the old man's hair.
When you go to church I'll tell you what to wear,
An old cotton dress and that's about the best;
An old lint sack, grease all around,
An old leather bonnet with a hole in the crown,
An old leather bonnet with a hole in the crown.

For some Missourians this was life as it had been east of the
Mississippi, or as it might be in faraway Texas, but not in the Missouri
they knew, certainly not in the Missouri along the river. For them
such a frontier phase had passed quickly. The gold rush, which began
three years after Stephen Cleaver's death, gave rise to "Joe Bowers,"
a song in which the humor has a slightly different cast:

My name it is Joe Bowers,
I have a brother Ike;
I came from old Missouri,
Yes, all the way from Pike.
I used to court a pretty girl
By the name of Sally Black.
I asked her to marry me,
She said it was a whack.

But says she to me, "Joe Bowers,
Before we hitch for life,
You'll have to get a little house

To keep your little wife."
I said, "Sally, oh, Sally,
It's all for your sake;
I'll go out to California
And try to raise a stake."

At length I went to mining,
Put in my biggest licks;
Fell down upon the shining
Just like a thousand bricks.
I worked both late and early
In rainstorm and snow;
It was all for my sweet Sally's sake;
Oh, yes, the same to Joe.

At length there came a letter;
It was from my brother Ike;
It was from old Missouri,
Yes, all the way from Pike.
It had some of the goldarnedest news
A fellow ever heard
That Sally had married a butcher
And the butcher had a red beard.

There was something more in that letter
That would make a fellow swear,
That Sally's got a baby
And the baby's got red hair.

In the Cleaver language, as it survived in Texas, to tell a whack was to tell a lie.

On September 20, 1840, Stephen Cleaver made his last will and testament, "written with my own hand." General items in the will were brief and to the point: "that my body be buried in a Christianly manner" and "that all my debts if there be any at my decease be punctually paid." To his son Thomas he left the land on which he lived with the exception of one-third, which, including the house, was to be his wife's dower for life. Also to his wife he left one-third of his slaves plus one-third of all his estate including horses, cattle, household furnishings, farm utensils, and cash to do with as she pleased. The fifth item is terse: "The advances I made to my son Jacob in his lifetime and to his heir and widow since his death, I consider to be a full share of my estate."

The remainder was to be divided equally among five of his children: William, Henry, Charlotte Jones, Ellender Cobbs, and Rebeckah Glasscock. As executors he appointed his son Thomas and his son-in-law William Jones.

Annexation of Texas became an angrily debated issue. Antislavery forces saw it as another extension of slave territory. Proannexation forces saw possibilities that an independent Texas would become aligned with England or France. All expected annexation to bring war with Mexico. In March 1845, Congress passed a joint resolution for the annexation. Mexico immediately broke off diplomatic relations with the United States and began strengthening her armed forces. Through 1845 there was rattling of swords on both sides of the Rio Grande. Then on May 1, 1846, Mexicans in force crossed the Rio Grande and laid siege to Fort Texas. The United States declared war against Mexico on May 11, 1846.

Stephen Cleaver died on May 30, 1846. From early childhood he had heard the call to arms, to guard Friend's Fort from the Indians. From early youth he himself had answered the call to service that gave him as much as anyone the right to be called Indian fighter, soldier. Again young men were going off to fight, Again there was a new war song to march to:

> My pretty little pink I once did think
> That you and I would marry,
> But now I'm off to the Mexican War
> And have no time to tarry.

> I'll take my knapsack on my back
> And musket on my shoulder,
> And march away to Old Mexico
> And fight like a valiant soldier.

> Where coffee grows on whiteoak trees
> And rivers flow with brandy,
> And the rocks are painted all over with gold
> And the girls are sweeter than candy.

Stephen Cleaver was given a Christianly burial in what was called the "Cornfield Graveyard" at the foot of the hill from his house. He was dressed in his military uniform. The graveyard was shared by the Cleaver and Dabney Jones families. On February 22, 1852, Patrick Lyons was paid fifty dollars by the estate to erect a tomb.

On August 5, 1846, three appraisers presented an official appraisal of his estate to the clerk of the Ralls County Court. The items listed, close to two hundred in all, showed that he had accumulated wealth and lived well. Among the household goods there were the usual bedroom furnishings and kitchen ware. There were also pieces of brass, pewter, silver, cut glass, and a silver watch.

There were two slaves: a man named Nelson, appraised at $450.00, and a woman named Lyda, appraised at $200.00.

There were also some books, among them, as listed, were Nelson, *On Infidelity;* Butler's *Geography & Key to Popery,* or *Reformation in Europe;* and Henry Clay's *Life.* These say something of his interests as well as his biases. He had lived long enough to see his hero, Henry Clay, unanimously nominated for President by the Whig National Party at Baltimore, and then defeated by James K. Polk.

When the estate was finally settled, on September 2, 1856, apparently after the death of Mary Hays Cleaver, the residue was $7,151.52. His executor, Thomas Cleaver, once pleaded guilty to playing cards and was fined $5.50, but that did not interfere with his services as executor. Records of receipts and expenditures were meticulously kept and dutifully rendered to all the heirs, including William and Henry, first in Alabama and then in Arkansas.

Stephen Cleaver left another legacy, a legacy that as time passed melded into the common frontier experience. His eighty years spanned times of danger, times of hardship. His wilderness wanderings took him across the high Alleghenies in his youth and then the broad Mississippi when he was growing old. A hard worker, a believer in work, he surveyed land, plowed land, became a soldier when fighting was needed, ruled from a judge's bench, deliberated with the body that set governing principles for a new state. To many a document he set hand and seal, but not to one that recorded his own story. Documents get buried in the accumulations of years. Actual names, recorded facts are lost, and past happenings, if they are recalled at all, survive in the stories that make up the "they say" of a people.

In his old age Stephen Cleaver took to telling his stories to anyone who would listen, with others like him trying to set the record and set it straight. But by then the danger and hardships of the wilderness had become blurred in the memories of the old. The young, listening to vague searchings for the right time, the right names of place and people, often dismissed true stories as tall tales, the works of minds no longer in touch. Thus it was with Stephen Cleaver. Third-generation keepers of his tales often regarded them as tales only—as the fantasies of a man turned windjammer at last.

Still his legacy remains. It is the history of his time, truly recorded in documents, and just as truly recorded in the winnowings of time remembered in "they say."

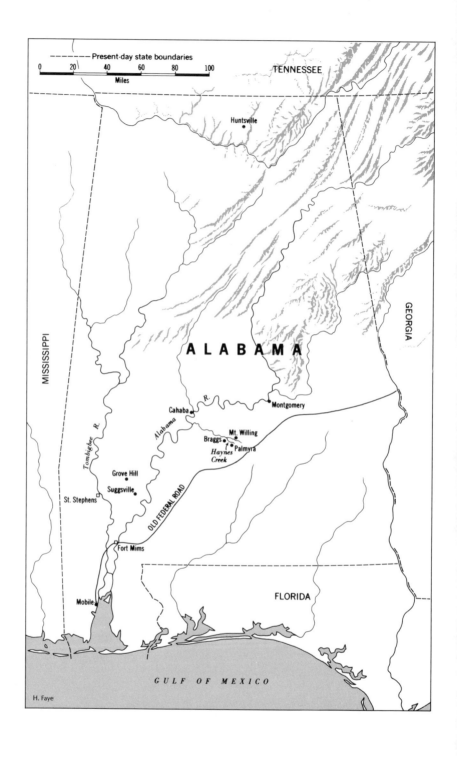

Alabama

I N 1789, THE YEAR IN WHICH GEORGE WASHINGTON WAS INAUGU-
RATED FIRST PRESIDENT OF THE UNITED STATES, ALABAMA WAS A
WILDERNESS OWNED IN PART BY THE UNITED STATES, IN PART BY
Spain. In 1819, thirty years later, Alabama was admitted to the Union
as the twenty-second state. For most whites in the region this was the
result of logical and legitimate expansion; for most Indians it was
land-grabbing in its cruelest form.

Alabama is an Indian name. Before the coming of the white man
the territory was dominated by four tribes: Creeks, Choctaws, Chickasaws, and Cherokees. These were the ones who greeted the first
European among them, Hernando De Soto, who with his men appeared on the Coosa River in 1540. The reception was friendly, but
the Spaniards' demands for supplies and for Indians to become their
serving men soon alienated the Indians. The conflict grew at last into
a battle in which the Spaniards attacked the Indian fort at present-
day Mobile, a battle that lasted nine hours, the first and bloodiest on
Alabama soil, and one of the fiercest in all warfare between Indians
and white men. De Soto won the battle but his men were so exhausted, their morale so low that after another skirmish or two, the
Spaniards passed on from the Alabama territory.

In 1702 French explorers founded Mobile and began a policy of
friendship and trade with the Indians. The British, who succeeded
the French in Alabama, at first had trouble with the Indians, but in
1765, by treaty with the Choctaws, they secured the first strip of land
ceded to whites in Alabama. In the same year the Creeks ceded to
them a strip of land along the coast extending twelve miles inland.
These treaties were the initial steps that in seventy-three years resulted in the removal of the Indians from Alabama.

[201]

After the Treaty of Paris, in 1783, Spain owned both East and West Florida and claimed a part of the Mississippi and Alabama territory. They originally claimed latitude thirty-two degrees, twenty-eight minutes, as their northern boundary, but in a treaty with the United States in 1795 they accepted thirty-one degrees. Thus the Spaniards followed the British and were the last Europeans to occupy Alabama territory and to influence Indian relations. Few Indians lived in the Spanish territory then, but the Spaniards were able to use them as well as some from outside their territory for trade and for a buffer against American expansion toward the Mississippi. In the terms of the Louisiana Purchase in 1803 no mention was made of East Florida or West Florida, though many, including President Jefferson himself, assumed that West Florida was included. Eager settlers had little regard for ownership, Spanish or Indian.

Many white settlers came into the Tombigbee and Mississippi basins during the period from 1790 to 1800, with the approval and aid of the federal government. In a treaty with the Creeks the Government secured the right to maintain forever a horse path through their territory. In addition, the Creeks agreed not to molest settlers on this path and to provide them with ferries and houses of accommodation. Settlers came in such numbers that this path soon turned into a road. The federal government also secured the right of a horse path through the Chickasaw lands from Colbert's Landing on the Tennessee River to St. Stephens, a white settlement on the Tombigbee. Pressure on the Indians continued and expanded. On October 17, 1802, the Choctaws accepted claims of the United States to ownership of the land they had ceded to the British in 1765. On November 16, 1805, they ceded an additional five million acres of land extending along their southern boundary from the settlement at Natchez to the settlements on the Tombigbee, for $5,000 in money, $3,000 in goods, $500 to each of the three head chiefs, and $50 annually to each as long as he remained chief. A part of this land lay in Alabama, in present Clarke and Choctaw counties.

The two horse paths, one from Nashville to Natchez, the other from the Ocmulgee River to St. Stephens, called federal roads before 1811, were still hardly more than trails in 1812. But settlers beat their way over them, so that there were some twenty thousand whites in the territory, most of them at Natchez and in the settlements along the Tombigbee. Indians saw that what they had granted as horse paths were becoming routes of invasion and occupation.

In 1811, at the time that General William Henry Harrison was moving against the Shawnees in Indiana Territory, their chief, Tecumseh, was in the Old Southwest for the purpose of arousing the Indian tribes there to join in exterminating the whites. According to tradition, he met in debate the powerful Choctaw chief, Pushmataha, before an assemblage of Choctaws and Chickasaws. Tecumseh described American atrocities against Indians. Pushmataha talked of the kindnesses white settlers at St. Stephens had shown his people. Pushmataha ended the debate by offering Tecumseh safe passage out of Choctaw territory.

On June 19, 1812, President Madison declared war on Great Britain. A year later a militant part of the Creeks known as "Red Sticks" engaged in a general uprising along the southern part of the frontier. Indians scalped and pillaged; whites armed themselves and built stockades. On July 27, 1813, some white settlers and militiamen attacked some Indians camped on Burnt Corn Creek, about eighty miles to the north of Pensacola. In retaliation the Creeks on August 30, 1813, attacked Fort Mims, on the east bank of the Alabama River about thirty-five miles above Mobile, just at noon when the drum beat was calling the soldiers to dinner. There was no help or hope for the people inside, for the women and children, the sick and feeble. Of the five hundred and fifty or so inside, two hundred and fifty were massacred and many others were burned to death. At about five o'clock the Indians ended their carnage. They had won what was the first battle of the Creek War.

As has been related before, news of the massacre reached General Andrew Jackson in Nashville. As major general of the Tennessee militia he organized a force of two thousand volunteers, most of them from Tennessee with some from Georgia and from settlements in Mississippi Territory. There were encounters between whites and Indians during the remainder of 1813. Then in 1814 Jackson with three thousand troops marched into the Upper Creek territory. On March 27 he attacked their fortifications at the Horseshoe Bend on the Tallapoosa River. It was a great victory for the whites. About nine hundred warriors were killed; about three hundred women and children were taken prisoner. The Creeks sued for peace. At the Treaty of Fort Jackson, signed on August 9, Jackson made a harsh bargain. The Creeks ceded two-thirds of their land to the United States and agreed to withdraw from the southern and western part of Alabama.

Andrew Jackson, appointed commander of the military district that included Mobile and New Orleans, on November 7 invaded Spanish Florida and seized Pensacola. Two weeks later he was on his way to what became the battle of New Orleans.

The Creek War left the Indian tribes in a weakened condition. The time had come, the whites reasoned, to push all the tribes to western lands. Andrew Jackson became a chief instigator, and a reason was ready at hand. The British fort that they had built on the Apalachicola River in Florida in 1812 was now occupied by Seminole Indians and had become a refuge for runaway slaves and renegade Indians. A United States force destroyed the fort and started a conflict with the slaves and Indians. On December 26, 1817, Andrew Jackson assumed command of the force and on January 6, 1818, wrote to President Monroe, "Let it be signified to me through any channel . . . that the possession of the Floridas would be desirable to the United States and in sixty days will be accomplished." He was as good as his word.

Meanwhile the trickle of settlers swelled to a flood. As in earlier migrations the first routes were along Indian trails running east to west. They were also along rivers that flowed from the mountains to the north down to the Gulf of Mexico. Though not as difficult as passage across the Alleghenies, these routes were difficult enough, especially the ones that required crossing rivers—by fording or by rafts built on the spot, sometimes from cane, sometimes from logs. Settlers from the Ohio Valley came down the Ohio and Mississippi to Natchez, and from there to the Tombigbee country by way of the Natchez Trace. The first federal road built in Alabama Territory, the Natchez Trace joined the Nashville Trace at Nashville. The Nashville Trace went on to Maysville, Kentucky, where it joined the National Road to Columbus and Wheeling and on to Philadelphia.

The greatest number of settlers came from southern Virginia and the Carolinas. They entered Alabama by way of the Tennessee and Alabama rivers. The Alabama was reached by the horse path negotiated in 1805 and expanded into a road by federal troops in 1811. It went by way of St. Stephens on the Tombigbee and ended at Mobile.

Two distinct classes of settlers came, two distinct social structures came with them, and two economic classes as well: the white plantation owners with their slaves; and the poor whites, already labeled "po' white trash." And two cultural strains came: the romantic idea of feudalism, drawn from England through much reading of Sir Walter Scott, reinforced by young men schooled in England; and the folkways, also drawn from England, oral not written, a culture of song and story and language handed down by word of mouth. These two cultures were European. By the time settlers reached Alabama a third had been added, the Afro-American—a blending of the European and the African in a setting belonging to neither but to America.

Why did they come? Cotton—"King Cotton" they eventually called it—was a major factor. Cotton had been grown by Indians before the coming of the white man. It was a money crop for white planters and they took up the cultivation, mostly with slave labor. The problem was that separating the lint from the seeds was done by hand and was tediously slow. A slave with nimble fingers could produce only a few pounds of lint in a day. Then Eli Whitney, a Connecticut Yankee studying law on a Georgia plantation, designed a cotton gin. With the improved model that he built in 1793 a slave could separate fifty pounds of lint in a day. The impact on Southern migration was instantaneous. Plantation owners saw in the rich lands of Alabama a chance for wealth beyond measure, especially in a broad strip between the mountains in the north and the wet coastal plain. Farming had become marginal on the worn-out lands of the states to the east. Alabama soil would grow cotton high as a man's head.

Travel into the wilderness, even as early as 1814, was by wagon train, the master's family riding in carriages, household goods and supplies in wagons, slaves following on foot, sometimes just walking to keep up, sometimes driving livestock. Arrived on their land, these plantation owners began at once clearing and planting and building —as early as possible firing brick, hewing timbers, raising roofpoles for mansions, and along with this building square log cabins for their slaves.

Poor whites came on foot, and the way was hard. An item in the Augusta *Chronicle*, September 24, 1819, shows how they traveled:

Passed through this place from Greenville District (South Carolina) bound for Chatahouchie, a man and his wife, his son and his wife, with a cart but no horse. The man had a belt over his shoulders and he drew in the shafts; the son assisted his father to draw the cart; the son's wife rode in the cart, and the old woman was walking carrying a rifle, and driving a cow.

Those fortunate enough to own a pony or an ox had an easier time of it. They packed their goods in a hogshead with trunions set in the ends and shafts hooked to the trunions. In this way some settlers rolled their belongings from as far as Edgefield District in South Carolina to Clarke County, Alabama. They traveled either the Upper Road or the Fall Line Road, both of which began in Virginia, crossed North and South Carolina, and intersected at Montgomery, Alabama. On either road, settlers who could no longer endure the hardships of travel stopped and squatted where they were.

In 1817 Mississippi Territory was divided. The western part was admitted to the Union as Mississippi, a slave state. The eastern part was organized as Alabama Territory, with St. Stephens as the seat of government. By this time it was the most important town in Alabama, with good trade in cotton and other products down the Tombigbee to Mobile, and with an academy for the education of young ladies.

Settlers continued to pour in:

The flood-gates of Virginia, the two Carolinas, Tennessee, Kentucky, and Georgia, were now hoisted, and mighty streams of emigration poured through them, spreading over the whole territory of Alabama. The axe resounded from side to side, and from corner to corner. The stately and magnificent forest fell. Log cabins sprang, as if by magic, into sight. Never, before or since, has a country been so rapidly peopled.

Admission of Alabama as a state could be expected, but the question of slave or free was inevitable. In December 1818, the territorial legislature passed a resolution petitioning for admission and forwarded it to Congress. On the following March 2 Congress passed the Enabling Act authorizing the people of Alabama Territory to frame and adopt a constitution. Though this constitution had some traces of frontier liberalism, it more generally reflected the conservatism of the older Southern states. On December 14, 1819, President Monroe signed the resolution admitting Alabama. The number of states now stood at eleven slave, eleven free.

Haynes Creek

THE STREAM OF MIGRATION that peopled the Old Southwest flowed out of Virginia and the Carolinas, into Georgia and through Georgia into Alabama and Mississippi. It was a Southern migration but it drew men, especially young men, from other parts of the nation. Among these were William and Henry Cleaver, sons of Stephen, who left home in Missouri and struck out on their own to a part of this new frontier—Alabama. They no doubt had the itching heels common to young men on the frontier. They also may have been affected by rumors of "Alabama fever," which had spread farther and farther with every report of fortunes to be made in slaves and cotton. They could have heard about Alabama through Benjamin Linn, the Separate Baptist preacher, their neighbor on Beech Fork in Kentucky, who had migrated to Madison County in 1810; or from James and Hannah Linn Cleaver, who apparently went ahead of them from Missouri.

Whatever their reasons, their going changed the courses of their lives and drastically affected the lives of their children and their childrens' children through at least four generations. They became Southern, not in the tradition of the poor whites who walked the roads and spread into the hilly regions, but in the tradition of the Southern gentlemen who came in wagon trains with Negro slaves to clear the land, plant the crops, build homes stately if possible, at least comfortable if they had to be modest. It was a period of Greek revival and houses with white columns rose on spacious grounds shaded by oaks and magnolias. There were names like "Gaineswood" and "Thornhill." Plantations called "Waverly" connected Alabama and Mississippi with the Scottish border.

[207]

When they arrived in Alabama William Cleaver was thirty, Henry was twenty-one. Both were single, both propertied to a degree, but not compared with the men who brought the makings of a plantation in a wagon train. Whether they traveled together is not known, or the route they took. They could have taken a boat down the Mississippi and traveled overland from Natchez. They could have come by way of Kentucky and down the Nashville Trace. However they came, for a time their paths separated. Henry settled in Dallas County, in the part that is now Lowndes, and William in Clarke, above Mobile on the Tombigbee River.

The land that Henry Cleaver took up was at the edge of the area called the "Black Belt" because of the rich black earth. Later it was called the Black Belt because the population was almost half slave. Later still, with all of Alabama and much of the South, it was called the "Bible Belt."

The wife he took was Nancy Ann Coleman, also on deeds as Ann A., daughter of Frank Coleman of Dallas County. Henry was born on March 18, 1805: Nancy Ann, on June 18, 1811. He was about twenty-two when they were married; she about sixteen. The Colemans had come by wagon train from Edgewater District in South Carolina in 1817 and settled to the north of present-day Greenville.

From deed records the house that Henry and Nancy Ann Cleaver lived in must have been in the Palmyra community, north of Greenville, south of Mount Willing, not far from the Butler County line. It would have been on the headwaters of Haynes Creek, a few miles from Bragg's Store, now called Braggs, a few miles from the Church of Christ to the east of Braggs. It is possible that the name Palmyra came from Palmyra, Missouri, a town that had been a part of Henry Cleaver's boyhood. Once a thriving community, it has dwindled away and finally disappeared from the road maps.

The Cleavers and Braggs were neighbors and members of the same Church of Christ. Thus began a family relationship remarkable in its closeness, in its years of sharing birth, marriage, war, death. The first Peter Newport Bragg, a Revolutionary War soldier, moved from Virginia to Spartanburg, South Carolina, in 1783. There his son Peter Newport, called Newport, married Martha Crook. In 1829 the Braggs moved to Lowndes County, where they operated a general store and where the first Peter Newport died on May 21, 1841.

As it is the children who eventually carry the story forward, their names and dates of birth are important. The first child of Henry and

Nancy Ann Cleaver was Mary Rebecca, born on March 26, 1829; the second, Martha Charlotte, born on February 24, 1831. Two children died in infancy, and then Missouri Ann was born on December 22, 1835. Her name, given in honor of relatives in Missouri and of Stephen himself, was unusual but not bizarre for the times. Another grandson of William and Hannah Cleaver had named his daughters South America and North Carolina. Their next child, a son, was born on August 15, 1837, while Stephen Cleaver was visiting in Alabama. As both Stephen and Henry were admirers of Henry Clay, they named him Henry Clay Cleaver, the name itself a wish for greatness.

The children of Peter Newport and Martha Crook Bragg were Walter Lawrence, Junius Newport, Virginia C., and Anthon.

Both the Braggs and the Colemans had been brought up in the Southern tradition. Henry Cleaver adjusted to it apparently without difficulty. The children knew no way of life except the Southern, the Southern way as it was practiced by people with education and with enough slaves to provide at least some leisure time. They all worked, men and women, boys and girls, but the hard jobs and the menial jobs were left to slaves, called servants. Women and girls did not go to the fields as they did on small farms where there were no slaves. Theirs were the lighter duties of the household, especially making cloth and clothing. They picked the lint from the seed, carded it, spun it into thread, dyed it with the colors of bark or berry, and wove on looms rarely idle. Women made their own clothes, their children's, and often their husband's.

Religion, predominantly evangelical religion, dominated their lives. It is believed that Nancy Ann was Roman Catholic. She may have been. Her children, however, were brought up in the Church of Christ, apparently from an early age. These were fundamentalists, followers of Alexander Campbell. Around them there were Methodists, Baptists, Cumberland Presbyterians. For them all, religious fervor reached its height in summer camp meetings or in protracted meetings under brush arbors, where the preachers held forth on the evils of this world, the glories of the next, where the congregation sang and prayed, danced and shouted.

The preachers were often not educated but they could reach heights of oratory that would stir the soul, at times curdle the blood, especially when they preached on such subjects as "Uncapping Hell." The sermon would go on for an hour or more and then the penitents would be invited to come up to the mourners' bench to be prayed over, exhorted over till the spirit broke through. Then there would be shouting and dancing and falling down in trances. Children yielded easily to pressure of preacher and family. Preachers went after hardened sinners.

One preacher when he saw an old sinner start for the mourners' bench put in words a summer experience known all over the South:

> Thank the Lord, bruthrin, here comes the Devil's mail-rider. Who'll back him up? Brother Grover, come work with this po' repentunt sinner. Don't ye leave a patchin o' the old Satun in him. Show him all his dev-lish life, and how he's making devuls o' the youngsters a-fallerin' in his tracks. And then he prayed: "Oh Lord we've come ter Thee ter wras-le fur a blessin', and we 'low ter have it afo' we let Thee go. Father, dump us in Thy washpot an' bile the ol' Adum clean out'n us. Beat us on Thy battlin'-board 'tel not ser much es a scrapin' o' dirt is left. Wash us an' rench us an' wring us, an' make us whiter'n crimson, skyarlit snow."

Such a sinner, converted, might dance and shout, "He took my feet out'n the miry clay and set them on solid rock, hallelujah."

Such church meetings were summer social events. So were the singing schools devised to teach young people church singing and to add to the income of the singing school master. The standard books were *The Missouri Harmony,* published in 1822, and *The Western Harmony,* published in 1824. The music was written in shaped notes and the instructions printed at the beginning of the book rudimentary indeed. The notes were sounded *fa, la, sol,* and *mi* and the master had his pupils "sol fa" each song until they were familiar with the tune before they sang the words, with each pupil "beating out the time" with his right hand. The effect was modal, even primitive, but an improvement over church singing that had no musical accompaniment and depended on the memory of the singers for words and tunes.

This was slave country and slaves were beginning to organize their own churches and use their own spirituals, or modified versions of white spirituals. Modification in words can be seen in two versions of "Old Ship of Zion." One of the white versions follows:

> What ship is this that will take us all home?
> O glory hallelujah,

'Tis the old ship of Zion,
Hallelujah, hallelujah,
'Tis the old ship of Zion, hallelujah.

A Negro version follows:

'Tis the old ship of Zion,
'Tis the old ship of Zion,
'Tis the old ship of Zion,
Get on board, get on board, yes, get on board.

It will take us all to heaven,
It will take us all to heaven,
It will take us all to heaven,
Get on board, get on board, chile, get on board.

Modifications in melody and rhythm cannot so easily be shown.

Separation of white and black congregations affected the creation of spirituals. While the whites were working to make their spirituals conform to a printed standard, the blacks, with no controls imposed by reading and writing, could sing and make up songs unhampered.

For a great number of people, white and black, religion was a summertime thing. With the coming of cold weather, no matter how vociferous their conversions, no matter the preachers' warnings, they turned to drinking, gambling, horse racing, and fighting. Young people who had danced for the Lord in the summer danced just as joyfully to the fiddle in winter.

Season in, season out, the religious held the greater sway on the Alabama frontier. It became the "Bible Belt" because the Bible was the final authority for so many people in so many things, political as well as religious. With it the Alabamans could defend white supremacy as well as the "peculiar institution" called slavery.

Alabama was in the heart of the land of cotton and Henry Cleaver took King Cotton as the rule of life. He planted corn for bread and feed but cotton was the crop that brought money. To make cotton pay he had to have land and slaves to work it. He took up land of his own, at least three quarter sections, four hundred and eighty acres, and he bought land from other grantees. On September

14, 1835, he and George L. Womack of Butler County bought a three-quarter-section tract from William Edward Hayne of Charleston, South Carolina. For it they paid twenty-three hundred and forty-one dollars and fifty cents. This had been a good cotton year and they had money to spend. Cotton brought more than seventeen cents a pound and living was easy. There was money left over to buy more land, more slaves.

Then came the panic of 1837 and Henry and Nancy Ann Cleaver sold some small tracts of land. Her name last appears on a deed as of January 12, 1837, when she signed herself Ann A. Cleaver.

Nancy Ann must have died soon after August 15, 1837, probably in her twenty-sixth year. She left four children, the oldest eight years old, the youngest an infant. Henry married for his second wife Christian or Christiana, who was born on February 10, 1800, and was five years his senior. By family tradition her name was Womack and she was Nancy Ann's cousin. She bore four children, two of whom survived: Allen Womack, born on September 7, 1839, and Abner Mitchell, born on February 12, 1847.

Tombigbee River

SOME TIME, SOMEHOW, William Cleaver made his way to St. Stephens in Clarke County on the Tombigbee. Though St. Stephens had lost out to Cahawba, and eventually to Montgomery, as the capital of Alabama, it was still a center of activity, with a general land office, a bank, and the first steamboat company organized in Alabama. Though not as rich as some other parts of Alabama in timber, farming land, or minerals, Clarke County was strategically located at the confluence of the Alabama and Tombigbee rivers. At the time Alabama was admitted to statehood it had a population of sixteen thousand, or one-fifth of all white residents in the state.

When William Cleaver arrived there Clarke County already had a considerable history. Organized in 1812, it had served as a center for territorial government. It had survived Indian wars and sicknesses, malaria, endemic, and yellow fever, sporadic. The county seat was moved to Grove Hill in 1832. At the time the other villages were Suggsville, Jackson, and Coffeeville, with Suggsville regarded as the cultural center of the county.

William Cleaver's name first appears in Clarke County on December 20, 1832, when he was married to Lucy Finch, whose family lived in a cedar-pole house south of Suggsville. This must have been one of the more impressive houses in the region. It had two stories and was built high off the ground with a broad verandah across the front. At one end there was a limestone and brick chimney with wide white spaces where people could leave their initials and dates.

The Finch family had also come from the Carolinas. Thus William, like Henry Cleaver, was brought under the influence of the Old South. He became landowner, slaveholder, sheriff in Clarke County

[213]

at a time when the Old Southwest was booming and roaring and distilling the raw humor that wagged the dog's tail when it was not being wagged by preachers and revival meetings.

The record was kept, enhanced as well, by Joseph Glover Baldwin, who at the age of twenty-one left his home near Winchester, Virginia, and set out to make a career for himself in the law in the Old Southwest, attracted by accounts of "most cheering and exhilarating prospects of fussing, quarrelling, violation of contracts, and the whole catalogue of *crimen falsi. . . ."*

In both Mississippi and Alabama he found crime aplenty:

> What country could boast more largely of its crime? What splendid role of felonies! What more terrific murders! What gorgeous bank robberies! What more magnificent operations in the land offices! Such . . . levies of black mail, individual and corporate! Such flourishes of rhetoric on ledgers auspicious of gold which had departed forever from the vault. And in *Indian Affairs*—the very mention is suggestive of the poetry of theft—the romance of a wild and weird larceny! . . . Swindling Indians by the nation! Stealing their land by the township!

What is a major effort of frontier humor is to some the telling of tall tales, to others plain lying. In either case art was required. Of the practitioners Baldwin found none better than Ovid Bolus, Esquire:

> Some men are liars from interest; not because they have no regard for the truth, but because they have less regard for it than for gain: some are liars from vanity, because they would rather be well thought of by others, than have reason for thinking well of themselves: some are liars from a sort of sense of virtue: some are enticed away by the allurements of pleasure, or seduced by evil example and education. Bolus was none of these: he belonged to a higher department of the fine arts, and to a higher class of professors of this sort of Belles-Lettres. Bolus was a natural liar, just as some horses are natural pacers, and some dogs natural setters. What he did in that walk, was from the irresistible promptings of instinct, and a disinterested love of art. His genius and his performances were free from the vulgar alloy of interest or temptation. Accordingly, he did not labor a lie: he lied with a relish: he lied with a coming appetite, growing with what it fed on: he lied from the delight of invention and the charm of fictitious narrative. It is true he applied his art to the practical purposes of life; but in so far did he glory the more in it. . . .

Alabamans, having proved adept at taking land from the Indians, could only applaud the move to take Texas from Mexico. People in Clarke County had a more personal interest. William B. Travis, one of their neighbors and a promising young lawyer, had answered the call for volunteers. He led the Texas colonists who seized the Mexican garrison at Anahuac on June 30, 1835. Along with Davy Crockett he was massacred at the Alamo on March 6, 1836. Word of his death was followed quickly by news of Santa Ana's defeat at San Jacinto and Texas independence.

During the excitement over the Texas Revolution a new Creek war broke out in Alabama. Orders came from Montgomery to Clarke County for men to volunteer to march against the Creek Nation. At a rally at the courthouse one hundred names were added to the roster. On May 30 the volunteers assembled at the courthouse wearing their own clothes, carrying their own squirrel rifles. After a short patriotic address and the shouting of a large crowd assembled to see them off, they were on their way.

With more flurry than action the war was soon over and the volunteers came marching home again. On Friday, August 12, Clarke County gave a dinner for the returning heroes, at which seventeen toasts were offered. Two of these show the temper of the times:

Our guests, who at the sound of the warwhoop nobly seized their arms and went to the rescue.

Texas. May her government be free and enlightened as her troops were brave and chivalrous at the battle of San Jacinto.

At a dinner the following Thursday at Suggsville, again honoring the returning heroes, nine toasts were offered. Of these, four stand out:

The Union of the United States. May it ever continue.

Our virtuous fair. Always lovely, but most so in the domestic circle.

Texas. May Texas continue as she began, and never cease until she is free.

The noble fabric of our Republic. Reared by the hands of sages, cemented by the blood of patriots, may it last till the dissolution of all earthly governments.

Certainly those dealing with the Union had some political motivation. During the new Creek War federal and state governments came into open conflict over the question of states' rights, specifically of Alabama's jurisdiction over Indian lands belonging to the Creeks by right of treaty with the United States. The matter was complicated by the possibility that federal troops would be used to enforce the treaty, to the extent that civil war became a possibility. Alabama preferred secession to yielding. In the long run it was the federal government that yielded and the danger was averted.

The argument left the federal and state governments in agreement on one thing: the Indians had to go. In 1817 General Andrew Jackson had proposed a plan through which Indians would give up their lands in Georgia and Alabama and be resettled on government lands to the west. The plan had little support at the time but as President of the United States Jackson was in a position to force it through. During his two terms the Creeks, Choctaws, and Chickasaws in the Old Southwest signed treaties of evacuation to Arkansas Territory. By the end of 1833 only the Cherokees retained their land. The Choctaws and Chickasaws departed peaceably. Creeks resisted and were hunted down and sent west in chains. In December 1835, the Cherokees were persuaded to sign the Treaty of New Echota, in which they ceded all their lands to the United States for $5,600,000 plus free transportation to their new homes. Evacuation began in 1836 and did not end until December, 1838, when federal troops were used to drive them west. Their departure left five million acres of their land open for sale to the speculators.

The story of the Cherokee evacuation, soon known as the Trail of Tears, has been told often, the tragedy of a proud people laid bare. Fully as tragic are the accounts of small bands of Choctaws, Chickasaws, and Creeks moving slowly across Alabama and Mississippi. A young army officer kept a vivid account of the removal of the Creeks:

The necessity of their leaving their country immediately was evident to everyone; although wretchedly poor they were growing more so every day they remained. A large number of white men were prowling about, robbing them of their horses and cattle and carrying among them liquors which kept up an alarming state of intoxication. . . . Public indignation was strong against them, and no doubt the most serious consequences would have resulted, had not immediate measures been adopted for their removal. . . .

The train consisted of forty-five wagons of every description, five hundred ponies and two thousand Indians. . . . The marches for the first four or five days were long and tedious and attended with many embarrassing circumstances. Men, who had never had claims upon these distressed beings, now preyed upon them without mercy. Fraudulent demands were presented and unless some friend was near, they were robbed of their houses and even clothing. . . .

The distance traveled by this party was eight hundred miles by land, four hundred and twenty-five by water. Of the two thousand who started, twenty-nine never saw the western lands. Many of those who survived had little to start a new life on: "They were poor, wretchedly, and depravedly poor, many of them without a garment to cover their nakedness."

Back in Alabama people could confidently return to their homes. The Indians were gone.

The Indian problem solved, the slavery issue came to the fore. The abolitionist movement had developed new strength with the organization of the New England Anti-Slavery Society in 1831 and the American Anti-Slavery Society two years later. Abolitionists sent so many antislavery publications to the South that local postmasters refused to handle them and serious efforts were made to deny mailing privileges for such incendiary material. Church denominations North and South debated slavery as a moral and Christian issue, to the extent that Methodists and Baptists divided themselves along sectional lines. Slaveholders had their say. One Alabama body passed a resolution: "Our right of property in slaves is fixed and guaranteed by the Federal Constitution, and we regard the acts of the Anti-Slavery Society at the North as a fearful crime and as treason against the Union."

In the states' rights conflict over Creek lands Alabama had won an easy victory. A similar victory over the question of slavery seemed certain.

In the meantime new territory was opening up in Arkansas. Land—good cotton land—could be had cheap. As early as 1837 thirty families assembled in Clarke County and in a wagon train started west. That was a year of panic, and though cotton prices held up well, there was general concern about future prices. The concern was justified. In 1842 cotton of a middling grade sold for as low as three and one-quarter cents a pound in Alabama.

The Cleavers and Braggs in Lowndes County began looking toward Arkansas. William Cleaver in Clarke County depended less on cotton prices. He had income from his office as county sheriff. He had honor if not income from his appointment as major in the Alabama State Militia. Before 1843 was over they had all decided to sell out and go.

Present-day state boundaries

0   25   50   75   100
Miles

MISSOURI

Pea Ridge ×

Fayetteville

OKLAHOMA

White R.

Black R.

Fort Smith

Arkansas R.

TENN.

Mississippi R.

A R K A N S A S

Little Rock

White R.

Helena

Arkadelphia

Arkansas Post

MISSISSIPPI

Washington

Ouachita R.

Poison Spring ×

Camden

Two Bayou

Red R.

TEXAS

LOUISIANA

H. Faye

Arkansas

ARKANSAS WAS TO HERNANDO DE SOTO THE FIRST TIME HE SAW IT, IN 1541, "A FAIR AND PLEASANT LAND." IN TWO YEARS OF WANDERING FROM A BAY ON THE GULF COAST OF FLORIDA TO A BLUFF overlooking the Mississippi River he and his men had seen much land, good and bad, had suffered hardship and disease and death, had watched their conquering band dwindle from six hundred well mounted, well supplied explorers to some two hundred stragglers, poor, hungry, naked except for clothing made from skins of animals, their dream of gold from the Indians fading, their treasures lost, including two hundred pounds of mussel pearls they had collected and the wine and wafers for celebrating mass. But Arkansas lay before them, to their sight a fair and pleasant land, waiting for them to cross over.

From June to the middle of October De Soto and his men worked their way up through Arkansas as far as present-day Hot Springs, with delays to visit prosperous Indian villages, where there were groves of pecans and persimmons and fields of corn, beans, and squash. They themselves planted the first cross in Arkansas and claimed the land in the name of the Spanish king.

With the approach of winter they turned south and eventually built a stockade on the lower Ouachita River. There they suffered from starvation and malaria and waited for spring. In March 1542, they moved on again, this time toward the east. De Soto died and his men, to keep his body from being mutilated by hostile Indians, reportedly buried him under the waters of the Mississippi. His men, left to struggle on as they could, made their way to the Gulf and finally disembarked from rough-made boats at a small Mexican village.

They left behind them in Arkansas legends of buried treasure, legends based enough on historical fact to inspire men even to the present day to go out digging. Not legend but fact were the hogs that escaped from De Soto's men, to run wild, to increase, generations later, to provide settlers with the meat of Arkansas razorbacks, the state with an emblem.

In March 1682, well over a hundred years later, La Salle came down the Mississippi and, in a dense fog, put ashore when he heard the drumming and singing of an Indian war dance. To their relief the Frenchmen found that the Indians were working themselves up to fight not them but other Indians. As acquaintances, these Indians, who called themselves Quapaws, were both friendly and hospitable, so much that the Frenchmen named them Les Beaux Hommes. Here in the country called Akansea by the Indians, La Salle also planted a cross. He took the land in the name of the King of France and called it Louisiana.

In 1762, in the secret Treaty of Fontainebleau, France ceded to Spain all French territory west of the Mississippi River and added the city of New Orleans. In 1800, again by secret treaty at San Ildefonso, Spain returned the territory to France, at the urging of Napoleon Bonaparte, who wanted to revive the French colonial empire in America. His plan, when it was discovered, created considerable apprehension on the western frontier, so much so that President Jefferson entered into negotiations for a part of the territory. In May 1803, Louisiana was purchased for approximately fifteen million dollars. By acquiring this tract, which lay between the Mississippi River and the Rocky Mountains, Jefferson doubled the area of the United States.

For several years before the Louisiana Purchase settlers from the western frontier had squatted on land west of the Mississippi River but migration had not been encouraged. As a matter of fact, inducements from the Spanish government were low and Roman Catholic leaders openly opposed admission of Protestants. Even after the purchase there were impediments, in Arkansas as there had been in Missouri, partly because the land still had to be acquired from the Indians, partly because of the long distances from the older settlements. In 1808 the Osage Indians gave up their claim to Missouri and the northern half of Arkansas; in 1817 the Quapaws ceded the remainder of Arkansas and a strip of land between the Arkansas and Red River in what is now Oklahoma. With these lands open for speculation, changes were rapid, especially in the organization of state and local government and the encouragement of new migration.

In 1806 the District of Arkansas came into being and by 1810 there were one thousand and sixty-two white residents within its borders. In 1815, the federal government ordered a general land survey and local land offices were set up to accommodate the onrush. Settlers in numbers came first from Kentucky, Tennessee, and North Carolina. They were soon followed by settlers from Virginia, Georgia, Alabama, and Mississippi, many of them planters bringing their slaves with them.

Wherever they came from, they soon learned enough of Arkansas geography to know that a line drawn from the northeast boundary to the southwest boundary would divide the land for both soil and crops: the upper part hilly, at times mountainous, good for small farms at best; the lower, lightly rolling or level plain, excellent for cotton plantations and slave labor. Without plan, other than the fact that pioneers often sought new land like the old land they had left behind, this line became a divider between the people drawn from the southern mountain and the southern lowland states—dividing them geographically, economically, culturally, and, in times of crisis, politically.

In 1819, when the population had grown to approximately fourteen thousand, the settlers, as they had on most of the western frontiers, demanded self-rule. Congress, acceding to their demand, created the Territory of Arkansas, with the seat of government at Post of Arkansaw, on the Arkansaw River. Settlers continued to come, in such numbers that the roads west and southwest out of Memphis were crowded and wagon trains had to wait their turns at river crossings. Within a decade the population had grown to the point that there was talk of statehood. In 1835, when the population had grown to seventy thousand and settlements stretched all the way to Fort Smith on the western border, the talk changed to demand. Independent as an Arkansas razorback, the members of the territorial legislature, not waiting for the slow progress of an enabling act through Congress, formed their own constitution and presented it to Congress for approval. In the tension over the slavery question a long fight could have developed. Luckily for Arkansas, the Territory of Michigan applied for statehood at the same time: Congress could maintain a balance, one slave, one free. On June 15, 1836,

Arkansas became the twenty-fifth state and the second carved from the Louisiana Purchase.

From the beginning the state, called "Arkansaw" at home, had a character of its own. So did the residents, "the Arkansawyers," a character perpetuated in one form in a dialogue called "The Arkansas Traveler." This is a dialogue that can be learned by heart, or can be added to or subtracted from—made up as the teller goes along. The basic story remains the same. A man traveling through the Ozarks stops at the cabin of a squatter and asks for a place to stay the night. The squatter is sitting on the end of a whiskey barrel and sawing away at a fiddle. From then on the teller is free to bring in any of the devices of frontier humor: the canny backwoodsman versus the dumb furriner, bad grammar, misunderstood meanings, and so on. Early in some versions the Arkansawyer explains that he cannot take the traveler in because his roof leaks. This leads to the following:

> TRAVELER: Why don't you finish covering your house then, and stop the leaks?
> ARKANSAWYER (stopping his fiddling): Hit's been a-rainin' all day.
> TRAVELER: Why don't you do it in the dry weather, then?
> ARKANSAWYER: Hit don't leak, then.

One passage of this dialogue could bring a laugh from Cleavers generation after generation:

> TRAVELER: Do you know how far it is to Little Rock?
> ARKANSAWYER: Cain't say I do, but they's some damn' big ones down on the hindside o' pa's field.

Arkansawyers have square-danced thousands of miles to this breakdown tune, still called "The Arkansas Traveler," and they affectionately call themselves razorbacks.

The razorback was an honest if not an elegant choice as an emblem. Having survived the wilderness, root hog or die, from the time his ancestors escaped from De Soto's men, he had grown lean, tough, wily, and afraid of neither man nor beast—qualities not unlike those of Arkansawyers. The vanguard of Arkansas settlers had survived one—sometimes two or three—frontiers before they crossed the Great River. Some were adventurers who had moved on by choice; some were outlaws and renegades who had left on the run with a gun at their backs. Some had escaped from feuds but had not left their feuding ways behind—ways they had learned in the mountains of Carolina or Kentucky or Tennessee. Nor had they left behind their mountain talk, their mountain ways, or the ease with which they could slip into or out of their religion.

Like razorbacks, they were laughed at by sleeker breeds outside, the butt of many a backwoods joke. Not easily put on they made their own jokes and laughed back:

"What do you do when a young'un ain't smart enough to make a living in Arkansaw?"
"Make him a schoolteacher and send him down to Texas."

Last laugh or not, their joking ways helped them endure a frontier time as tough as any their ancestors had come through.

Two Bayou

IN 1844, William and Henry Cleaver set their wagon train toward southwestern Arkansas, to start over again on a new frontier. Henry was then thirty-nine, William forty-eight. Eighteen years before they had come to Alabama, single men, in search of a new way of life. They had prospered. Both were now married and heads of large families. Both knew the hardships facing them on the road, especially with small children, hardships they had been through on the way to Missouri, their wives had been through on the way from Carolina to Alabama. They could make travel a little easier by going together.

It may be that Peter Newport Bragg and his family went with them. A church letter shows that they were leaving Alabama about the same time:

The Christian Church, near Bragg Store, to the brethren of like faith, where our beloved brother and sister Bragg's lot may be cast, we the members assembled on this the 29th day of October A. D. 1843 at the church above named, take great pleasure in saying that they have demeaned themselves as Christians for near four years since which time they have been members of this church, we bid them a reluctant farewell, and hope that (by their Christian walk and Godly conversation) they may prove a blessing in the land of their destination.

EVAN S. WILEY, ELDER

Apparently their lot had not been cast toward any particular locality but they ended up in Arkansas near Henry and William Cleaver.

Whether they traveled together or not, their lives and their children's lives became so intertwined that for a whole generation it

[228]

is not possible to tell the story of one family without the other. Names
of Bragg children and Cleaver children run through the narrative,
at times as participants, at times as counterpoint. The Braggs also had
known other frontiers, from South Carolina to Alabama. Reasons for
their migrations are made clear in a letter from J. B. Bragg, Lowndes
County, Alabama, to P. N. Bragg, Ouachita County, Arkansas, dated
September 25, 1845: "We have had no letters from South Carolina I
think since May, but understand that they are not making a support
this year. Many people we understand emigrating west on that account, better for them I expect in the end." His was another way of
saying that the land was worn out and a living was not to be made
on it.

    This does not explain why the Braggs and Cleavers were willing
to leave a comparatively comfortable life in Alabama and start all
over again in Arkansas. They had no doubt heard of rich land, good
for cotton, good for a man with slaves, to be bought for next to
nothing. They may have heard of gold nuggets picked up along
swift-flowing streams, of emeralds and other precious stones abound-
ing—lures for the adventuresome. The charms of Arkansas had been
well advertised in newspapers, and also in song:

> They say there is a stream
> Where crystal waters flow
> That'll cure a man sick or well
> If he will only go.

Settlers from Missouri, Kentucky, Tennessee, and other states responded to the refrain:

> We're coming, Arkansas,
> We're coming, Arkansas;
> Our four horse teams will soon be seen
> On the road to Arkansas.

Others—merchants, professional men, speculators—came from as
far away as New York and New England.

    Whatever their reason for going, the Cleavers joined forces with
others and headed their covered wagon train west, taking with them
their families, their slaves, their livestock, their household goods,
their tools for building and farming. Women and children rode in the

wagons. Slaves drove the livestock. Out of Alabama and across Mississippi the roads were good enough in dry weather for wagons, especially if they followed the Natchez Trace and crossed the Mississippi River in the vicinity of Gaines Landing. From then on there was not even a marked trail. The land remained much as Cephas Washburn, a missionary to the Cherokees, described it in 1819: "At that time Arkansas was a perfect *terra incognito*. The way to get there was unknown; and what it was, or was like, if you did get there was still more an unrevealed mystery."

It must have seemed so to Henry Cleaver as he faced heavy forests threaded by streams that had to be crossed, spotted with swamps impassable except in the dryest times in the year. But, like his father and grandfather before him, he had to move on, and he was the one who had to take the lead. Taking some whites and blacks to help him, he went ahead and blazed the route. Another crew followed and cut and opened the road. Last came the wagons and teams, the oxen plodding slowly along, the women walking to lighten the load, the children racing ahead or falling behind. At night they all came together again to camp and rest against the next day's traveling.

Their destination was Camden, the county seat of Ouachita County, located at the head of navigation on the Ouachita River. Officially named Camden when the county was organized in 1843, it was still called Ecore Fabre, Fabre's Bluff, for a Frenchman who had settled there as early as 1805. When the Cleavers arrived it had one storehouse, twelve by fourteen feet, made of hewed logs, with a few dry goods and no groceries to sell.

Henry Cleaver selected for his home site a place about six miles southwest of Camden, not far from Two Bayou and close to the places selected by his brother William and the Braggs, and began the work of clearing and building. It was now the winter of 1844, a remarkably warm winter but very wet. The land, never before packed down by human feet, was soft and boggy. Here he threw up some half-faced houses for shelter against the rain. Then he built cabins and unloaded his wagons for the first time since leaving Alabama. Food was a daily problem for his family and his slaves. From a settler there ahead of him he bought a scant supply of corn for bread. For meat, game was plentiful. He often shot bear, deer, and turkey in sight of the camp.

They had come to Arkansas at a good time, he soon knew. He had missed the roughest part of Arkansas frontier life and the conflicts that had been a part of achieving statehood, some of which ended in duels and death. The Indians had been pushed on into the Indian Territory, out of reach, out of mind except for stories told to children at night. It was a good time for clearing and planting and building. The house he built for his family was probably of the type called two pens and a passage—two front rooms with an open hall in the middle—with other rooms strung out behind. It may have been more pretentious, like the Braggs'—a Southern mansion, less imposing than mansions in Lowndes County, but with its high ceilings, wide floor boards, and broad verandah unmistakably built for gracious Southern living.

In education Arkansas was more backward than either Alabama or Missouri. There was no schoolhouse for the Cleaver children the first year, and no teacher. Children old enough to work had to work, the boys in the fields and woods, the girls in the house, part of their time given over to carding, spinning, and weaving. Not so much the heavy work for either. That was left for the slaves.

Henry Clay Cleaver, who was seven when they moved to Camden, left an account that reflects somewhat on the life of the times. At first there was only one mill in the whole country and that was a horse mill in Camden. Then in 1845 B. F. Jordan settled seven miles south of the Cleaver homestead and put up a horse mill. Soon after the mill was in operation Henry Clay was put on a horse with a sack of corn under him and told how to get to the mill. After a long ride he heard the sound of many axes ahead of him. Then he came to an open place where a number of slaves were clearing land. Henry Clay rode up to the white man who was overseeing their work.

"Good morning, young man," the man said.

"Good morning, sir."

"But who are you? And where do you come from? Who lives off in that direction?"

"My name is Henry Clay Cleaver. I am the son of Henry Cleaver, who lives across the two bayous."

"Are you not lost? Where are you going?"

"No, sir, I am hunting Mr. Jordan's mill."

"Well, sir, my name is Jordan and I have a mill. I expect I am the man you are looking for. But what are your politics? Are you a Whig or a Democrat?"

"I am a Whig, sir."

"A Whig indeed! And what is your daddy?"

"A Whig."

"Well, sir, I am a Democrat, and my mill is a Democratic mill, and will not grind Whig corn. So if you get any meal, you will have to change your politics. What do you say to that?"

"I cannot do it, but will take my corn back home and make it into hominy. Good bye, sir."

He started off toward home but Jordan called him to stop.

"I guessed that you were a Whig from your name and only meant to test your firmness. I, too, am a Whig. Come, we will go to the house and I will grind your corn. I wish the country was full of such boys as I take you to be."

In the fall of 1846 the Cleaver children of school age—Missouri Ann, Henry Clay, Allen, and possibly Martha—started to a school typical of those on earlier frontiers. The house was a pole cabin ten by twelve feet with a puncheon floor and benches made of split logs. To reach it the children had to travel two miles through thick woods with no guide except notches cut in trees. The teacher was Xeno Clouch and there were six to eight pupils, at least half of them Cleavers. Terms, adjusted to farm work, started late in the fall and ended early in the spring. Teachers rarely stayed more than a term, if that long, and the teaching was chiefly in reading, writing, and arithmetic. But the attitude at home—for Cleavers and Braggs alike —was for education, for professional education for some of their sons.

Arkansas, if not the land of milk and honey, allowed both William and Henry Cleaver to prosper. In time, Henry Cleaver acquired title to fifteen hundred acres of land and a number of slaves to work it. Cotton crops were good: in 1854 Henry Cleaver sold fourteen bales at one time. There was a ready market when it was picked, ginned, and baled. There were cotton gins but not enough to separate all the lint from the seeds. Slaves had to work in their cabins at night, pulling the locks apart, putting the seeds in one pile, the lint in another. When a slave had filled his shoe with seeds so that he could not get his foot in it he was allowed to quit for the night. When there were not enough slaves of his own to do all the work, Henry Cleaver leased from others: in one case a boy named James from September to Christmas for what he was worth and a pair of shoes.

Within ten years of its founding Camden became a fairly important river port where bales of cotton began the journey down the Ouachita to the Red, the Mississippi, the Gulf, and on to the New England markets; where goods from New Orleans could be unloaded. Cotton money went into better homes, and acquiring things like pianos and fine furniture.

It was also a period of comparative calm. The Mexican War came and went and few Camden lives were touched by it except that it opened up ten years of greater prosperity. The California gold rush, in territory acquired in the settlement after the Mexican War, tempted few to try their luck, or to look on the waters of the Pacific, possible now that Manifest Destiny had been achieved.

For the Cleaver and Bragg children it was a quiet time of growing up, of work and school and simple country pastimes: church meetings, Sunday-night singings, play-parties where they chose partners and danced and sang:

> Buffalo girl, won't you come out tonight?
> Won't you come out tonight?
> Won't you come out tonight?
> Buffalo girl, won't you come out tonight
> And dance by the light of the moon.

That, and "The Girl I Left Behind Me," which could be a fiddle tune or play-party song or just a song for singing:

> Oh, the girl, the pretty little girl,
> The girl I left behind me,
> With rosy cheeks and yellow curls,
> The girl I left behind me.

Christmas was the best time of the year, for white and black alike. Slaves had time off to go into Camden for what they called "jubilee." Year after year Henry Cleaver promised that Christmas would last till the backstick burned out. Year after year the boys would go down to the Ouachita bottom, find the biggest sweetgum they could, and cut a backstick from it. Then they would bury it in oozy mud and leave it there till their father announced the first day of Christmas. By then, no matter how high the fire roared, the backstick was so waterlogged that it could last as long as two weeks—two weeks of all play, no work. This without forgetting the why of Christmas, and remembeing it in song and verse. One that was said by Missouri Ann—she may have made it up—went down to her children and her children's children:

Will Christians remember this eve of December
When Christ the little Bethlehem babe
Was pillowed by stranger
In the lowliest of mangers?
No fortune was there, neither pride nor parade,
And He was as poor as the barefoot that wanders tonight.

At such times rumblings of antislavery trouble seemed far away, even improbable, to young people on the Ouachita.

Cotton prices were good in the decade following 1850. Plantation owners could endow daughters and provide land for sons who wanted to build their own plantations. There was also money to train sons in professions. Peter Newport Bragg was a lawyer and practiced law in Camden until his death in 1855. His son Walter followed him in the law. He studied law at Harvard University and then set up his office in Camden. Junius Newport went to medical school and returned to Camden to practice.

William Henry Cleaver also turned to the law and studied at the University of Virginia. After about two years of study he returned to Camden but not to practice there. He had made up his mind to move on to Texas. On December 23, 1858, he married Virginia C. Bragg. In October 1859, he was chief justice of the Angelina County Court and owned houses and lots in Homer, the county seat now a part of Lufkin. Records show that he had slaves and household goods sufficient for comfortable living. He also owned a library extensive for the day. In addition to numerous law books he had dictionaries in English, Latin, and French, and works by such writers as Virgil, Cervantes, and Milton. There were also readings in philosophy, theology, and criticism.

Henry Clay Cleaver's story is fully known. In 1852, when he was fifteen, he heard the lectures of an evangelist, Elder Sallee, and was converted to the Church of Christ. In 1855 he went down the Mississippi to New Orleans and then up to Hannibal, where he worked for his cousin William, Jacob's son, in the Cleaver and Mitchell machine shop. He was there long enough to learn the art of working iron and steel. As William lived across the street and less than a block from the Clemens home, Henry Clay likely crossed paths with Samuel. In November 1856 he returned to Camden and then went to Texas, probably to Waco, where Ellender Cleaver Cobbs was living. In

January 1857 he entered Arkansas College at Fayetteville. Robert
Graham was president of the college at the time. In October 1858 he
began the study of law under the Honorable David Walker in
Fayetteville. In 1859 he entered the law department of Cumberland
University, in Lebanon, Tennessee. In 1860, when he was twenty-
three, he was licensed to practice, and set up an office in Camden.

Antagonism between the North and South over the slavery question, after twenty years of quiet but steady growth, became alarming
with the acquisition of the territory from Mexico after the Mexican
War. When on March 12, 1850, California applied for statehood with
a clause in the constitution barring slavery, the question was again
in Congress, with anger and bitterness on both sides. John C. Calhoun led the Southern attack: "I trust we shall persist in our resistance until the restoration of all our rights, or disunion, one or the
other, is the consequence."

But the country was not ready for civil war and the Compromise
of 1850 was arrived at after months of bitter debate. Certain measures were of special significance to the South: California was admitted as a free state and the old balance of power was upset; New
Mexico was organized into a territory without restriction on slavery;
the Fugitive Slave Act placed fugitive slave cases under exclusive
federal jurisdiction. The last measure put the federal government in
the business of capturing fugitive slaves and returning them to their
owners. Given the anger North and South, sectionalists on both sides
could use this act to create more bitter division.

Other events during the same decade were the passage of the
Kansas-Nebraska Act, a compromise destined to lead to "bleeding
Kansas," the Dred Scott decision, and the election of 1856. This
election and outbreaks in Kansas made Southerners believe that the
Union had seen its best days and that civil war was inevitable. For
this they blamed the Northern drive to rule and ruin. At the same
time they defended themselves with the statement that the South
did not invent slavery and the charge that guilt lay with the Yankee
slave traders.

In May 1860 the Republican Party, young, little known in Arkansas, little regarded, nominated Abraham Lincoln as its presidential
candidate. By July his opponents in Arkansas were beginning to talk
of "Black Republicans" and his election as another step toward the
destruction of the South. For some, election day, November 6, 1860,

was the most important day since July 4, 1776. As they feared, he was elected, partly because of splits in party lines over slavery. Henry Cleaver watched the Whig Party, to which he had been devoted, and his father before him, emerge with a Northern wing, called "Conscience Whigs" on one hand, "Cotton Whigs" on the other, and a Southern wing simply called "Southern Whigs," as there were now Southern Methodists and Southern Baptists, and splinterings in his own church, the Church of Christ. He saw Abraham Lincoln, born near him in Kentucky, four years his junior, at the head of a government dedicated, so the fire-eating abolitionists said, to the destruction of slavery, of freedom—southerners said. He had listened to months of debating unionism or disunionism. Now the time had come to accept or reject the Union and the bitter consequences either way.

Events moved rapidly. On December 20, 1860, the South Carolina state convention met at Columbia and voted an ordinance that stated that "the union now subsisting between South Carolina and the States, under the name of the 'United States of America,' is hereby dissolved." Other states followed apace into what in 1861 became the Confederate States of America: Mississippi, on January 9; Florida, January 10; Alabama, January 11; Georgia, January 19; Louisiana, January 26; and Texas, February 1. On February 4, 1861, delegates from these states met in convention in Montgomery and framed a constitution that provided for both slavery and states' rights. They also elected Jefferson Davis of Mississippi as the provisional president of the provisional Confederacy.

Secessionist feeling ran high in Arkansas, especially in the cotton areas. Disunionists held mass meetings in which the rabid opinions in the seceded states were echoed by the reckless, the hotheads, the fire-eaters. Unionists in the northwestern part of the state countered with mass meetings aimed at the preservation of the Union. Pressure mounted for a referundum for the election of delegates to a convention that would decide the issue. The referendum, held on February 18, 1861, showed a majority of those voting in favor of the convention, and the date was set for March 4.

In the meantime secessionists were taking matters into their own hands. Rebels forced the seizure of the Little Rock Arsenal on February 8 and the United States Stores at Pine Bluff on February 12. On February 22, 1861, Jefferson Davis took the oath of office at Montgomery, Alabama, and a new flag was lifted on the breeze.

Secessionists in Arkansas strengthened their argument: better to secede and join their neighbor states in a common cause than to remain in the Union and submit to Black Republican rule.

Though the movement for disunion was growing, the conservatives still spoke out. The Camden *Eagle*, for instance, editorialized, "Select no office seekers, no excitable and inconsiderate men . . . let the calm voice of a free and independent people go up in favor of their right in the Union. . . ." Leaders spoke out for the election of delegates who had the good of their country at heart.

Delegates were elected. The convention met in Little Rock on March 4, with something of a carnival atmosphere, with the galleries and lobbies crowded and disorder on the convention floor, with secessionists applying to unionists such invectives as "abolitionist tool." Judge David Walker, a conservative from Fayetteville, under whom Henry Clay Cleaver had studied law, was elected president of the convention.

Two leading questions were before the convention: secession from the Union and recognition of the recently organized Confederate States of America. Walter Bragg was a spokesman for the secessionists, a representative from the inside. He was also subject to pressures from outside Arkansas. His uncle, A. B. Crook, wrote of him from Greenville Court House, South Carolina, on March 17, 1861:

I am glad to see he is on the right side. Those politicians in your state and elsewhere that excuse their fogyism and cowardice by abusing South Carolina will in the end have to succumb. If they would fairly meet and answer and compute the doctrine South Carolina preached, they would be entitled to some consideration and respect. But so long as they seek to overthrow the best interests of their country and keep themselves in power by lying, slandering, misrepresenting and abusing South Carolina their eminence in the future history of the country will be *unenviable*. . . .

Tell Walter I saw and read with great pleasure his address to the people of Arkansas as chairman of the committee. That was decidedly an able paper and the best I have seen from him. . . .

Arkansas will repudiate the milk and cider, timid, hesitating political leaders.

This letter ably, though perhaps unwittingly, points up the conflict within Arkansas itself—in its largest dimensions a conflict between the small farmers of the hilly regions, where slaves were not profitable, and the plantation owners on the rich plains. It also indicates the kind of pressure being applied from outside Arkansas, and ignores a point Bragg made: the problems the agricultural South would face in a war against the industrial North.

But the convention was not yet ready for secession. Unionists were so much in control that a secessionist spokesman could say, ". . . Remarkably strong Union sentiment which prevails in this convention, leaves no hope of the secession of the State of Arkansas from the Federal Union." The delegates, after ten days of argument, agreed to a compromise that would submit the question to the people of Arkansas in a referendum to be held on August 5. The convention adjourned on March 21.

Ironically, Abraham Lincoln himself played a direct role in forcing Arkansas into secession. After Fort Sumter fell to the Confederates on April 12–14, 1861, Lincoln called for seventy-five thousand militia and proclaimed a blockade against the seven Confederate states. Arkansas was called upon for a quota of seven hundred and eighty men, a request that was refused with the words, "The people of this commonwealth are free men, not slaves, and will defend to the last extremity their honor, lives and property against northern mendacity and usurpation."

The question was suddenly reduced to secession or coercion. The response was immediate: secessionists demanded immediate separation. Companies of volunteers assembled, and filled the streets with the martial music of fife and drum. Out of his own life Lincoln could have predicted this response. His ancestors had crossed the mountains. They had been part of the fiercely independent people who conquered the Kentucky frontier, a people who would never be "put on" by anybody. He could have predicted that the men would start collecting weapons, the women sewing uniforms; that the bold, rash, violent actions that had characterized the frontier would again come to the fore.

The secessionists demanded that the state convention be reconvened, and it was, on May 6. By his one act Lincoln had changed the temper of the convention. Spectators filled the hall for the excitement and they were rewarded. Secessionists presented a list of grievances of the state of Arkansas against the federal government as preamble to a resolution that declared Arkansas "is in full possession and exercise of all the rights and sovereignty which appertain to a free and independent State." Southern oratory was opened to flood as delegate after delegate prefaced his vote with a peroration for secession. When Judge Walker's turn to vote came the count was sixty-four for, five against. Conservative, Unionist, he stated that if it was "inevitable that Arkansas . . . secede . . . let the wires carry the news to all the world that Arkansas stands as a unit. . . ." The vote for secession thus became unanimous.

Arkansas was now officially in the fight. Those strongly opposed could move on to some new frontier, possibly the Indian Territory. Others could remain and take part in an action that most thought would take only a few weeks.

The military board, soon after the convention adjourned, called for ten thousand volunteers. By the end of the year over twenty-one thousand were in service. They had little to fight with: not enough rifles to arm half the volunteers, and some thirty pieces of artillery all told. There were no lead mines nearer than Missouri and few factories that could be retooled for ordnance. Volunteers were expected to furnish their own clothing, guns, and, when they could, horses. Still the spirits ran high. It was generally believed that one Rebel could handle ten Yankees. Hadn't they proved that at Fort Sumter. To fight the "milk and cider" Lincoln, volunteers rushed themselves into units raised locally by lawyers, planters, sometimes preachers—almost anyone who wanted to ride at the head of an outfit and lend it his name.

When war came to the Cleavers and Braggs death had already taken its toll among the older generation. William and Lucy Cleaver were both dead and buried at Two Bayou. So was Christiana Cleaver. So was Peter Newport Bragg, in the family graveyard. Martha, his widow, had to rear their minor children and look after the plantation. Henry Cleaver had two sons at home and the responsibility for both William's minor children and estate. Both had received final settlements under the terms of Stephen Cleaver's will and their estates in land and slaves were fairly large for southwestern Arkansas.

The older children of the three families had started their own families or careers, in some cases both. Three were in law: William Henry Cleaver in Texas, Walter Bragg in Camden, Henry Clay Cleaver in Camden. Junius Newport Bragg was practicing medicine in Camden. Allen Cleaver had married Helen Butcher and settled on a farm near Camden. Missouri Ann and Jesse Herndon James had four small children and a farm near the Cleaver place. Abner Cleaver and Anthon Bragg were younger, but not too young to look forward to becoming soldiers.

In these three families, already bound by ties of friendship and

marriage, these named are the children fated to be bound inextrica-
bly in a war which they could not escape—two to die, the others to
survive, maimed, some in body, all in spirit. Junius Newport Bragg
became their scribe, their poet, and his words run like a Greek
chorus through four years that began in pride and ended in despair.

In Camden the beginnings of war were highly romantic, as they
were in many parts of the South. Imbued with reading and declaim-
ing Sir Walter Scott, their sense of loyalty and valor drawn at least
in part from *Ivanhoe* and *Marmion*, somewhat less from the Greek
classics, men and women alike plunged into the excitement. Soldiers
all over the South were calling themselves "The Knights of the
Golden Circle." Volunteers in Camden organized themselves into a
unit that they called "The Camden Knights," and also "The Red
Jackets" for the color of their tunics. Dressed in uniforms sewed by
mothers, wives, sweethearts, they drilled and paraded and talked of
the Yankees they would kill. Allen joined "The Camden Knights,"
called officially Company G, Eleventh Regiment, Arkansas Infantry,
a part of the state militia. So did Junius Bragg.

On May 15, 1861, nine days after Arkansas seceded, Henry Clay
Cleaver closed his law office and joined Company H, Sixth Arkansas
Infantry. At first opposed to secession, he was more opposed to coer-
cion. He was also loyal to Arkansas and the South. Walter Bragg
joined the same unit and, when orders came, they marched off to
Little Rock, no doubt to the tune of "Dixie."

"Dixie" was a widely popular minstrel song just before the war
and as many as twenty different versions appeared during the conflict, some with words for the North, some for the South. Albert Pike,
Arkansas schoolmaster, poet, politician, soldier, had revised the
words to make them more patriotic:

> Southrons, hear your country call you!
> Up, lest worse than death befall you!
> To arms! To arms! To arms! In Dixie!
> Lo! all the beacon fires are lighted—
> Let all hearts be now united!
> To arms! To arms! To arms! In Dixie!
> Advance the flag of Dixie!
> Hurrah! Hurrah!
> For Dixie's Land we take our stand,
> And live or die for Dixie!
> To arms! To arms!

And conquer peace for Dixie!
To arms! To arms!
And conquer peace for Dixie!

The flag they were called upon to advance may have been The Stars and Bars, the first national flag of the Confederate states, or The Battle Flag, the one more widely known as the Rebel flag, or The Bonnie Blue Flag, an unofficial flag that inspired a favorite Southern military song:

We are a band of brothers, and native to the soil,
Fighting for the property we gained by honest toil,
And when our rights were threatened, the cry rose near and far;
"Hurrah for the Bonnie Blue Flag that bears a single star.
"Hurrah! Hurrah! for Southern Rights, hurrah!
"Hurrah! for the Bonnie Blue Flag that bears a single star!"

Whichever flag they followed, it took some of the Camden men to Little Rock, some on to Pocahontas, in either place to be discharged from the service of Arkansas and enlisted with the Confederate regulars. Allen Cleaver became a regular at Little Rock on July 23, 1861, two days after the first battle of Manassas, or Bull Run. Three days later Henry Clay Cleaver and Walter Bragg were enlisted in the Army of the Confederate States of America by Colonel Thomas C. Hindman, a politician turned soldier, at the time in command of military operations in Arkansas.

A strange mixture of volunteers answered the call, from professional men to day laborers. Some had uniforms of bright color and fancy cut; most wore their civilian clothes. Many had long hair, which they dressed with bone marrow. Their weapons were whatever they could bring from home: muzzle loaders, six-shooters, squirrel rifles, a few of the last equipped with bayonets. The men were not trained in the simplest rudiments of warfare, and the officers were not much better. But they had faith that their cause was right and their courage was strengthened by a sense of righteousness. Of these qualities, they believed, the Yankees could have but little. Junius Bragg expressed a general sentiment when he wrote, "I have seen some of the enemy. They have fine horses and pretty uniforms, and they are well drilled. They are better in all of these particulars than our soldiers, but they are cowards."

After less than adequate training, after much exercise in preaching and prayer meetings, often led by their officers, Arkansas troops were marched from Little Rock to Tennessee, to protect Memphis from attacks by Yankee gunboats. During their period of training two significant things had happened: the Confederate capital was moved from Montgomery to Richmond and the Confederates suffered their first battle death.

Then on August 10, 1861, a full-scale battle—called Oak Hill by the Confederates and Wilson's Creek by the Federals—was fought across the border in Missouri. The Arkansas Cleavers missed this fight, but not the Missouri Cleavers.

The Cleavers who had remained at Hannibal were strong secessionists, in a state where unionists had enough strength to prevent secession. Missourians were left bitterly divided and highly susceptible to the kind of guerrilla warfare they had known in the Kansas dispute. John Stephen, Thomas Cleaver's oldest son, stirred by the Rebel cause, enlisted as a Confederate soldier in May 1861. At the time the tests for enlisting consisted of three questions: Is your heart on the Southern side? Are you physically able to march and carry your pack and gun? Can you see well enough to aim a gun?

For John Stephen Cleaver the questions were easy; the actual enlisting not so easy. Union forces were in control of northern Missouri and they closely guarded ferries across the Missouri River to keep men of military age from crossing to join the Rebel forces to the south. John Cleaver and some others, his cousin M. J. Jones probably among them, arranged to meet at Vandalia, Illinois, and plan their slipaway. His parents approved his enlistment but his mother made him promise not to attend the Vandalia meeting and to go alone if he had to. Keeping his promise, he and two others rode toward the Missouri River. The ones who met at Vandalia were ambushed by Union soldiers and killed.

John Stephen crossed the Missouri and, aided by Southern sympathizers along the way, soon joined Generals Sterling Price and Ben McCulloch. This was the slaveholding General Price who had fought in the Mexican War, whose reputation as a Rebel soldier would soon be recorded in a song made for people to dance to:

> General Price made a raid,
> Made a raid, made a raid;
> General Price made a raid
> Down in Alabama.

John Stephen was soon uniformed as a private and set to drilling.

He first saw action some ten weeks later at Oak Hill, near Springfield, Missouri. The Confederates were led in the fight by General Price, wearing a high hat and frockcoat instead of a uniform because Missouri had not seceded. John Stephen did not see much action, because his unit, the 140th Missouri Volunteers, was in reserve. He was close enough to see General Lyon, the Union commander, ride out on the field trying to rally his men. Just as the general appeared a Rebel soldier shouted above the noise of musket fire, "Look at the damned fool officer! He's sure to be shot!" Almost with the words, they saw the general and his horse fall to the ground.

The body was taken to a private home in Springfield, now held by the Confederates, for preparation for temporary burial. A request for help came and John Stephen was one of the squad sent. When they entered the home they were escorted to the parlor. The body and coffin were already in a rough wooden box, and a woman stood alone, weeping in deep grief. After they had stood silent for a moment she said, "Gentlemen, you are burying a good and noble man and a great soldier."

At once a Rebel blurted out, "Yes, ma'am, and right now I guess he's in hell, drillin' little red divils!"

"Silence!" the Rebel sergeant roared.

It was the only word spoken. They carried the coffin to an orchard on the place and buried it, to await a transfer home to Connecticut.

The battle was over, the Confederates had won—with troops half armed, briefly trained, short on military supplies and food.

Away from their home territory the Camden Knights began to see themselves through the eyes of others, not as conquering heroes but as ordinary soldiers. A complaint written by Junius Bragg to his mother from a camp near Memphis was fairly general:

> While women, children and cowardly men are alarmed and frightened for their own as well as the safety of their friends, the poor soldier, scorned and reviled, was not worthy to be the peer of respectable stay-at-home people; looked upon as the synonym of debauchery and meanness. . . .

There had been a decline in popularity in the towns where large detachments were camped, and with reason. Though the soldier had volunteered to fight for the people, to lay down his life if necessary, he had to have food and often had to live on the land, often when there was not enough food to go around. Troops provided escorts for young ladies at parties and dances and occasional church meetings, but the behavior of some more befitted the camp than the parlor. Junius Bragg shows how friction between soldier and civilian could arise:

> Ned Warren went to town yesterday, and as usual got drunk. After making a fool of himself generally, he was arrested and put in the Military Guard house. His cousin, the handsome "Frog" went down to effect his liberation, of course he failed. Then Jim Whitfield went down to release him and *he* got drunk. . . .

Army officers held preaching and prayer meetings for their troops to warn them of the evil of drink and the sin of dancing.

Problems with slaves affected civilians and soldiers alike. Young Southern gentlemen took body servants with them to the army as they had taken them to college or on their travels. Some remained faithful. Some, joining the growing unrest, ran away and hid in the towns until they could work their way North. Junius Bragg wrote to his mother, "Ned's niger Sutton gets drunk as often as his master. Ned fears to use rough language toward Sutton, lest he should avail himself of the 'Underground Rail Road.' I rather think I shall make a *striking* distinction between him and the whites before long." He had apparently not yet learned that from the Northern point of view the war was to erase this "*striking* distinction."

Blandishments from the North had begun to draw the slaves off in number, some to join the Northern army, some to sample the promised freedom. Southern masters, civilian and soldier alike, were unable to stop them. Flight was easier than it had ever been, and there were no fugitive slave laws under which they could be captured and brought back. The race toward freedom was infectious but some of the slaves elected to stay and wait for their freedom in the South. "Kingdom Coming" became their song of exultation:

> Oh, darkies, have you seen the massa this morning
> With the mustache on his face?
> He was all dressed up this very morning
> Like he's a-gwine a-leave this place.

REFRAIN:
Oh, the massa's ranned away,
And the darkies stays at home.
It must be now that the kingdom's comin'
In the year of Jubilo.

He's five foot one weighs six foot the other,
And he weighs five hundred pounds;
His coat's so big that he cain't pay the tailor,
And it won't meet half way around.

The massa saw the smoke way up the river
Where the Lincoln gunboats lay;
And he picked up his hat and he left in a hurry,
And I think he's ranned away.

Massa lives in a big white house,
And the darkies on the lawn.
They'll move their things up to massa's parlor
To keep it while he's gone.

There's wine and cider in the smoke house cellar,
And the darkies they'll have some.
I think they'll all be confiscated
'Fore the Lincoln soldiers come.

Still the morale of the Camden Knights held up. They were
guarding on the Mississippi watching for Federal gunboats. Allen
Cleaver, according to reports, was quite well and had not yet been
in combat. There was general concern about the shortage of arms but
not about the final outcome of the war. Junius Bragg expressed the
prevailing thought:

I would not have you think for a moment that I regret having enlisted,
or that I am tired of soldiering, not a bit of it! If I was at home today, and
perfectly free, I would volunteer in less than a week, just as soon as I could
join a company. If I was at home I could not rest easy.

On September 7, 1861, a call for volunteers was inserted in the
Austin *State Gazette,* signed by W. L. Robards:

I am authorized by Gen. Sibley, Gov. Clark, and the Adjutant General to raise a company of Cavalry, to be mustered into the Confederate service, and attached to Gen. Sibley's Brigade. It will consist of one Captain; one first Lieutenant; two second Lieutenants; four Sergeants; four Corporals; one Farrier; one Blacksmith; two Buglers, and sixty-four privates minimum, one hundred and fourteen maximum.

Volunteers are required to furnish themselves with a good horse, saddle, bridle and blanket; a good double barrel shotgun or rifle certain, a bowie knife and six shooter, if the latter can possibly be obtained. All necessary camp equippage will be furnished at San Antonio. . . .

At his home at Homer, Angelina County, Texas, William Henry Cleaver responded to the call and in only nine days raised a company called first the Captain William H. Cleaver's Company, or the Angelina Troops. On September 16 he wrote from Alto, Cherokee County, Texas, to General J. L. Hogg, in Rusk, Texas:

Enclosed find muster roll of Angelina Troop rank and file 78 which is hereby tendered for Gen. Sibley's Brigade. If you have not received the five companies I would be proud to know that Angelina will be represented. We are expecting to be able to move from this County two weeks from tomorrow.

Your Obt Servt
W. H. CLEAVER
Capt. Angelina Troop

Connivance for speed in getting the brigade on the road is obvious. On the same day, from Alto, General Hogg wrote to William Byrd, Adjutant General of Texas:

I have the honor to report Capt W H Cleaver's Company of "Angelina Troops" Cavalry. The muster roll whereof is hereto appended. The service is for during the war unless sooner discharged. I have ordered them to march with the greatest dispatch from Homer Angelina County on or before (if Possible sooner) the 30 inst to San Antonio Texas and there report to Gen Sibley.

I have the honor to be Very Respectfully

Your Obt Servt
JAMES L. HOGG
Aide-de-Camp
5 Dist Texas

Apparently both communications were written and signed by the same hand.

In a will made in Homer and dated October 1, 1861, William Henry Cleaver left all his estate to his wife, Virginia C. Cleaver. In the preamble he stated the circumstances clearly, angrily: "I William H Cleaver . . . being about to submit my mortal body to the uncertainties of the present unholy war waged against the Confederate States of America under the auspices of the usurper and despot Abraham Lincoln. . . ." He was then twenty-six years old.

The campaign under way, still little known because it was so far from the main theater of war, grew out of strong pro-Southern sentiment in parts of the territory lately acquired from Mexico, especially in the southern parts of states later organized as New Mexico and Arizona. As a matter of fact, at conventions held in March 1861, pro-Southern delegates had seceded from the Union and created the Territory of Arizona, following the example of Texas, which had passed a secession ordinance on January 28, 1861. Thus a vast territory was added to the Confederacy, and a considerable burden in defense, a burden soon shifted to the shoulders of Henry Hopkins Sibley. Sibley, a West Point graduate from Natchitoches, Louisiana, had been commissioned a brigadier general in the Confederate army and instructed to raise a brigade to drive Union forces from New Mexico Territory.

Sibley arrived at San Antonio on August 12 and set up his headquarters. Fifteen days later the first volunteer unit reported for duty and was sworn into the service "for the war." Other units arrived and training was under way, in the tactics of both cavalry and infantry. At twenty-six, William Henry Cleaver was the youngest officer in his company. His first lieutenant was forty-three, one of the second lieutenants fifty-six. His muster roll for October 24, 1861, shows thirteen commissioned and noncommissioned officers and sixty-one privates. Though two of the privates were in their forties, most of them were between eighteen and twenty-three. On October 26 the brigade reached full strength in men but it was sadly lacking in uniforms, weapons, and other equipment. Sibley had counted on patriotism and it was there in plentiful supply. On November 7, after the officers had put them in shape through rigorous training, they were on their way to New Mexico. Unit after unit marched through San Antonio, to the sound of fife and drum and the farewell salutes of ladies waving white handkerchiefs.

William Henry Cleaver was on his way to his own date with destiny. Virginia Cleaver had watched him go with the mixture of trepidation and cheerfulness characteristic of Confederate women. She remained at their home at Homer one week and then went back to Camden to wait out the war.

By the beginning of 1862 much of the earlier optimism in the South disappeared with the knowledge that the war would be longer, harder than anyone had thought. For the civilians, flour and salt were in short supply. So were chewing tobacco and medicine. Henry Cleaver helped people at Camden somewhat by organizing wagon trains to haul flour and other supplies from Jefferson and Marshall, Texas. He was used to doctoring his family and slaves. With most of the doctors away in service, people came to him and he gave them medicine as well as he could: blue mass and calomel, both mercury compounds, for purging; quinine for malaria; teas made of foxglove or snakeroot or watermelon seeds for miseries as he diagnosed them. For the troops, there were no axes, water barrels, pillow cases, clean clothes. Civilians and soldiers alike boosted morale as well as they could, the troops with singing "Dixie" and "The Girl I Left Behind Me," the civilians with prayer meetings and repetitions of the belief that their cause was just and God on their side.

As the situation worsened, protestations became more fervent. Junius Bragg wrote to his mother from New Madrid, Missouri, on January 25, 1862:

Placing our trust in the Great God who doeth all things well, and who controls the destinies of all things earthly, and knowing that with us is Victory and Death, let each and every man be ready and firm, and look danger full in the face. Our *all* is staked on the one issue of this conflict, and we must be *men* or fall forever. I thank God I was nurtured by one, who like a Spartan mother had rather not see her sons return from battle unless they do so with honor.

Greater fortitude was needed. While William Henry Cleaver was marching toward New Mexico John Stephen Cleaver was retreating in Arkansas. Before the Battle of Oak Hill, General Price had turned command of his Missouri troops over to General McCulloch, who had made a reputation for himself as a Texas Ranger. The

Confederates won that fight but McCulloch failed to take the advantage and press on into Missouri. Partly because of this failure Missouri was left unprotected from a bloody guerrilla warfare between the Northern jayhawkers and Southern bushwhackers, a kind of feuding warfare that left civilians tortured or dead, their homes burned. While he hesitated the Union forces were building up strength. McCulloch decided to withdraw into Arkansas. During the winter the Yankees kept pressure on the retreating Rebels with rear-guard skirmishes, but there were no significant engagements. Then at the end of February 1862, the Southern force, now some twenty thousand strong, including Cherokee, Choctaw, and Chickasaw Indians under General Albert Pike, decided to stop the Federal advance into northwestern Arkansas. Again the Indian war whoop would sound, mingled this time with the Rebel yell, described by some as a high yip: *ki-yi-yi-yi.* In bitter winter weather they made their stand at Pea Ridge, and there, on March 7 and 8, John Stephen Cleaver had his first taste of real combat. It was a bloody battle, fought at close range, with disastrous results for the South.

On March 10 the Union commander could report the following to Washington:

> The Army of the Southwest . . . after three days' hard fighting . . . has gained a most glorious victory over the combined forces of Van Dorn, McCulloch, Price, and McIntosh. Our loss in killed and wounded estimated at 1,000; that of the enemy still larger. . . . Our cavalry in pursuit of the flying enemy.

The "Southrons" had indeed lost heavily. Three generals had been killed, among them McCulloch and McIntosh, plus a number of field and staff officers. On March 9 General Van Dorn had sent a message to the commanding officer of the Union forces:

> In accordance with the usages of war I have the honor to request that you will permit the burial party whom I send from this army with a flag of truce to attend to the duty of collecting and interring the bodies of the officers and men who fell during the engagements. . . .

The response came not from the commanding general but from an acting assistant adjutant general. Permission was granted and facilities offered, on condition that such accommodations would also be granted by the Confederates. Then a statement reminiscent of earlier frontiers was added:

The general regrets that we find on the battle-field, contrary to civilized warfare, many of the Federal dead who were tomahawked, scalped, and their bodies shamefully mangled, and expresses the hope that this important struggle may not degenerate into savage warfare.

A later dispatch, signed by the commanding officer, Brigadier General Samuel R. Curtis, adds more information:

General Pike commanded the Indian forces. They shot arrows as well as rifles, and tomahawked and scalped prisoners.

Confederates deplored that Albert Pike had not been able to control his Indian warriors, but they also reported atrocities, of Southern prisoners killed in cold blood by Yankee soldiers. Hatred of Yankees increased. Rebel soldiers talked of revenge, and more quietly, of doubt. Their attitude shows in a letter from Junius Bragg to his mother: "If it is our fate to be conquered, which I do not believe, I want to kill a Yankee, and then lie down and die."

General Curtis, who was graduated two years after Robert E. Lee at West Point, became the subject of a Rebel song, a fragment of which still is sung in the South:

Oh, who is prized to fight him,
Somebody I don't know;
It surely is old Curtis—
I hear his cannon roar.
He just up and scattered fast,
But still he did not know;
But all that lay on Curtis's mind
Was a little lump of lead.

At Pea Ridge the opportunity to advance into Missouri had again been lost. General Price saw his troops defeated, dispersed, never again to fight in Missouri except as bushwhackers in guerrilla warfare. The Confederates who survived began a slow, laborious withdrawal, following a line diagonally across Arkansas toward the southeast, over wretched roads that made transportation of supplies almost impossible. Rivers, hills, swamps, sickness—much malaria, threats of cholera—harassment from Northern units—all of these left the soldiers with a low opinion of Arkansas and uncertainty about their future. John Stephen Cleaver knew he had Cleaver relatives in Camden he could call on but their route never came close. In early spring they finally crossed east of the Mississippi and joined other Southern forces in the general area west and south of Corinth.

While John Stephen Cleaver was retreating across Arkansas, Allen was serving in the defense of Island Ten in the Mississippi River —a desperate defense as Fort Donelson had surrendered, Nashville had been evacuated, and Island Ten was already marked as a point of siege in the campaign to drive the Confederates from the upper Mississippi. Henry Clay Cleaver had been wounded in a skirmish in Tennessee, and had been evacuated, probably to the military hospital in St. John's College, Little Rock. Walter Bragg had been wounded but had been able to rejoin his unit, now stationed near Corinth.

General Grant had decided on Corinth as his next point of attack, but the Confederates attacked first, on April 6, in a battle that lasted all day and left the Union forces close to defeat. At night Union reinforcements, some under General Lew Wallace, arrived. At dawn the battle began again and raged all day. At night the Confederates were compelled to withdraw but the Federals were too weakened to follow. Losses were high on both sides, thirteen thousand for the Federals, eleven thousand for the Confederates. The battle, called Shiloh, was both bloody and inconclusive.

That night twenty-three hundred Yankee prisoners were marched to Memphis to be guarded by the local militia. They all walked to their prison whistling "Yankee Doodle." The Rebels retorted by calling them Goths and Vandals. But damage had been done to the Rebel cause. Nightly in the camps there was the sound of praying and preaching, of calling on God to help them in their fight. Morale among the troops became a serious problem. There was a marked increase in the number of desertions. A Camden Knight, not from Camden, went over to the Union. The remedy ordered was to the point: deserters would be shot.

Junius Bragg, with a surgeon's freedom of movement, went to Corinth to see for himself and stayed three days with the Sixth Arkansas Regiment. He found Walter and wrote to his mother:

I was somewhat fearful that my brother was killed or wounded. This was not the case, but he narrowly escaped. Several bullets penetrated his clothes. I was very much surprised at the the appearance of Walter. Instead of the stout, robust man of last summer, full of fun and humor, I met a thin and emaciated creature, whose countenance was care worn and solemn. He had on a pair of old shoes, such as may be seen lying in the gutters of cities; a pair of coarse grey pants, such as negroes wear; an old brown slouched hat, a flannel shirt trimmed with red and the same coat he wore away last summer. He said they had never drawn any pay, that he had long since loaned his original money to his friends in the company. Poor fellow! Ragged as he was and sick besides, having only returned from Atlanta two days previous to the battle, he tramped seven miles through mud and water and slept five nights in the rain without even a blanket for shelter and nothing to eat for thirty-six hours.

This was the proud Harvard man, the successful lawyer, the ardent spokesman for secession. Still a private, after a year as a soldier, he had endured both illness and hardship; he had had ample time for reflection, to see how desperate his situation, how endangered the Confederate cause. Yet for him, as for thousands like him, there was no thought of turning away from duty.

To make morale worse, on April 10, 1862, about six Confederate regiments were captured at Island Ten in the Mississippi, including the Eleventh and Twelfth Arkansas—all of the Camden Knights in those units except eleven who were in the hospital. Allen Cleaver was among them. They were sent to Camp Douglas in Illinois and no one in Camden could learn their fate.

The war had taken a bad turn in Arkansas. St. John's College in Little Rock was overflowing with sick and wounded from Pea Ridge and Shiloh. Yankee troops were within the state and there were not enough Rebels to hold them back. Military supplies were low, so low that people dug up the dirt from the floors of their smokehouses and leached out the saltpeter to make gunpowder. There was disillusionment accompanied by grim humor. On May 25 Junius Bragg wrote from Camden:

The Federals at Searcy and in that region generally are said to number about twenty three thousand. They carry pillage and destruction wherever they go. It is thought they will come on to Little Rock. Rector and Roane have five or six thousand men at L. Rock. It is not to be supposed that this force will give the enemy an open fight, if it fights at all. I rather think that as soon as the Federals reach L. Rock there will ensue a spirited footrace. Since running has become a Confederate fashion. There is no knowing when we shall see the last of it. When the Yankees out-general as they generally do, then we exhibit to them our superiority in the art of running.

Bitterness rose to a certain extent from the feeling of Arkansaw-yers that they had been left to fight their own battles, after their best troops had been sent east of the Mississippi. Daily the division be-tween East and West in the Confederacy became more pronounced. The Confederate capital had been moved to Richmond. The war was being generaled far from the western sector. Yet the western sector was needed, Arkansawyers knew, and more troops would have to be raised. On June 3, 1862, Confederate conscription was instituted. In an irony that made them especially bitter, Confederate troops, volunteer or conscripted, knew there was a chance they would face in battle runaway slaves, in the Yankee Army, wearing the hated blue.

Then there was great excitement in Camden. Some of the Camden Knights had escaped from the Federal prison, Allen Cleaver among them. He was making his way to Hannibal and then home. Another Knight, not from Camden, had escaped with him but he died at Hannibal, where he had been cared for by secessionists, Cleaver relatives.

For the moment all the Cleaver and Bragg men were accounted for except William Henry, who was still out West on the New Mexico campaign.

Then in July the Braggs and Cleavers received a message that stunned them: William Henry was dead, killed on July 1 by Mexican Feds in an ambush while crossing the Rio Grande in the Mesilla Valley, New Mexico. Details were scanty. His horse was shot from under him and fell. He fought for his life, standing in the river, until he was brought down by a bullet. Of the seven on the scouting party with him only one boy escaped.

The gloom cast over his family and friends at home gradually reached his relatives in the service. Junius Bragg wrote his mother on August 30, 1862:

When I think of poor Bill—of our associated boyhood—how we grew up together, and entered upon the race of life—of our friendship, never marred by a harsh word—and last by our relationship. When I think of his bright future—of his high hopes, that the coming time was sure to fulfill; When I think, (worst picture of all) of his wife—my sister, who was anxiously looking for, and happy in the expectation of his return, but whose hopes are now, not only blighted for a season but for all time to come, it almost—it *does* make me play the woman. I can give Virginia no words of consolation, I have none to give. As for me, I try to swallow up the bitter part of my grief in my patriotism—in my love of country. I try to feel as if I would be willing to sacrifice myself and all my kindred upon the altar of my country. But the bitterness is only to be tasted, when the matter is put to the test. I feel perfectly reckless of my own life. I feel—at least I try to do so, about Bill, in the language of Halleck:

> We tell thy doom without a sigh,
> For thou art freedom's now and fame's
> One of the few, the immortal names,
> That were not born to die.

On August 1, 1862, William R. Cleaver, a cousin from Munford-ville, Kentucky, enlisted as a Yankee soldier and began a journal of his experiences in the South.

As 1862 wore on the war took a heavy toll on both sides, with mounting numbers of battle deaths and deaths from fevers that hung like a plague over the South. Every day the situation became more bitter, more desperate. Yankee newspapers called for putting down the rebellion even if it meant killing every man, woman, and child in the South. The Rebels were willing to fight back, to wipe every Yankee from the face of the earth. The picnic air of the early days, when Yankee and Rebel officers, classmates at West Point, kept up a kind of camaraderie, when troops North and South swapped songs at night across narrow streams, had vanished.

Though people in the South could still be stirred by a band playing "Dixie," a new kind of song had come into being, a song like "This Cruel War," which came closer to the feelings of the time:

> Dearest one, do you remember
> When we last did meet?
> How you told me how you loved me
> Kneeling at my feet?
> Oh, how proud you stood before me
> In your suit of grey;
> When you vowed for me your country
> Ever to be free.

Weeping sad and lonely,
Sighs and tears how vain,
When this cruel war is over
Freeing them to meet again.

But our country calls you loved ones,
Angels guide your way;
While you Southern boys are fighting
We can only pray.
When you strike for God and freedom,
Let all nations see
How you loved your Southern banner,
Emblem of the free.

If amid the line of battle
Nobly you should fall,
Far away from those who love you,
None to hear you call.
Oft in dream I see you lying
On the battle plain,
Lonely, wounded, even dying,
Calling but in vain.

Among the Northern soldiers, "Yankee Doodle" began to give
way to songs of loneliness and of death on the battlefield. Songs for
the North or South crossed battle lines as easily as they crossed
mountains and rivers. Though the words might be propagandistic,
the feeling, as in "Brother Green," was universal:

Oh, Brother Green, do come to me,
For I am shot and bleeding;
The Southern foe has laid me low,
On this cold ground to suffer.

Stay, Brother, stay and lay me away
And write my wife a letter;
Tell her that I'm prepared to die
And hope we'll meet in heaven.

Oh, Sister Nancy, do not weep
For the loss of your dear brother,

For he's gone home with Christ to dwell,
To see his blessed mother.

Two brothers yet I can't forget,
They're fighting for the Union,
And one dear wife—I'd give my life
To put down this rebellion.

And two little babes, I love them well,
Oh, could I once more see them,
I'd bid them all a sad farewell
Till we might meet in heaven.

Oh, Mary, you must treat them well,
And bring them up for heaven;
Teach them to love and serve the Lord
And then they'll be respected.

Oh, father, you have suffered long
And prayed for my salvation,
But now I'll be to home at last—
Farewell, farewell, temptation.

Chaplains like Brother Green, North or South, had more and more work to do.

Then on January 1, 1863, Abraham Lincoln issued the Emancipation Proclamation declaring that all slaves in areas still in rebellion were "then, thenceforward, and forever free." News of the proclamation traveled slowly through the Confederate states, reaching Mississippi on May 8 and Texas on June 19. Negroes made these their emancipation days to be celebrated from then on—"Eight o' May" in Mississippi, "June 'teenth" in Texas. Among Southern slaveholders the proclamation caused anger and concern, but they did not free their slaves, as they considered themselves outside the sovereignty of the United States. For this separation they had fought and would continue to fight what they called the War for Southern Independence. Lincoln to the contrary, the slaves were theirs and they would hold on to them, though they had to admit to each other that more and more were walking away and that they were powerless to stop them.

To Southerners, what the Yankees called the War of Rebellion had now become more than a matter of life and death on the battlefield; it was extermination for all who held Southern beliefs. On all fronts the Yankees were pressing, on too many the Rebels were retreating. Reports of casualties were grim. On both sides desertions were high—about ten percent. Because of their smaller manpower reserve the Rebels could ill afford such a rate. Executions, now not a threat but a reality, took place in camp after camp, strong deterrents to troops standing in formation to watch.

Grant's primary objective was to complete Union control of the Mississippi River, the great highway in the West for men, munitions, and supplies. Yankee pressure had been relentless: Grant had taken Cairo, Illinois; Farragut took New Orleans on April 24, 1862; Memphis was captured on June 6, 1862. Only Vicksburg was left to the Confederates. That captured, the West would be entirely cut off from the East. Knowing the gravity of their situation, the Southerners had prepared the best defense they could, with forts and breastworks against land attack, cannon batteries on the river bank.

Union strength had been slowly increased until the advantage in numbers of troops and availability of supplies clearly belonged to the North and the hordes of Northmen, as the Rebels bitterly called them. On March 29, 1863, Grant crossed the Mississippi with twenty thousand troops, marched down the Louisiana side to the south of Vicksburg, and crossed again to the east side. There he met resistance, but it was a weakened resistance. In three weeks of continued pounding away in well-planned, well-manned, and superior artillery attacks he won five battles against the Confederates and slowly pushed them back into Vicksburg.

John Stephen Cleaver was at Champion's Hill, the last heavy combat before the Rebels were shut up inside Vicksburg. For him this battle was the hardest in all his soldiering. His company, reduced in previous fights and by sickness, began the engagement with only forty men, or two-fifths of a full complement. When the battle ended they numbered three—the others all killed, wounded, or captured. He had never received an officer's commission but here he was a captain for a short time. As Stephen Cleaver had done at St. Clair's defeat, John Stephen led his company—the other two survivors—out and they made their way to Vicksburg.

Then the siege of Vicksburg was on, not to end for about six weeks—six weeks of starvation, of irregularly timed attacks, of fighting back when fighting seemed hopeless. Early in the siege Grant attempted to storm the Rebel breastworks but the attempt was a bloody failure. The Rebels had prepared well and were waiting. When the attack came it was expected, as the artillery fire had been much heavier than usual. Then the Federal soldiers ran across open ground that had been well cleared by the defenders, the charge aimed at the section defended by John Stephen's unit. As most of the Rebels were armed with muskets—only a few had rifles—they held their fire until the enemy was in range, in plain sight. John Stephen was tall, tall enough to peer over the earthen wall that was their defense. Two shorter men loaded the muzzle-loaders and passed them up for him to shoot. His aim was good. No Union soldiers got inside their section.

Then the siege was on in earnest, to starve them out. The Rebels had days and nights of waiting, with now and then an incident to remind them that the war was still on.

Early one morning John Stephen saw a young Confederate officer with field glasses looking over the wall toward the enemy line. John Stephen said to another soldier, "Look at that simpleton. The sun shining on that spy glass makes it a good target for a sharpshooter." Soon after he had spoken, a rifle bullet pierced the officer's skull.

Another day, a very warm day, enemy cannon shells were coming over. A chance shell exploded and tore away their plank-covered shelter while they hugged the earth wall. There was a lull in the shelling, and the heat from the sun beating on them was intense. Back of them a short distance and in the open was a tree. A soldier went back to the shade of the tree and was soon asleep. Suddenly the cannon fire began again and a shell exploded near the tree. A tremor passed over the sleeping soldier. The war was over for him.

As the siege went on, food became very scarce, and they were under orders not to steal from Vicksburg civilians. Then the soldiers were reduced to a ration of mule meat for two meals a day. One day they saw a cow in a pasture and saw a way to supplement their ration. Their plan, well laid, went wrong. John Stephen stood ready with his knife well sharpened. He heard the shot, saw the cow fall, and ran, but he was too late. She had been carved up and taken away before he could get to her.

The supply of fish and bullfrogs in a brook behind the fortifications was soon exhausted, but one hungry Johnny Reb had an idea. He made a large, loose ball of wild grapevine and tied an old soup bone in the center, with some gristle remaining. He left this in the shallow water a while, quickly pulled it out, and caught a few crawfish. Each one yielded a piece of "inland shrimp" the size of a thimble.

As the siege wore on the morale got lower and lower. Still the soldiers crowded together in the darkness could whistle and sing "The Girl I Left Behind Me."

At last they were starved out and on July 4, 1863, they surrendered. Yankee soldiers showed no ill will or bitterness toward them as they passed out real food in generous quantity. Yankees could afford to be generous, the Rebels knew. Confederate resistance on the Mississippi and in the West had all but ended, except in Arkansas, Louisiana, and Texas. Vicksburg might have ended the war but it did not; the Rebels were determined to go on fighting even if Richmond, Mobile, and Charleston should fall. Neither did Gettysburg end it, though news of Lee's defeat there, also on July 4, shocked and embittered and, to some, brought grim despair.

Of Vicksburg Junius Bragg wrote from a camp at Delhi, Louisiana:

> I have been fearful that Vicksburg would fall, since the passage of the Gunboats, but I hoped for better things. It was a point of national pride, and national importance. Could it have been saved, as it should have been, it really seemed as though it would have been the first step towards peace. Now all is dark. Great God! I would have eaten mules and dogs and cats, and snakes, and grass and dirt, and old boots and shoes before I would have given up the place. If it was true that Vicksburg was surrendered after two meals of mule meat, and on the 4th of July at that, a nation's curse forever be upon the heads of those who gave up, thus ignominiously, the town. . . . We will not be over-run. But as certain as that God . . . sits enthroned in heaven, we will wade through blood to that goal for which we are striving.

John Stephen Cleaver survived on two meals of mule meat a day and with others like him had to give up. Loyalty to the Southern cause was not enough for them to withstand the superior power of the Union forces. For them it was either death or surrender. He surrendered.

The fall of Vicksburg opened the way for a sustained Union drive against Arkansas. Feeling neglected, even abandoned, but not defeated, the troops in Arkansas—recruited from Missouri, Texas, and the Indian Territory as well as from Arkansas—fought on. Their last significant fight against the Yankees, and that a draw, had taken place on December 7, 1862. Before Vicksburg, Arkansas Post and Helena had fallen. On the day Vicksburg surrendered, General Sterling Price, in a vain attempt to save Little Rock, attacked the Federal fortress at Helena with seven thousand men. They attacked courageously, but they were outnumbered and outgunned. They did manage to advance the Confederate flag—the last time it was advanced —and set it on a place ironically named Graveyard Hill. It was dislodged and Price was compelled to order his raggle-taggle army to retreat.

It was a slow and disorderly withdrawal. Many of the men were without weapons. Their homespun, home-dyed uniforms were in rags. Some limped along barefoot. Their rations exhausted, they foraged in the fields they passed through, eating raw the corn, peas, potatoes, and peanuts they found. There was despair and disaffection aplenty, lightened at times with flashes of humor, at times with wry laughter as they straggled along to the words and tune of a song like "Goober Peas":

Sitting by the roadside on a summer's day,
Chatting with my messmates, passing time away,
Lying in the shadow underneath the trees,
Goodness how delicious, eating goober peas!
      Peas! Peas! Peas! Peas!
      Eating goober peas!
      Goodness how delicious,
      Eating goober peas!
Just before the battle the Gen'ral hears a row,
He says, "The Yanks are coming, I hear their rifles now."
He turns around in wonder, and what do you think he sees?
The Georgia Militia—eating goober peas!

These were the soldiers Price had for the defense of Little Rock, against General Frederick Steele and his well-fed, well-supplied Union troops, some fifteen thousand strong. The best Arkansas soldiers were still fighting east of the Mississippi and there was no help to be expected from any quarter. Fortunately for Price, Steele made a slow, easy march. Price began his retreat on July 4. On September 6 Steele began maneuvering for a vantage point on the Arkansas

River to the south and east of Little Rock. Price used the time in between as well as he could to build fortifications and prepare his troops, but odds were against him. Five days earlier the governor had fled from Little Rock and set up his government at Washington. The people Price was committed to defend criticized him bitterly for wasting men and supplies in the futile attack on Helena. On the afternoon of September 9 Steele attacked. At eleven the next morning Price led his troops across the Arkansas River and through Little Rock, having elected retreat over surrender.

Five days later Lincoln appointed a provisional governor with authority to organize a Union government. Again Arkansas belonged to the Union, at least nominally, but not that section from Arkadelphia to Camden along the line of the Ouachita River. "Good" Yankees—that is, those Arkansawyers who had opposed the war in the first place—remained in their homes and took the oath. "Good" Rebels clogged the roads headed for Texas and escape. There was no way to tell how much longer the war would last, or what destruction lay ahead. Winter was coming on, a winter as harsh as Arkansas was likely to experience, with weeks of freezing temperatures, days of zero weather. One Arkansawyer described it in his scrapbook: "The weather is as cold as a Yankee's heart, and as disagreeable as his company; as blustering as he is before battle, and as dismal as he is after one."

The Cleavers, by luck, were not living in occupied territory, under what they would have thought the shame of Yankee rule, but they had their share of distress and want. By January everything seemed out of hand, with slaves running away, Yankee soldiers laying waste to areas they could not control. Henry Cleaver took the slaves he had left to Texas, reportedly to Montague County, gave each one hundred dollars, and set them free. Then, taking his son Abner with him, he refuged to Waco, Texas. Allen had returned home after his escape from the Yankee prison, rested for a little time, and reenlisted for service east of the Mississippi. When that tour was over he returned to Camden and finding that his wife had died, took his little daughter to Waco. Henry Clay, severely wounded on March 5, 1863, in the battle of Thompson's Station, north of Columbia, Tennessee, was returned to Camden as soon as he was able and appointed enrolling officer. He boarded in the home of John M. Brown, where they had bachelor fare, poor in the beginning, reduced to only hog and hominy as time wore on.

Jesse Herndon James, Missouri Ann's husband, was dead of a brain fever contracted while building wagons in a Confederate ordnance plant. He may have been the J. H. James, who was enlisted in Marshall's Battery, Arkansas Light Artillery, at Little Rock, on February 28, 1863, by Captain W. E. Woodruff. If so, he was probably assigned to the ordnance plant at Little Rock, though he might also have been assigned to Camden, where wagons were also built.

Missouri Ann at twenty-eight was a widow with four children to support and care for, and with only Old Mose to help, a slave who had stayed on after the others had left. She also had the house and land her father had given her. Like countless other Confederate women she had to turn to farming—to plowing, hoeing, gathering— to make a living. She was a strong woman, able as a man to take an ax to the woods or a plow to the field. Pioneer ways and pioneer stories had come down to her at least to the fourth generation and they were a part of her strength. But, for her, times were different. The women before her had followed the frontier to make a way of life. What she was doing, she felt, was to protect and preserve the way of life they had made.

So from daylight till dark she and her children worked in the fields. At first she had horses and mules to pull wagon and plow. After they were impressed by the Rebels or confiscated by the Yankees she made rope harness for cows and calves and worked them as well as she could. Then they were gone and everything had to be done by hand: a hole dug with a hoe or a stick, a grain of corn dropped in, the dirt leveled and tamped. A young child could drop the corn. Older ones could dig and hoe and gather, working in all seasons, for there was no school to keep them from work.

In the spring they followed fencerows looking for poke, wild lettuce, and wild onions for greens. In the fall they could hunt for hickory nuts in the woods or for chinquapins along the Ouachita. At any time of the year they might find that when a crop was ready for gathering, it might have been gathered for them by Yankee soldiers, jayhawkers, renegade Rebels, runaway slaves who stripped the fields or trampled them down out of meanness. By April 1864 the country around Camden had been stripped of everything and women and children were starving. Women without men, like Missouri Ann, had to barter, beg, or steal.

Salt was one of the items hardest to come by. The nearest works were at Arkadelphia, some twenty-five miles from where she lived, through woods or over roads traveled at times by renegades and Yankee soldiers. One morning she got on a broken-down nag, rode to the salt works, traded for a twenty-five pound sack to be shared with her neighbors, and started home. On a lonely part of the road she was suddenly stopped by Union soldiers and accused of being a spy.

"Where are the Rebel soldiers?" the Union captain demanded.

She told him that she did not know and had no way of knowing. She had gone to buy salt and had to get back to her children. The captain became threatening.

"I'll prick you with my bayonet," he said.

She stood her ground.

"Prick away," she said.

Then she saw a Union soldier sidling toward her.

"You got any baccy?" he asked.

Without a word she lifted her skirt, rolled down a stocking, took out a homemade twist, and gave it to him.

Suddenly she was free to go.

One day when they and all the women and children around them were desperate for food some Union soldiers came by on foot, driving a herd of cattle they had confiscated on farms farther out. She made a quick and dangerous decision. She got out the old muzzle loader, went out to the road and, without a word to the soldiers, shot and killed a steer. Again they threatened her but she told them she had to have food for her starving children. When they did not touch her she sent for the neighbor women and began the job of skinning. The soldiers watched her a little while and then went on, leaving her and the other women to cut up and divide the beef.

Then in April 1864 Camden itself became a part of the battlefield. On April 7, General Frederick Steele, commanding general of the Union forces at Little Rock, wrote from Elkin's Ferry, "Leaving here, I shall proceed directly to Camden with my whole force." Confederate soldiers were determined to keep up at least a delaying action, and did so with enough success for Steele to report, "We were bushwhacked, and attacked in front, rear and flank by Price's cavalry and twelve pieces of artillery."

There was fighting at the Little Missouri River crossing and then a battle at Prairie de Ann, in which the Confederates had to retreat. In both engagements the Federals lost heavily. Confederate losses were even heavier. Steele had to report, "Our supplies were almost exhausted, and so was the country." In the latter he was accurate. The country had been stripped of meat and bread and there was nothing left to stop crying children or feed a Union soldier. Steele continued to slog ahead. He considered Camden essential to Federal control of the trans-Mississippi region.

On April 15 people knew the worst. Yankee troops were in Camden and free to loot, pillage, burn. Rebel soldiers had to flee. So did men and boys of military age. Slaves who wished to could leave, and many did. Despair settled over the whites who had no way to escape, who saw their homes taken over by Union officers.

On April 17 the Federals sent out a foraging train of about two hundred and twenty-five wagons, guarded by about fifteen hundred men and four pieces of artillery. They took the road that went from Camden to Washington, the road that passed in front of Missouri Ann's house. She had nothing more for them to forage on, but she had another worry. A Confederate detachment under the command of General Sam Bell Maxey was waiting nearby for the Federals. She and her children were close to the line of fire and there was no place to go.

Early in the morning of April 18 she saw Union soldiers forming a battle line in front of her house. She made her children lie on the floor and spread feather beds over them. Then she went out to the Union captain and pleaded with him to move his troops a little farther down the road and spare her children. He agreed to do so and she went back to the house to wait in fear.

The Confederates attacked almost at once, in a battle close enough for Missouri Ann and her children to hear bullets striking the log walls of the house.

It was a victory for the Rebels, this Battle of Poison Spring. They captured the entire wagon train, the pieces of artillery, and a number of prisoners. The Federals left behind nearly five hundred dead, most of them Negroes, ex-slaves fighting against their former masters.

On April 24 the Federals quietly evacuated Camden and began making their way back to Little Rock. Contrary to expectations, they had burned no houses, harassed only a few people in Camden. Most paid for their food and lodging. Rebels took none of this into account as they mounted attack after attack on the retreating troops. It may have been out of revenge. It may have been out of the knowledge that though they had won a battle, they were inevitably losing the war.

For the remainder of 1864, though the Federals controlled the larger part of Arkansas, the Rebels were able to keep up almost daily harassments. Though they knew that victory was beyond their grasp, some thought that by keeping up the fight Arkansas could maintain enough strength to secede again, this time from the Confederacy, and become an independent state. Hadn't they defeated the Yankees at Poison Spring and stopped the Federal expedition up the Red River at Mansfield, Louisiana? These were the fire-eaters. The more level-headed could look back to Chickamauga, where the Confederates had made a splendid try and lost, and from there trace the gradual but dramatic deterioration of their forces: on May 5–7, Battle of the Wilderness; September 2, capture of Atlanta; December 15–16, Battle of Nashville, Tennessee; December 21, capture of Savannah, after the devastating march to the sea. Yet there were a few encouraging signs: growth of the Copperhead movement among Northern civilians weary of war; occasional acts of kindness from Copperhead Yankee officers in the South. There was even a slight hope that Lincoln would not be reelected.

Anti-Lincoln rumors circulated freely throughout the Confederacy, some of them no doubt fed by anti-Lincoln factions in the North. As the election day for his second term approached, the rumors increased in volume and intensity. On January 18, 1864, Junius Bragg wrote, "We have news that Abraham Lincoln is dead. I sincerely hope it is true. . . . The event if true will not change the aspect of affairs in the least. The whole generation of them are but types of Lincoln, and are as much bent on our subjugation as he is."

Before secession many Southerners firmly believed that the intent of Northerners was to rule or ruin. By now the belief was that they wanted to rule *and* ruin, Lincoln along with the rest. Better for him to be dead than elected.

Before the year's end the sad news reached Camden: Lincoln had been reelected. Their worst fears were to be realized. The war would go on until his will was imposed on the South. The last slave would be freed. Plantation owners would lose their land so that each ex-slave could be furnished forty acres and a mule. Equality of black and white would be the law of the land. Against such prospects those who could had to fight on, even though they knew that Grant was slowly closing in on Richmond. When there was nothing left but pride they still would have to fight on.

By January 1865, soldier and civilian alike knew that southwestern Arkansas would be at the center of the disputed ground, that therc the two armies would contend until the last shot was fired. Civilians would be the sufferers. If they could, it was better for them to flee the wrath, to take what slaves they had left, drive the sheep and milk cows they had been able to hide for themselves, and get across the Red River. There they would escape marauding soldiers and find provisions aplenty. On February 6 Junius Bragg wrote the following to his mother:

> If you wait for the Federals to come it will be too late. You will then be powerless. If you get what you have to Texas, it will support you and you have plenty of time so to do. Red River will not be given up. Get all your effects on the west bank of it, and you are "over Jordan."

Events marched inexorably on. On March 4 Lincoln was inaugurated. Columbia, South Carolina, was burned on February 17. On March 18 the last Confederate Congress adjourned. Lee surrendered at Appomattox Court House on April 9. On April 14, after having repeated his plea for conciliation, Abraham Lincoln was assassinated at Ford's Theater in Washington. There was no longer a Yankee but a nation of Yankees on whom the Rebels could pour their venom. They still had their capacity to hate but no longer to fight. Surrender came in stages but it came.

Confederates west of the Mississippi—faced with the imminent prospect of Yankees as masters, Negroes as equals—fought on as long as they could, preferring that to living in the mortification of defeat, to the self-chastisement of unworthiness. But there were a few officers and many soldiers who saw the futility of trying to hold on when by leaving at once they could get home in time to plant crops. Under this reasoning, desertion was easy. On the night of May 19 eight hundred at Marshall, Texas, deserted, and more than a hundred the next day. Seeing that resistance could no longer be effectively maintained, on May 26 General Kirby Smith yielded at New Orleans. The War for Southern Independence was over, and so was independence as the Southerners saw it. Only their pride was left. They had failed to emblazon C.S.A. on the sky, but it was seared into the soul, like a malignant-prone gene to be carried forward generation after generation.

Even then, after there was nothing left to hope on, some five hundred officers and men—Smith, Price, Shelby, Hindman among them—refused to surrender. Sorrowfully, defiantly, they carried their Confederate flags across Texas and at last into Mexico, where, as reports have it, they buried them.

The war was ended; so was Negro slavery as an institution, following by nearly one hundred years the abolition of the Crown and the established church—the costliest of the three in lives lost, bodies maimed, minds warped; in a nation disrupted, in a sectionalism not easily put down. Was it worth the price? The North said *yes*, the South said *no*. Compassionate men on either side said there should have been another way.

Of rejoicing there was little if any; only sadness and bitterness and hate as each tried to pick up the pieces of life. For the Cleavers the pieces were scattered but no more so than for many of their neighbors.

At about the time the war was over Henry Cleaver died at the home of Ellender Cobbs, his sister in Waco, and was buried in the Cobbs family graveyard. He never got beyond the frontier. It was with him from Kentucky to Missouri, from Alabama to Arkansas, and finally in Texas—sixty years of clearing and planting and building—and accumulating. Without the war he would no doubt have lived out his life in Camden, close to the six of his ten children who survived him.

Virginia Bragg Cleaver never went back to Texas to live, and from her husband's estate she received only the slave boy Harvey. She remained with her mother in the Bragg mansion, not entirely convinced that William Henry was dead, living in the hope that someday he would return, watching for him down the Camden road at sunset.

Allen Womack Cleaver, too restless to remain in Waco, enlisted for the third time, this time in Company H, Willis's Battalion, Ross's Texas Brigade. He took with him his brother Abner, who was just seventeen. They surrendered on May 4, 1865, and were paroled at Jackson, Mississippi, on May 13. They walked from Jackson to Waco, and at one point survived only because they killed and ate a crow.

Henry Clay Cleaver, at the end of four years of hard service, was lame, without a cent of money, with only one suit of clothes—and a prisoner. Captain Goodycoon, of the Union Army, kindly presented him with a dollar to pay for the privilege of restoring his loyalty to the Union. With that, at the age of twenty-eight, he was at liberty to begin life again. But what could he do? All around him lay desolation and ruin. Friends urged him to return to the practice of law. He replied, "I am too poor." One who had been more fortunate than most said, "If you will return to the practice of your profession I will build you an office and board you until you say your are able to pay me." Henry replied, "I am too poor to practice law and too proud to accept your kind proposition. I will go to the farm and in retirement and hard labor seek happiness that no public business promises to give." With that in mind he went to Texas to look after the small remnant of his father's estate that had been taken there during the war.

Missouri Ann survived the conflict but she remained embittered and ingrained with a hatred of Yankees that never abated. Except for her house and land, they had left her destitute. She had neither stock nor tools to make a crop and feed her children. But she had to go on, planting and cultivating by hand, making her children go to the fields with her as soon as they were big enough to swing a hoe or drag a cotton sack.

Stragglers came through, white and black, displaced by the war, and she had to share when she could. One afternoon, when she was working in the field with her children, a man appeared at the edge of the woods, a white man, they could see, though his face was blistered and his lips swollen and cracked from the sun. Hesitantly he came toward them and they knew he was a Union soldier, perhaps a deserter. He begged for food and water. She gave him all they had left: a fruit jar of sorghum molasses. He put the jar to his lips and drained it without stopping. Then he went back into the woods, leaving nothing of himself, not even his name, except an image of starvation that remained with the children the rest of their lives.

There were also jayhawkers and bushwhackers passing through. The guerrilla warfare that had been carried on extensively in Missouri and Kansas became prevalent in Arkansas during Reconstruction. The cause lost or won, depending on which side they had supported, these guerrilla bands roamed through the countryside, tortured or killed, robbed for gold, preyed upon the people for horses and food. Names of some of these bands became well known: Quantrill's Band, the Younger Brothers, the James Boys. Their names struck terror to the hearts of some. To others they were the avengers of wrongs, the friends of the poor. From among them came Jesse James, a kind of Western Robin Hood who robbed from the rich and gave to the poor, or so his worshipers believed. He was a special hero to Missouri Ann and her children. Was not her husband, their father, Jesse Herndon James, a cousin? They were ready to believe anything good they heard of him, and reject the bad. To them, "Jesse was a man who was known throughout the land. . . ."

Then they became involved in the myth. One fall, during cotton-picking time, a young man who called himself James Ally came to stay with them. Missouri Ann seemed not to question who he was, where he had come from, why he had come. She simply let him go along to the fields with them. He worked but he never seemed like a farmhand. Then one day he was gone, without explanation. The children never knew for certain but they began to take pride in the belief that he was Jesse James, and that they had helped him when he needed help. The belief was so strong that when Jesse's brother Frank was dying, Missouri Ann's son, Lawrence Cleaver James, rode in a wagon from Oklahoma to Texas to tell him good-bye.

Their Negroes came back—not all of them, but enough to create problems for their former masters. They came back, not yet franchised, dispossessed, with no one else to turn to. True, the Freedmen's Bureau was trying to give every ex-slave the promised forty acres and a mule, and was handing out relief rations to thousands of the starving. Soon it was clear that they could not live up to the promise, and that there was not enough Northern money to continue supplying the rations. Ex-slaves had to fall back on ex-masters, themselves victims of disruption and poverty. Arkansas was overrun with carpetbaggers and scalawags, most of them not above exploiting the hapless Negroes, or the plantation owners. Then the Reconstruction Act was passed and a period not of conciliation but of punishment, both legal and illegal, was on, a period that was to last until 1877. For a time ex-masters hired ex-slaves as day laborers. Then the sharecropper system was introduced, espoused by sharp Yankees who were acquiring plantations for themselves—a system by which a Negro was given a cabin, furnishings, and twenty acres of land to work. At harvest time the landlord took half the crop plus the cost of furnishings. In this system Negroes could exist; unscrupulous landlords could amass fortunes.

Negroes, disillusioned, angry, began their own rebellion, and as well an encroachment on what had been all white territory. The South had echoed to the sound of the war whoop and the Rebel yell. Now it was the "nigger holler" that came out of the darkness and left the whites chilled with fear. Rumors spread of the threats of Black

Republican government in Little Rock, of the dangers to Southern white womanhood, of black uprisings. Something had to be done, the whites said to each other.

Their answer was the Ku Klux Klan, truly an underground movement, designed for passive resistance and for staying the hand of the tyrant, whether white or black. Membership lists were secret. Meetings were held in the black of night. Their purpose and method were suggested in a poem published in a Memphis newspaper in March 1868:

> The wolf is in the desert,
> And the panther in the brake.
> The fox is on his rambles,
> And the owl is wide awake;
> For now 'tis noon of darkness,
> And the world is all asleep;
> And some shall wake to glory,
> And some shall wake to weep.
> Ku Klux.
> Thrice hath the lone owl hooted,
> And thrice the panther cried;
> And swifter through the darkness,
> The Pale Brigade shall ride.
> No trumpet sounds its coming,
> And no drum-beat stirs the air;
> But noiseless is their vengeance,
> They wreak it everywhere.
> Ku Klux.
> The misty gray is hanging
> On the tresses of the East,
> And morn shall tell the story
> Of the revel and the feast.
> The ghostly troop shall vanish
> Like the night in constant cloud,
> But where they rode shall gather
> The coffin and the shroud.
> Ku Klux.

In these words as in the methods there is a blending of forces that had been strong on the frontier for generations. In its names for

officers—"Wizard, "Cyclops"—in its sworn secrecy, in the sheets and
pillow cases members wore, organizers of the Klan had drawn
heavily on Freemasonry. At least some of their signals were derived
from Indian warfare. Ingenuity in putting it all together came from
the tensions of the times. Their targets were agents of the Freedmen's Bureau, Negroes who got out of place—almost anyone who
could be regarded as a threat to Southern womanhood as it was
known in antebellum days. Their membership increased till they
were bold enough to publish in a newspaper, "When shadows gather,
moons grow dim, and stars tremble, glide to the Council Hall, and
wash your hands in tyrant's blood."

They also were called night riders because they traveled country
roads late at night, their horses at a gallop, their sheets flowing out,
ghostly white. For a woman in Missouri Ann's position there was a
certain comfort to be drawn from what came to be known as the
protection of the Klan. For her children there was no comfort—only
fear at the sounds of night riders passing by.

For all—the war, the famine, the death—Yankees and only the
Yankees were to be blamed, and for the Yankees there was to be no
forgiveness, only futile, slow-burning anger. In stories to children
and grandchildren feelings were brought out, restated, given new
life eventually among those who had no memory of "that old war."
One man left a legacy of feeling in his will:

I have made several wills heretofore, when I had considerable property
to give my wife and children, but since the Yankees have stolen all my
negroes and robbed me of a great deal of my other personal property,
pillaging my house, breaking open all the doors, and stealing all the clothing
they wanted, I have very little to will. They stole a gold watch from me worth
about three hundred dollars, which was a bridal present from me to my wife
when we were married half a century ago. They threatened to shoot me if
I did not deliver my watch to them, and burn down my dwelling house,
presenting their pistols at me frequently, and I am an old man of seventy six,
that was too weak and old to defend myself. I therefore make this my last
will and testament, in manner and form following, viz: 1st. I give and bequeath to my children and grandchildren and their descendants throughout
all future generations, the bitter hatred and everlasting malignity of my
heart and soul, against the Yankees, including all the people north of Mason
& Dixon Line, and I do hereby exhort and entreat my children and grandchildren, if they have any love or veneration for me, to instill into the hearts

of their children and grand children and all future descendants, from their childhood, this bitter hatred and those malignant feelings, against the aforesaid people and their descendants throughout all future time and generations.

For all, existence after the guns of war stopped was tough enough without the recriminations and regrets, the violence and threats of violence that clouded their lives. Day in, day out they worked to keep themselves alive, holding on as well as they could to themselves and their land. That was the best they could hope for: there was no other way to hold their lives together. That and pride that would not accept defeat. The body could be conquered but not the spirit. Grimly they joked: "They can kill me but they cain't eat me."

Missouri Ann watched her children growing up not knowing how to read or write, because there were no schools. She could have taught them herself had there not been the constant round of back-breaking, soul-numbing work. She was too much alone; she had to have help.

She accepted for herself what men and women on the frontier had learned to accept. The first marriage might be for love. After that, marriage was more likely the joining of a man and woman, both widowed, in a union whose essential elements were working for a living, raising the children on both sides, adjusting themselves to getting along. Missouri Ann married a man named Webb, apparently soon after the end of the war, and lived with him until his death. Then, about 1869, she married a man named MeGehee, who fathered three children before his death.

Neither marriage improved her situation. Then, almost at the end of Reconstruction, she suffered one of the things pioneers feared most. She was forced off her land. She had lost three husbands and her oldest son. She was left with three children old enough to work, three under seven. Her only way to live, as she saw it, was to hire herself and her children out as day laborers, as she had seen her father hire out his slaves.

But not in Arkansas. There were too many destitute people in Arkansas. At last she looked to Texas. Hands were wanted to pick cotton in Texas.

Ironically, by this time newspapers began advertising Arkansas as a land of beauty and promise. It may have been so for people with money from the North. For those who had suffered destruction in war and destitution in defeat, the land of beauty and promise lay elsewhere. Still they were able to laugh. Still they were able to put new words to an old tune:

> They raise their baccer patch;
> The women all smoke and chaw;
> Eat hog and hominy and poke for greens
> In the State of Arkansas.

> We're leaving Arkansas,
> We're leaving Arkansas;
> Our four horse team will never be seen
> On the roads of Arkansas.

Present-day state boundaries

0 25 50   100   150   200
              Miles

OKLAHOMA

NEW MEXICO

Rio Grande

Red R.

ARKANSAS

See inset below

Texarkana

LOUISIANA

Dallas

Sabine R.

TEXAS

Waco

Homer
(Lufkin)

Austin

Houston

MEXICO

Rio Grande

GULF OF
MEXICO

H. Faye

OKLAHOMA

Red R.

Little Pine Creek

Pin Hook

Paris

Detroit

Blossom

Clarksville

Roxton

TEXAS

0   25
   Miles

Sulphur R.

Texas

F OR MORE THAN FORTY YEARS CROSSING THE RED RIVER INTO TEXAS HAD BEEN LIKE CROSSING OVER JORDAN INTO THE PROMISED LAND. MOSES AUSTIN, WHEN HE PASSED THROUGH KENTUCKY ON his way to Missouri in 1797, was on his way to a strange empire—of strange peoples, strange cultures. Missouri was but a stopping place, in Spanish territory. Rapidly Missouri changed hands from Spain to France, France to the United States. Moses Austin decided to move on. In 1820 he went to Texas and persuaded the Spanish authorities to allow him to settle three hundred families in Texas.

The grant was approved in 1821 but Moses Austin died before he could establish the settlement. His son Stephen took up the plans and in 1822 settled a colony on the Gulf Coast between the Brazos and Colorado rivers. In the interim Mexico had achieved its independence from Spain. Land grants continued to be made. Settlers arrived in great numbers, many legally, perhaps as many illegally— renegades, squatters, men of means ready to acquire land by grant or purchase.

Migration, a slow process on the older frontiers, was much faster into Texas. Steamboats from New York and New Orleans put settlers and their supplies ashore on Galveston Island and at other places along the coast. Wagon trains coming in from Missouri, Tennessee, and Mississippi did not have to cross rugged mountains and ferrymen waited for them at river crossings.

At first the motivation was no doubt the chance to take up cheap, rich land—the chance to start all over again. Soon the hope of empire was a strong factor in the motivation. These settlers were mostly of Anglo-Saxon origin. They had come through the United States, their

[277]

loyalty was to the United States, they began to see Texas as an extension of the United States. In many cases they swore their allegiance
to the Mexican government and joined the Roman Catholic Church
as steps toward acquiring land, but in their hearts they remained
Protestants and Americans to the bone.

Events moved rapidly. In 1835, thirteen years after they were
first let in legally, the colonists were in revolt against the Mexican
government. On March 2, 1836, delegates to a convention declared
themselves free and established a government. On April 21, 1836, at
San Jacinto they defeated the Mexicans in battle and made the
Republic of Texas a reality.

During the Texas Revolution sentiment in the United States
strongly supported the Texans. When they were free, sentiment was
as strong for annexation to the United States. Formal annexation
came in 1845. In the war with Mexico that followed, the United States
acquired full rights to Texas and to territory stretching all the way
to the Pacific. The dream of "manifest destiny" had come true.

Over the objection of antislavery forces in the North, Texas
came into the Union as a slave state. When the question of secession
arose, Texas, chiefly through the power of slaveholding plantation
owners in eastern Texas, elected to join the Confederate States of
America.

Texas furnished men and supplies to the Rebel army but was
never overrun by Yankee soldiers. As the conflict deepened, Texas
became a refuge, and people fleeing death and destruction got to the
Red River any way they could.

A song they had carried over the mountains and across the plains
was still with them, when they were alone or when groups came
together to get whatever they could to sustain them in their despair:

Where, oh, where are the Hebrew children,
Where, oh, where are the Hebrew children,
Where, oh, where are the Hebrew children?
Safe in the Promised Land.

They went through the flames and fire-a
Trusting in the great Messiah.
Holy Grace will lift them higher,
Safe in the Promised Land.

Little Pine Creek

FOR A TIME Missouri Ann was constantly shifting, but never shiftless. Her journey west, unlike the journeys of Cleavers before her, was a flight from the destruction of war—not a flight from worn-out land or toward adventure. Yet it was the journey of a pioneer woman. She had to leave her land. Everything else worth taking she could take with her. That was not much—not enough to fill a farm wagon, which she turned into a covered wagon by putting up wooden hoops and stretching a canvas wagon sheet over them. This would be their home for weeks, perhaps months.

It had to be a slow journey, with the older ones walking, the younger ones riding, with stops for cooking and sleeping, for the ponies to graze. It was a dry time and the wagon was old. Wooden felloes shrank away from the iron tires. To keep the wheels from breaking down she had to drive into a pool or creek and wait for the felloes to swell and tighten against the tires.

At last they came to the Red River and camped the night before crossing over, on low ground where there were mosquitoes and flies and enough discouragement to make them want to turn back. But they could not. They had nothing to turn back to. The next morning they crossed "over Jordan" and, still in Arkansas, not yet in the promised land, they went on with the feeling that the worst was over, that they would make it. They had come through a night to be remembered—a sleepless night with mosquitoes humming, with children crying from hunger, with the cry of a wildcat from the woods around them.

It turned out to be a long journey, the pace they traveled— ninety miles out of Arkansas, seventy-five more in Texas on the road

[279]

leading west from Texarkana. And a desperate journey. Time after time they stopped at houses along the road to ask for work, but there was no work. They were close to begging but she had too much pride to beg.

On and on they went, till at last they came to an open prairie, and then to Guest's Prairie, not far from Detroit. Here the cotton was white in the fields. Missouri Ann stopped her wagon in front of a house and a man came out.

"Need any cotton pickers?" she asked.

He could use some, if they wanted to camp out in their wagon. She reckoned they would have to. They had to have work.

Living in a wagon, picking from daylight till dark, they were worse off than Cleaver slaves had ever been, and as dependent. Unable to read or write, unable to tell weights on cotton scales, the children had to take someone else's word for what they had made in a day. The money they made was not much but it was enough to stave off hunger a little longer.

When picking ran out at Guest's Prairie, they moved on, past Paris, past Brookston, to the black land around Roxton. There they found good picking, but no one furnished houses for pickers. They still had to live in the wagon. Then the cotton was gone and winter was coming on. They drifted back to Detroit, where Missouri Ann found a place for them in the Red Oak community, sharecropping. This she had been brought to, sharecropping in cotton, corn, and black-eyed peas country.

Like pioneer women before her, she became like a beast of burden, working in the fields and woods, plowing and planting and gathering, feeding the horses, milking the cows, slopping the hogs. When she was not working outside she was cooking and sewing and scouring rough floors with a cornshuck broom. In mind she became more and more impoverished. There were so few to talk to. Her grown children still could not read or write. The younger ones were not learning. She turned to talking of the past—of the good life before the war, of suffering and sacrifice during the war.

She did have her pride left, and a few things saved from better times. She might have to go to church in a wagon, or walk, but she could put on a good dress, pin on a gold and mother-of-pearl pin, hang a gold locket around her neck, and go with her head held high. When she did, neighbors said not one of her "gal young'uns" could ever be as good-looking as she was.

They may not have been as proud in their walk but they were tall, strong women, hardened to work in woods and fields, ready as a man to pull a saw or swing a hoe. Like any man, they could work in rawhide shoes, or barefoot when they had no shoes. Like any of the Red Oak girls, they could carry their Sunday shoes till they were in sight of church and put them on to go inside, or they could "might nigh" wear them out at wedding or infare in their singing games.

Then Missouri Ann tried marriage one more time, to a man named Mires. When it did not work out she sold her land in Arkansas and bought a place at Pin Hook, up from Little Pine Creek. A house no better than her father's slaves had lived in, it was built partly of logs, partly of rough pine planks, with a roof of rough split boards. But it was close to the Pin Hook school. Her youngest might get some education.

So after two hundred years and six generations of westering, Cleavers came to Pin Hook, a place isolated enough for the gleanings of the many frontiers they had passed through to be kept. There was no mail delivery. The nearest post office was Blossom, nine miles away, a day's journey there and back. The outside world rarely reached Pin Hook. When the people talked at all, their talk was sprinkled with "they says."

When Missouri Ann could no longer handle the lightest kelly turning plow or Georgia stock she gave up her house and land and lived around with her four widowed children. To her grandchildren she became a teacher, as she could not be for her own. It was more than reading and writing and counting. It was the history of her people through telling over and over again the stories of what had happened to them. It was poetry, through the poems she remembered or made up, through the verses she helped them make up. It was teaching farming through beliefs such as planting root crops in the dark of the moon, leaf crops in the light. It was teaching religion through reading the Bible and singing songs. But there was another side to her. Bad luck had followed her most of her days. Bad luck had to be thwarted. Her mind was furnished with countless rituals, some from the Old World, some from the New. For example, it was bad luck to bring an ax into the house, but often necessary. A person could ward off bad luck by remembering exactly how many steps he took and how he carried the ax. Then he had to go out backward in exactly the same way.

A new frontier opened up across the Red River in the Indian Territory and her children caught frontier fever. She watched them go in their covered wagons and felt within her old stirrings for new country. On January 9, 1906, she wrote some of her feelings in a letter to Bertha James, a granddaughter:

Miss Berthie

Grandma got your sweet kind letter if I did have to push it on you to write me well do so again I am so glad to hear from you all now be a good smart girl cook pa plenty of good grub he will be oh so good to you don't have no beau but nice clever well standing fellows in the country Granma is coming to see you all if she lives long enough I am tired of this country tell all the children to write to me

I am glad you had a nice time Christmas I glad you are so well satisfied with the country where is Mr Roberson living now give my love to Mrs hews mrs furgison and nellie Tell them all I want to see them and I think they ought to write some in your letters to me I am glad you had so much good to eat ms burthie you be good to my baby kiss him for me tell Jesse and frank and loudie to be good children tell them granma is coming now berthie you write again tell me all you know this is a dull place

> your loving gran
> M. MIRES

She never made the trip. On May 7, 1907, she died in the home of a granddaughter, Jessie Ann Owens, the last words on her lips the request for the frontier song, "There'll Be No Dark Valley."

> There'll be no dark valley when Jesus comes,
> There'll be no dark valley when Jesus comes,
> There'll be no dark valley when Jesus comes
> To gather His loved ones home.

> To gather His loved ones home,
> To gather His loved ones home.
> There'll be no dark valley when Jesus comes
> To gather His loved ones home.

She did not live to see her grandsons, Jesse and Frank James, drafted in World War I to fight for the Union, or to read a letter Jesse wrote from the trenches in France:

I guess you have read of the St Mihiel Drive havent you? We were Both In that Drive and we Sure got Some Real experience It Sure was a great Battle. We came over the top at 5 o'clock AM Sept 12th Just at Break of day.

Our artilery behind us Started a bombardment at 1 o'clock the same morning. And It lasted untill 5 when we started over then they Showered down all the harder Shooting Just In front of us as we went there was the greatest Roar of cannons and Machine Guns that a person could emagine. The whole world seemed to Bee Electrified from the flashes from our artilery. It was great what good work our artilery did. Their Guns Seased about 4 P.M. the Same day. the Germans artilery Guns were Shooting Some But not verry mutch. their machine Guns were the Hardest for us to fight they tried to be wicked with their Machine Guns and Poison Gas. But we feared nothing when we started after them. We gave them the Best we had. And we are going to do that every chance we have for we have Realy got It In for them. . . .

Don't you all ever Be uneasy about us for I Think we will make It all rite as we have Been through one Battle and we know more how to do Next Time. It is going to Bee disagreable this winter if we have to Stay here In the Trenches But we will take It all In fun and do our Best. . . . It was a time that I will never forget from 1 o'clock untill 5 while we were standing In the trenches waiting for 5 oclock to come whe we would go over the Top. It was a steady down Poure of Rain and we were Standing In water up too our ankles. And a heavy Roar of Cannons To our Backs and the flashes from the Guns were like lightening We were there 4 hours waiting but The Time went like 30 minutes It was there That I thought of every Body and every thing that had ever happened and of Coarse I emagined that lots of Things would Happen Some of the Men Seemed to Bee down Hearted and would not talk verry mutch others seemed to Bee tickled others seemed to Bee Verry anxious to go over. And some seemed to be mad through and through. Frank was In my section I had a long talk with him he was in good Spirits and seemed To Think we would Bee luckey. he was Verry Cool headed and handled his Squad fine. He has made a good Soldier. . . .

After all my years of searching I came back at last to this letter, which throughout my boyhood had lain beside Missouri Ann's gold locket in my grandmother's clothes box, to be taken out, reread in times of remembering, pondered over. After my wanderings to so many places where the Cleavers had lived, I came back to Pin Hook, to two things Jesse wrote. Of the American soldiers he said, "We gave them the best we had." Of Frank he said, "He has made a good soldier. . . ." I came back to the letter with a broader knowledge of frontier geography, and of the frontier mind. Jesse's statements sound like mottoes to be hung on the wall beside "God is love" and "Home sweet home." Like mottoes, they suggest broad values— values set on a person's worth, not on such distinctions as man or woman, North or South, or red, white, or black.

Genealogy

The following genealogies are included more to aid readers in identifying Cleavers whose names appear in the text than as genealogical studies. They are incomplete, often because information was not available, as often because further research would have been too time-consuming. Because of lack of space, female lines have not been developed except in the case of Missouri Ann Cleaver. Names of children who did not survive infancy, where so identified, have been omitted.

In pioneer families Christian (christening) names are repeated from generation to generation, to the despair of historian and genealogist alike. Exact identification of some of the Cleavers appearing here was often difficult, at times impossible. Obviously a complete genealogical study is much needed.

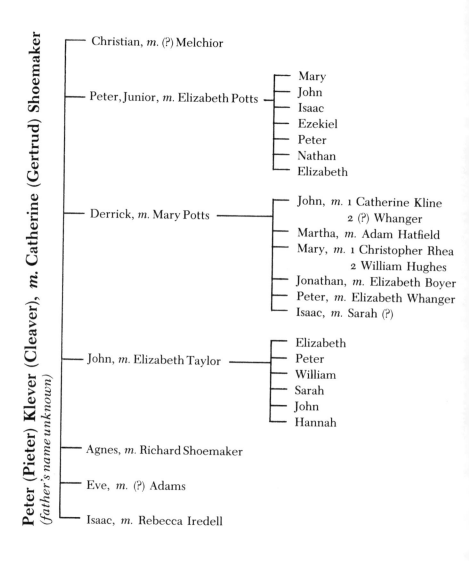

Peter (Pieter) Klever (Cleaver), *m.* Catherine (Gertrud) Shoemaker
(father's name unknown)

— Christian, *m.* (?) Melchior

— Peter, Junior, *m.* Elizabeth Potts
    — Mary
    — John
    — Isaac
    — Ezekiel
    — Peter
    — Nathan
    — Elizabeth

— Derrick, *m.* Mary Potts
    — John, *m.* 1 Catherine Kline
            2 (?) Whanger
    — Martha, *m.* Adam Hatfield
    — Mary, *m.* 1 Christopher Rhea
            2 William Hughes
    — Jonathan, *m.* Elizabeth Boyer
    — Peter, *m.* Elizabeth Whanger
    — Isaac, *m.* Sarah (?)

— John, *m.* Elizabeth Taylor
    — Elizabeth
    — Peter
    — William
    — Sarah
    — John
    — Hannah

— Agnes, *m.* Richard Shoemaker

— Eve, *m.* (?) Adams

— Isaac, *m.* Rebecca Iredell

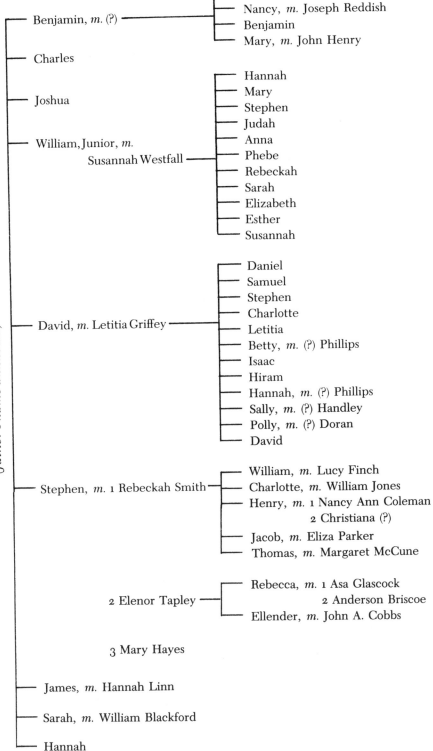

William Cleaver, Senior, m. Hannah (?)
(father's name unknown)

- Benjamin, *m.* (?)
  - Charles Cadle
  - Nancy, *m.* Joseph Reddish
  - Benjamin
  - Mary, *m.* John Henry
- Charles
- Joshua
- William, Junior, *m.* Susannah Westfall
  - Hannah
  - Mary
  - Stephen
  - Judah
  - Anna
  - Phebe
  - Rebeckah
  - Sarah
  - Elizabeth
  - Esther
  - Susannah
- David, *m.* Letitia Griffey
  - Daniel
  - Samuel
  - Stephen
  - Charlotte
  - Letitia
  - Betty, *m.* (?) Phillips
  - Isaac
  - Hiram
  - Hannah, *m.* (?) Phillips
  - Sally, *m.* (?) Handley
  - Polly, *m.* (?) Doran
  - David
- Stephen, *m.* 1 Rebeckah Smith
  - William, *m.* Lucy Finch
  - Charlotte, *m.* William Jones
  - Henry, *m.* 1 Nancy Ann Coleman
    2 Christiana (?)
  - Jacob, *m.* Eliza Parker
  - Thomas, *m.* Margaret McCune
  - 2 Elenor Tapley
    - Rebecca, *m.* 1 Asa Glascock
      2 Anderson Briscoe
    - Ellender, *m.* John A. Cobbs
  - 3 Mary Hayes
- James, *m.* Hannah Linn
- Sarah, *m.* William Blackford
- Hannah

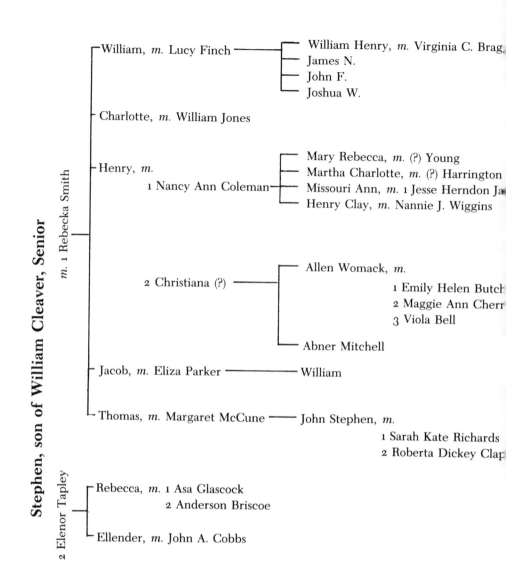

Stephen, son of William Cleaver, Senior

m. 1 Rebecka Smith

William, *m.* Lucy Finch
- William Henry, *m.* Virginia C. Brag
- James N.
- John F.
- Joshua W.

Charlotte, *m.* William Jones

Henry, *m.*
1 Nancy Ann Coleman
- Mary Rebecca, *m.* (?) Young
- Martha Charlotte, *m.* (?) Harrington
- Missouri Ann, *m.* 1 Jesse Herndon Ja
- Henry Clay, *m.* Nannie J. Wiggins

2 Christiana (?)
- Allen Womack, *m.*
  - 1 Emily Helen Butch
  - 2 Maggie Ann Cherr
  - 3 Viola Bell
- Abner Mitchell

Jacob, *m.* Eliza Parker ——— William

Thomas, *m.* Margaret McCune —— John Stephen, *m.*
  - 1 Sarah Kate Richards
  - 2 Roberta Dickey Clap

2 Elenor Tapley

Rebecca, *m.* 1 Asa Glascock
2 Anderson Briscoe

Ellender, *m.* John A. Cobbs

3 Mary Hayes

[288]

Henry Cleaver, son of Stephen

m. 1 Nancy Ann Coleman

- Mary Rebecca, *m.* (?) Young
- Martha Charlotte, *m.* (?) Harrington
- Missouri Ann, *m.* 1 Jesse Herndon James
- Henry Clay, *m.* Nannie J. Wiggins
  - John Young, *m.* Bettie May Jones
  - Richard Henry, *m.* (?)
  - James Bruce, *m.* Brunett Tatham
  - Mary Ella, *m.* Daniel Thomas Jones

2 Christiana (?)

- Allen Womack, *m.*
  - 1 Emily Helen Butcher — Mattie H.
  - 2 Maggie Ann Cherry
    - Viola G.
    - Eucratus
    - Thomas Bell
  - 3 Viola Bell
- Abner Mitchell

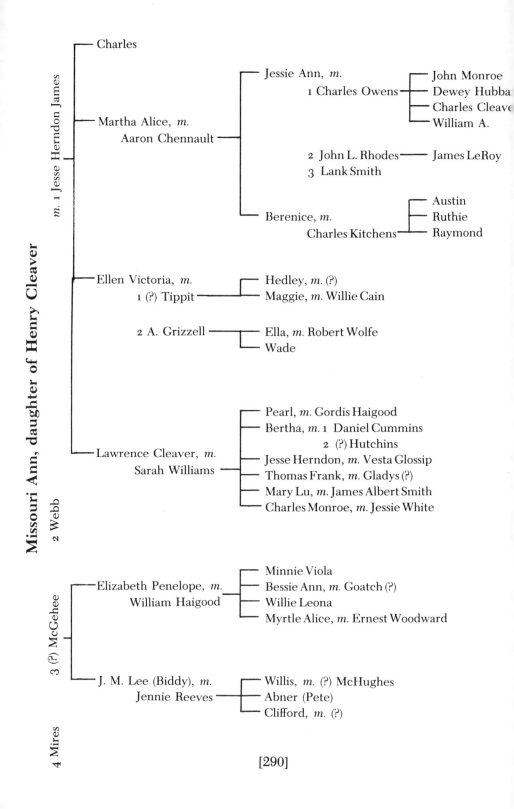

Missouri Ann, daughter of Henry Cleaver

m. 1 Jesse Herndon James
2 Webb
3 (?) McGehee
4 Mires

- Charles
- Martha Alice, *m.* Aaron Chennault
  - Jessie Ann, *m.*
    1 Charles Owens
    - John Monroe
    - Dewey Hubba
    - Charles Cleave
    - William A.
    2 John L. Rhodes — James LeRoy
    3 Lank Smith
  - Berenice, *m.* Charles Kitchens
    - Austin
    - Ruthie
    - Raymond
- Ellen Victoria, *m.*
  1 (?) Tippit
  - Hedley, *m.* (?)
  - Maggie, *m.* Willie Cain
  2 A. Grizzell
  - Ella, *m.* Robert Wolfe
  - Wade
- Lawrence Cleaver, *m.* Sarah Williams
  - Pearl, *m.* Gordis Haigood
  - Bertha, *m.* 1 Daniel Cummins
    2 (?) Hutchins
  - Jesse Herndon, *m.* Vesta Glossip
  - Thomas Frank, *m.* Gladys (?)
  - Mary Lu, *m.* James Albert Smith
  - Charles Monroe, *m.* Jessie White
- Elizabeth Penelope, *m.* William Haigood
  - Minnie Viola
  - Bessie Ann, *m.* Goatch (?)
  - Willie Leona
  - Myrtle Alice, *m.* Ernest Woodward
- J. M. Lee (Biddy), *m.* Jennie Reeves
  - Willis, *m.* (?) McHughes
  - Abner (Pete)
  - Clifford, *m.* (?)

Notes

Since the research for this book has been unusually far-ranging for a family history, no attempt has been made to list all the books and documents consulted—only those which have direct bearing on the text or those which appear useful to others in their research. Likewise, explanatory notes have been kept to a minimum.

Though the research was directed more toward history than toward genealogy, many genealogical sources were used, especially United States censuses, military records in the National Archives, military and civil records in the various state libraries, and records of deeds, marriages, and wills in county courthouses. To the trained genealogist the genealogical information may seem fragmentary. It is necessarily so, partly because of the volume of items, partly because documentation has not been completed. The trained genealogist may be justly critical of the fact that the gap between William Cleaver, Senior, and his forebears was not bridged. Every effort was made to do so, but to no avail. In the absence of documentation no claim has been made, except that in its final form the book depends for its worth more on the Cleavers as people than on the Cleavers as a genealogical succession.

Much documented genealogical information has been included in the text. Additional details, perhaps of less interest to general readers, appear in the notes. All this information now becomes available to the several persons actively at work developing Cleaver genealogies. No doubt a complete one will be forthcoming.

In the following notes the first figure refers to the page number and the second figure, to the paragraph number. An incomplete paragraph at the beginning of a page counts as the first.

3.1   See Edwin B. Bronner, *William Penn's "Holy Experiment": The Founding of Pennsylvania, 1681–1701* (New York and London, 1962), 6–20.

4.2   Dates are given in the New Style (Gregorian) Calendar. The British used the Old Style (Julian) until 1752. In the Old Style the New Year began on March 25. Hence dates between January 1 and March 25 were rendered doubly, i.e., 1682/1683. Quakers further complicated the calendar by substituting numbers for what they considered the pagan names of months and days. In their system March was the First Month, February the Twelfth. Sunday became First Day.

4.4   Catherine Owens Peare, *William Penn* (Philadelphia, 1957), 247.

5.4   See Hannah Brenner Roach, "The Planting of Philadelphia," *The Pennsylvania Magazine of History and Biography*, vol. 92 (1968), for details on land divisions and buildings.

6.2   Bronner, 39–42.

8.1   Samuel Whitaker Pennypacker, *The Settlement of Germantown, Pennsylvania, and the Beginning of German Emigration to North America* (Philadelphia, 1899), 1–6. Referred to hereafter as *Germantown*. Germantown charter (1691), printed in *Pennsylvania Archives*, 1st Ser., vol. 1, 111–15.

9.3   Jane W. T. Brey, *A Quaker Saga* (Philadelphia, 1967), 217.

9.4   Marion Balderston, ed., *James Claypoole's Letter Book, 1681–1684* (San Marino, Calif., 1967), 223.

9.5   Samuel Whitaker Pennypacker, *Historical and Biographical Sketches* (Philadelphia, 1883), 30. Referred to hereafter as *Sketches*.

10.5   Germantown *Grund und Lager Buch*, The Historical Society of Pennsylvania.

11.3   Pennypacker, *Germantown*, 19, 136–40, 144–47.

11.5   Pennypacker, *Sketches*, 46. Among those applying for naturalization was Reyneir Hermanns Van Burklow.

12.2   Germantown *Rathbuch*, The Historical Society of Pennsylvania.

12.5   Richard Frame, quoted in Pennypacker, *Sketches*, 47.

12.6 Franz Loeher, *Geschichte und Zustände der Deutschen in America,* quoted in Pennypacker, *Sketches,* 48.

13.2 Pennypacker, *Sketches,* 42–44.

13.3 Pennypacker, *Sketches,* 35.

14.3 Minutes of Abington Monthly Meeting.

14.4 William Caton, quoted in Joseph Besse, *Sufferings of the People Called Quakers,* vol. 2 (London, 1753), 453.

15.3 Minutes of the Abington Monthly Meeting.

15.5 Pennypacker, *Sketches,* 50–51.

16.2 Germantown *Rathbuch.*

16.5 Christian, b. 1/2C/1695–96; Peter, Junior, 10/28/1697. See Thomas Maxwell Potts, *Historical Collections of the Potts Family in England and America* (Cannonsburg, Pa., 1901).

17.2 Germantown *Grund und Lager Buch.*

17.5 Pennypacker, *Sketches,* 57.

19.2 Potts: Derrick, b. ca. 1702; John, b. ca. 1705; Eve, b. ca.; Agnes, b. ca.; Isaac, b. ca. 1710. See also Mrs. Thomas Potts James, *Memorial of Thomas Potts, Jr.* (Cambridge, Mass., 1874).

19.4 Brey, 178–79.

19.5 John Bakeless, *Daniel Boone* (New York, 1939), 5.

20.3 Howard M. Jenkins, *Historical Collections Relating to Gwynedd,* Philadelphia (1897), 411.

20.4 Minutes of the Gwynedd Monthly Meeting.

20.5 Minutes of the Abington Monthly Meeting.

21.2 Benjamin Franklin, Works, New York, 1904, 240.

21.3 The children of Peter Klever married as follows: Christian, m. (?) Melchior; Peter, Junior, m. Elizabeth Potts; Eve, m. (?) Adams; Derrick, m. Mary Potts; John, m. Elizabeth Taylor; Agnes, m. Richard Shoemaker; Isaac, m. Rebecca Iredell.

22.2   The Peter Klever will is filed in the Philadelphia County Court House.

23.6   The inventory is filed with the will.

25.2   Thomas Maxwell Potts, 854.

25.3   Ray Billington, *Western Expansion*, 3rd ed. (New York, 1967), 90–92.

26.2   J. Dalrymple map, printed 1751, now in possession of New York Public Library: the Great Philadelphia Wagon Road extended to Winchester via Lancaster, York, and the Williams Ferry; distance from Philadelphia to the Yadkin River via Staunton Court House was 435 miles. Also Charles A. Hanna, *The Wilderness Trail* (New York, 1911).

26.3   Jenkins, 73–82.

30.1   These day books are now the property of the Pine Forge School at Manatawny.

30.3   George Boone's letter was reprinted in the Pennsylvania *Archives* 1st Ser., vol. 1, 217–18.

31.1   This petition appears in Pennsylvania *Archives*, 1st Ser., vol. 1, 213.

31.2   *Minutes of the Provincial Council of Pennsylvania*, vol. 8 (Harrisburg, 1840), 432.

31.5   Minutes of Exeter Monthly Meeting; Jenkins, 373–74.

32.2   Minutes of Gwynedd Monthly Meeting.

32.4   Minutes of Exeter Monthly Meeting.

33.2   Minutes of Exeter Monthly Meeting.

34.2   Minutes of Exeter Monthly Meeting.

34.5   Bronner, 235–49.

36.2   Derrick Cleaver's will is in the Berks County Court House.

37.2   Derrick and Mary Cleaver may have had as many as nine children. Information is available on six: John, m. 1 Catherine Kline, 2 (?) Whanger; Martha, m. Adam Hatfield, January 1, 1742; Mary, b. 1740, m. 1 Christopher Rhea, July 16, 1757; 2 William Hughes, June 7, 1774;

Jonathan, m. Elizabeth Boyer; Peter, m. Elizabeth Whanger; Isaac, m. Sarah (?).

41.2   Billington, 35–56.

42.2   Richard L. Morton, *Colonial Virginia*, vol. 2 (Chapel Hill, 1960), 446–48.

43.5   Thomas Perkins Abernethy, *Three Virginia Frontiers* (Baton Rouge, 1940), 58 ff.

45.1   Morton, vol. 2, 546–48.

45.2   Morton, vol. 2, 542–44.

46.3   Billington, 80–81.

47.2   Morton, vol. 2, 488.

48.4   Thomas Chaukely quoted in Alvin Edward Moore, *History of Hardy County of the Borderland* (Parsons, W. Va., 1963), 13–14. Also in Samuel Kercheval, *A History of the Valley of Virginia*, 3rd ed. (Woodstock, Va., 1902), 42–43.

50.1   W. W. Henning, ed., *The Statutes at Large: Being a Collection of All the Laws of Virginia from the First Session of the Legislature in the Year 1619*, vol. 1, 532–33.

50.3   Deed, Frederick County Court House.

50.3   Deed, Frederick County Court House.

51.1   Morton, 643–48.

52.2   Public Records Office, London

52.4   Public Records Office, London.

54.2   Billington, 139–40.

55.3   Ezekiel Cleaver's letter is in the Friends Library, Swarthmore College.

57.1   E. L. Judy, *History of Grant and Hardy Counties, West Virginia*, 1–20.

58.2   Excerpts from George Washington's diaries quoted in Moore, 16–19.

59.5   The Nicholas Friend deed is recorded in the Hampshire County Court House.

60.4   Petition of the House of Burgesses, *Journal of the House of Burgesses* (Richmond, 1754), 192.

61.2   Deed in the Augusta County Court House.

61.3   George Washington, *The Writings*, vol. 1, edited by Worthington Chauncey Ford (New York and London, 1899), 197–98.

61.4   Washington, vol. 1, 249.

62.1   Moore, 27.

62.3   Jonas Friend was a sergeant from the present Pendleton County in the French and Indian Wars, 1754–60. His father, Jacob, owned land on Friend's Run, near the present Franklin.

63.3   Survey is in the Virginia State Library.

64.1   Deed is in the Virginia State Library.

65.3   Will has not been found. Inventory is in the Hampshire County Court House.

66.2   Hu Maxwell, *History of Randolph County, West Virginia* (Morgantown, W. Va., 1898; reprinted Parsons, W. Va., 1961), 180–81.

67.4   David Crouch, *Calendar of the Kentucky Papers of the Draper Collection of Manuscripts*, 12CC, 225–29.

69.1   William A. Owens, *Swing and Turn: Texas Play-Party Games* (Dallas, 1936), 65.

69.2   William A. Owens, *Texas Folk Songs* (Dallas, 1950), 157.

70.3   Letter from Samuel Allen as quoted in James Morton Callahan, *History of West Virginia Old and New*, Vol. 1 (Chicago and New York, 1923), 122–25.

71.2   Children of William Cleaver, Senior: Benjamin, b. January 1751; Joshua; Charles; William, Junior, b. 1761; Stephen, b. May 1766; David, b. ca. 1768; James, b. ca. 1770; Sarah, declared herself over twenty in declaration for marriage license, 1820; Hannah, single in 1807.

73.2   Owens, *Texas Folk Songs*, 283.

74.2   Bishop Francis Asbury, as quoted in Moore, 45.

74.4   Asbury as quoted in Moore, 47.

75.1   Owens, as recalled from brush arbor singing, Lamar County, Texas, ca. 1918.

78.5   Billington, 152.

78.6   Maxwell, 39–46; Billington, 165–68.

79.4   Maxwell, 182–84.

80.2   Colonel William Fleming's *Journal*, quoted in Reuben Gold Thwaites and Louise Phelps Kellogg, *Dumore's War* (Madison, Wisc., 1905), 281–88.

81.2   Thwaites and Kellogg, 343–46.

81.5   Military Records, Virginia State Library.

81.6   Thwaites and Kellogg, 433–34.

82.2   Thwaites and Kellogg, 361–62.

84.3   John Murray, Lord Dunmore, quoted in Thwaites and Kellogg, 371–72.

85.4   Maxwell, 47–49.

87.3   Public Records Office, London

88.3   William Cleaver, Junior, affidavit, National Archives.

88.5   Maxwell, 50–51.

89.2   Maxwell, 183.

90.2   Petition owned by Virginia State Library.

91.3   Lyman Chalkley, *Chronicles of the Scotch-Irish Settlement in Virginia: Extracted from the Original Court Records of Augusta County, 1745–1800*, vol. 1, (1912), 204.

91.5   Chalkley, vol. 3, 153.

91.6   Francis Asbury, *The Journal and Letters*, vol. 1, edited by Elmer T. Clark et al. (Nashville and London, 1958), 462–63, 576–78.

97.1   Richard H. Collins, *History of Kentucky*, vol. 1, (1874; reprinted Frankfort, K., 1966), 247–50; Bakeless, 82–84.

98.3   Collins, vol. 1, 16; Bakeless, 89.

99.2   Collins, vol. 1, 249; Bakeless, 102–3.

99.5   Collins, vol. 1, 18.

100.2   John Murray, Lord Dunmore, Thwaites and Kellogg, 371.

101.1   Billington, 170–71.

103.4   Sarah B. Smith, *Historic Nelson County* (Louisville, 1971), 15–18.

104.3   George William Beattie and Helen Pruitt Beattie, "Pioneer Linns of Kentucky," *Kentucky History*, vol. 20, 18–36.

104.3   George Rogers Clark, *Diary*, quoted in Bakeless, 154.

105.2   Land Office Treasury Warrants, Virginia State Library.

105.4   Original deed to William Cleaver in Virginia State Library.

106.2   Willard Rouse Jillson, *The Kentucky Land Grants* (Louisville, 1925), 36.

107.4   Bakeless, 117–20.

108.2   Bakeless, 124–36.

108.5   Bakeless, 142.

109.2   John Cowan, in Beattie, 140.

109.3   Bakeless, 153–54.

110.2   John Bowman, in Beattie, 145.

113.4   See Collins, vol. 1, 20, for organization of these three counties; and vol. 2, 643–5C, for Nelson County.

114.2   Smith, 17–24.

114.3   Bakeless, 256–57.

115.1   Beattie, 242–43, 31.

115.3   John Floyd, quoted in *History Quarterly*, vol. 15, 16.

116.2   Military records of Benjamin and William Cleaver, Junior, National Archives.

116.3   Collins, vol. 1, 20 and 253–54.

117.2   Bakeless, 261–65.

117.3   Benjamin and William Cleaver, Junior, affidavits.

117.5   DeHaas, 372–80.

118.4   Billington, 190–91.

120.3   Certificate in Virginia State Library.

121.2   Collins, vol. 1, 20–22.

122.2   Frank A. Masters, *A History of Kentucky Baptists* (1953), 24–26. Samuel Haycraft, *A History of Elizabethtown, Kentucky, and Its Surroundings* (Elizabethtown, 1960), 14.

122.4   Masters, 25.

123.2   Owens, recalled from brush arbor meetings in Lamar County, Texas, ca. 1918. See George Pullen Jackson, *Spiritual Folk Songs of Early America*, 2d ed. (Locust Valley, N. Y., 1953), song nos. 167 and 202, for variants and for note on use of refrain made by Julia Ward Howe.

123.3   Masters, 26–27.

124.2   Beattie, 242–43.

124.3   J. H. Spencer, *A History of Kentucky Baptists* vol. 1 (1866), 22–23.

124.4   Asbury, vol. 2, 631.

125.2   Asbury, vol. 1, 632.

125.3   Asbury, vol. 1, 632.

125.4   Asbury, vol. 1, 638.

125.5   John Taylor, *The History of Ten Baptist Churches*, 135.

125.6   Asbury, vol. 2, 760.

126.2   Barton W. Stone, quoted in Masters, 165–66.

127.2   Minutes quoted through the courtesy of the Southern Baptist Seminary, Louisville.

127.4   Taylor, 153.

128.2   Samuel Davies, as quoted in Morton, vol. 2, 488.

128.4   Taylor, 69.

129.1   Minutes courtesy of the Southern Baptist Seminary.

129.1   Minutes courtesy of the Southern Baptist Seminary.

129.2   Taylor, 100.

129.4   Owens, *Swing and Turn,* 43.

130.2   Smith, 39.

131.2   Original of this writ now in possession of The Filson Club, Louisville.

132.3   Orders copied from a typescript courtesy of The Filson Club.

134.4   Moses Austin's diary as it appears in *The American Historical Review,* vol. 5, 525–26; original in the Eugene C. Barker Texas History Center, The University of Texas.

135.4   Collins, vol. 1, 21–23.

139.5   Nelson County marriage records.

139.5   Benjamin Cleaver's children: Charles Cadle; Nancy, m. Joseph Reddish, August 9, 1802; Martha, m. John Henry, February 4, 1806; and probably William.

139.6   William Cleaver, Junior, m. Susannah Westfall, June 30, 1790. Children: Hannah, b. March 23, 1792; Mary, b. February 7, 1794; Stephen, b. January 5, 1796; Judah, b. October 29, 1797; Anna, b. November 23, 1799; Phebe, b. July 31, 1802; Rebeckah, b. February 2, 1804; Sarah, b. February 25, 1806; Elizabeth, b. March 26, 1808; Esther, b. January 14, 1810; Susannah, b. April 20, 1812. Susannah Westfall Cleaver d. April 28, 1812. William, Junior, d. 1836. Information from Sarah Cleaver McGrew Bible.

140.3   David Cleaver m. Letitia Griffey, November 17, 1793; d. July 2, 1829. Will lists children: Isaac, Stephen, David, Samuel, Hiram, Betty Phillips, Hannah Phillips, Sally Handley, Polly Doran, Letitia, Charlotte.

140.5   James Cleaver's children: no information available.

142.4   Billington, 223–24.

143.1   John M. Oskison, *Tecumseh and His Times* (New York, 1938), 24, 27.

143.2   Billington, 224; Haycraft, 48–49.

144.4   Stephen Cleaver quotation from account given Cleaver family by
         John Helm in Hannibal, Mo.

144.5   John Helm Memoir. Printed broadside. Draper 27CC1–2.

146.1   Collins, vol. 1, 275–81.

147.5   Nelson County marriage records.

148.2   Hardin County Order Book.

148.3   John Bradford, *The General Instructor: Or the Office, Duty, and
         Authority of Justices of the Peace, Sheriffs, Coroners, and Consta-
         bles* (Lexington, Ky., 1800), 124–25.

148.6   Hardin County Order Book.

149.2   Hardin County deed records.

149.5   Harrison D. Taylor, *Ohio County, Kentucky, in the Olden Days*
         (Louisville, 1926), 42.

149.6   Hardin County Order Book.

150.2   McDowell A. Fogle, *The Fogle Papers: A History of Ohio County,*
         19.

150.4   Ohio County Order Book.

150.5   Bradford, 118.

150.6   Haycraft, 45–46.

151.3   Bradford, 123.

151.4   Bradford, 70, 167.

151.6   Ohio County Order Book.

152.3   Hardin County Deed Book A, 244–45.

152.4   Ohio County Deed Book A, 16–18, 34–35; Deed Book C, 23–28.

152.6   Haycraft, 42–43.

153.3   Harrison Taylor, 42.

154.2   Asbury, vol. 1, 405.

154.3 Harrison Taylor, 43–46.

154.4 Asbury, vol. 2, 248.

154.6 Ohio County Deed Book D, 268.

155.3 Ohio County Deed Book A, 16–18, 34–35, 165–66, 336–37. Deed Book B, 157–60.

155.4 Ohio County Circuit Court Order Book 1, 117.

155.5 Order Book 1, 131–32.

156.3 Order Book 1, 143–44.

156.4 Ohio County Order Book.

156.4 Hardin County military records.

157.1 Randolph County, West Virginia, Minute Book No. 1, 66.

157.2 Nelson County Will Book.

158.3 Report of Stephen Cleaver, executor; Nelson County Court House.

159.5 Washington Irving, "The Early Experiences of Ralph Ringwood," *The Crayon Papers*, vol. 10 (New York and London), 441–74.

161.1 Stone, quoted in Masters, 151–53.

161.4 Billington, 277–78.

162.3 Oskison, 153.

164.3 Billington, 284.

164.4 Harrison Taylor, 218.

164.5 See Bennett H. Young. *The Battle of the Thames*, The Filson Club (Louisville, 1903), 139, 245.

164.6 Billington, 287–89.

165.3 Thomas S. Woodward, *Reminiscences of the Creek, or Muscogee Indians* (Montgomery, 1859; reprinted Tuscaloosa, 1939), 85–86. As an introduction to this statement Woodward claimed he had been a neighbor of Stephen Cleaver. The statement was written twelve years after Stephen Cleaver's death, and Woodward may have relied on a statement made by Stephen's son William, who was in the battle.

167.2   Haycraft, 146.

169.4   Ohio County marriage records. Elenor Rogers McFarland Tapley was the widow of Hosea, the mother of Breen. By her Stephen Cleaver had two daughters, Rebecca and Ellender.

169.4   Carl Sandburg, *Abraham Lincoln, The Prairie Years,* vol. 1 (New York, 1926), 15 ff.

175.1   Edwin C. McReynolds, *Missouri: A History of the Crossroads State* (Norman, Okla., 1962), 13–28; Eugene Morrow Violette, *A History of Missouri* (Kirksville, 1918; reprinted, 1960), 2–32.

176.5   Floyd Calvin Shoemaker, *Missouri's Struggle for Statehood,* (Jefferson City, 1916), 10.

177.2   Duane Meyer, *The Heritage of Missouri—A History* (St. Louis, 1963), 122.

177.5   Bakeless, 356–64; Violette, 63–64.

178.2   Meyer, 134.

178.3   *Western Pennsylvania Historical Magazine,* vol. 3, 113.

179.3   John Megown, manuscript memoir of Stephen Cleaver, courtesy of Virgil E. Megown, County Clerk, Ralls County.

180.5   Copy provided at Ralls County Court House.

181.3   Violette, 74.

181.4   Meyer, 149.

182.2   Shoemaker, 81–87.

182.3   Meyer, 150.

182.5   McReynolds, 77–78; Billington, 351–52.

183.3   *Journal of the Missouri State Convention* (St. Louis, 1820), 3. Referred to hereafter as *Journal.*

183.4   Violette, 114–18.

184.2   *Journal,* 4.

184.3   *Journal,* 34.

185.2   *Journal,* 46, 43.

186.2   *Journal,* 26–27.

186.4   McReynolds, 85.

186.5   Meyer, 763.

186.6   Ralls County Deed Book A, 179, 482, 501, 565.

187.4   *Missouri Historical Review,* vol. 20, 452–55.

189.5   Circuit Court records, Ralls County.

190.3   Ralls County Deed Book A, 109; B, 34, 462; C, 71; D, 155, 431.

190.4   Ralls County marriage records.

190.5   Richard Morris, *Encyclopedia of American History* (New York, 1953), 193.

191.2   Owens, *Texas Folk Songs,* 222.

191.2   Owens, *Texas Folk Songs,* 107.

193.2   Ralls County Wills.

195.3   Ralls County records.

201.1   Albert Burton Moore, *History of Alabama* (Tuscaloosa, 1951), 35–63.

202.2   Billington, 310–12.

203.2   Billington, 234, 285–86.

204.2   Andrew Jackson, *Correspondence,* vol. 2, edited by John Spencer Bassett (Washington, D.C., 1929), 346.

205.4   Item in Augusta *Chronicle* quoted in Moore, 77 ff.

206.4   Billington, 324.

207.1   Beattie, 157.

208.3   Children of Henry and Nancy Ann Coleman (b. June 18, 1811) Cleaver: Mary Rebecca, b. March 26, 1829; Martha Charlotte, b. February 24, 1831; Stephen William, b. October 14, 1832; Henry Thomas, b. September 10, 1834; Missouri Ann, b. December 22, 1835; Henry Clay, b. August 15, 1837. Stephen William and Henry Thomas apparently died in infancy.

209.2   The 1850 census for Ouachita County, Arkansas, lists the Bragg family as follows: J. N., 50; Martha W., 43; Walter L., 15; Virginia C., 13; Junius N., 12; Florence M., 7; Anthon J., 5; Albert P., 2.

210.2   Moore, 153.

210.3   Moore, 156–57.

210.4   Negro version recorded by Owens, Franklin, Tex., 1938.

211.5   Lowndes County deed records, Dallas County deed records.

212.3   Children of Henry and Christiana (b. February 10, 1800) Cleaver: Allen Womack, b. September 7, 1839; Virginia Thomas, b. December 12, 1841; Adelia Caroline, b. October 19, 1844; Abner Mitchell, b. February 12, 1847. Virginia Thomas and Adelia Caroline apparently died in infancy.

213.1   T. H. Ball, *A Glance into the Great South-East,* or *Clarke County, Alabama, and Its Surroundings, from 1540 to 1877* (Grove Hill, Ala. 1882; reprinted Tuscaloosa, 1962), 180–194; John Simpson Graham, *History of Clarke County* (Birmingham, 1923), 5–10.

213.3   Clarke County marriage licenses.

214.2   Joseph Glover Baldwin, *The Flush Times of Alabama and Mississippi* (1853; reprinted, William A. Owens, ed., New York, 1957), 34.

214.3   Baldwin, 2.

215.3   Ball, 200–201.

216.4   J. T. Sprague *Journal* quoted in Lucille Griffith, *History of Alabama, 1540–1900* (Northport, Ala., 1962), 86–87.

217.2   Sprague, 89.

217.4   Moore, 190.

218.2   Alabama State Archives.

223.1   John Gould Fletcher, *Arkansas* (Chapel Hill, 1947), 10–37.

225.4   Fletcher, 24–25.

228.2   Letters to Peter Newport Bragg and wife Martha Crook Bragg, microfilm, Arkansas History Commission, Little Rock. Hereafter referred to as Bragg Papers.

228.3   Bragg Papers.

229.2   Owens, *Texas Folk Songs,* 236.

229.3   Cephas Washburn as quoted in Boyd W. Johnson, *The Arkansas Frontier* (1927), 9.

231.3   Memoir of Henry Clay Cleaver, typescript, by courtesy of Curtis L. Cleaver, Fort Worth, Tex.

232.8   John W. Brown, *Diary,* July 4, 1852–July 13, 1865, microfilm, in possession of the University of Arkansas.

233.3   Owens, *Swing and Turn,* 290.

233.4   Verse as recalled by Jessie Ann Chennault.

234.4   Alumni Records, University of Virginia.

234.5   Henry Clay Cleaver, Memoir.

235.2   *John C. Calhoun: Basic Documents* (State College, Pa., 1952), 298–324.

235.5   Jack B. Scroggs, "Arkansas in the Secession Crisis," *Arkansas and the Civil War,* edited by John L. Ferguson (Arkansas History Commission, n.d.), 26–28.

236.2   Morris, 228.

237.2   Editorial in the Camden *Eagle* as quoted by Scroggs, 27.

237.4   Bragg Papers.

238.2   Scroggs, 33.

238.3   Scroggs, 38.

238.5   Scroggs, 41.

240.3   Henry Clay Cleaver military record, National Archives.

240.3   Walter Lawrence Bragg military record, National Archives.

240.4   Albert Pike's "Dixie" as quoted in Ferguson, 326.

241.2   Ferguson, 327.

241.3   Allen Womack Cleaver, military record in the National Archives.

241.4   The letters of Junius Newport Bragg contain a remarkable record of Confederate sentiment and experience. Many of them were printed in *Letters of a Confederate Surgeon,* edited by Helen Gaughan. The entire collection was made available by the Arkansas History Commission, in the Bragg Papers. All the Junius Newport Bragg letters that follow are to be found in that collection.

242.4   The Reverend Ben Hill Cleaver, Cape Girardeau, Mo., manuscript life of John Stephen Cleaver.

242.6   Owens, *Swing and Turn,* 32.

244.3   From a recording sung in 1938 by Lemuel Jeffus, Lovelady, Tex., made by William A. Owens.

246.2   Martin Hardwick Hall, *Sibley's New Mexico Campaign* (Austin, 1960), 33.

246.3   William Henry Cleaver military record, National Archives.

246.4   William Henry Cleaver military record, National Archives.

247.2   William Henry Cleaver will in the Angelina County Court House.

249.1   Ben Hill Cleaver.

249.2   Ferguson, 81.

249.3   Ferguson, 86.

250.3   As sung by Rod Drake, Silsbee, Tex., 1953, and recorded by William A. Owens.

251.2   Walter L. Bragg military record, National Archives.

252.4   Allen W. Cleaver military record, National Archives.

254.2   William R. Cleaver military record, National Archives.

254.4   Owens, *Texas Folk Songs,* 273.

255.2   Owens, *Texas Folk Songs,* 274.

257.5   Ben Hill Cleaver.

260.3   Ferguson, 328.

260.4   Ferguson, 182–87.

262.3   As recalled by Missouri Ann Cleaver's daughter, Martha Alice James Chennault.

263.3   Ferguson, 218.

270.2   Owens, *Texas Folk Songs,* 112.

270.2   As recalled by Missouri Ann Cleaver's granddaughter, Bertha James Hutchins.

270.3   Fletcher, 214.

271.4   Fletcher, 216.

271.4   J. D. G. Brown's will is in the Hanover County Court House.

273.3   Owens, *Texas Folk Songs,* 236.

Index

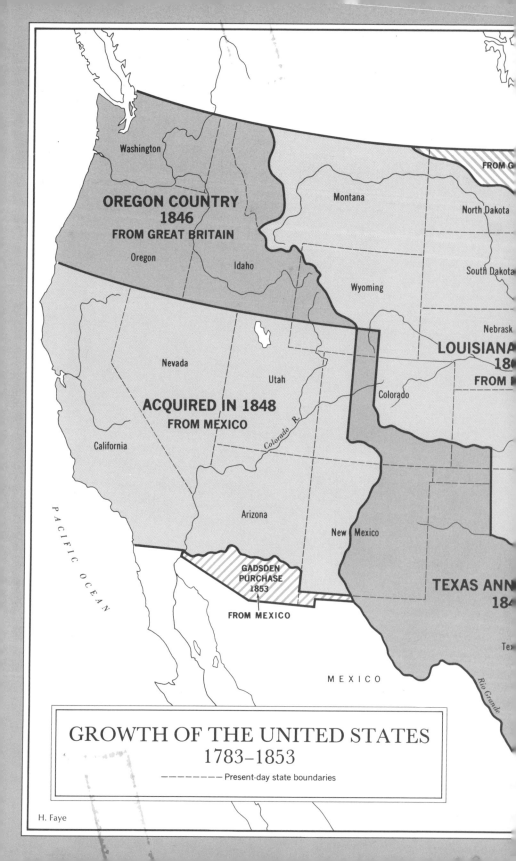

Washington

OREGON COUNTRY
1846
FROM GREAT BRITAIN

Oregon

Idaho

Montana

North Dakota

South Dakota

Wyoming

Nebrask

FROM G

LOUISIANA
18
FROM

Nevada

Utah

ACQUIRED IN 1848
FROM MEXICO

California

Colorado

Colorado R.

Arizona

New Mexico

GADSDEN
PURCHASE
1853

FROM MEXICO

TEXAS ANN
18

Te

PACIFIC OCEAN

MEXICO

Rio Grande

GROWTH OF THE UNITED STATES
1783–1853

--------- Present-day state boundaries

H. Faye